Pierre Corneille Revisited

Twayne's World Author Series
French Literature

David O'Connell, Editor

Georgia State University

TWAS 874

PIERRE CORNEILLE, natif de Rouen, s'est rendu celebre par quantité de pieces de Theatre, et par la traduction fidelle en vers François du liure incomparable de l'imitation de Iesus Christ.

1643 ENGRAVING BY MICHEL LASNE OF PIERRE CORNEILLE

Courtesy of Bibliothèque municipale de Rouen Cliché Didier Tragin/Catherine Lancien

Pierre Corneille Revisited

Claire L. Carlin

The University of Victoria

Twayne Publishers
An Imprint of Simon & Schuster Macmillan
New York

Prentice Hall International
London • Mexico City • New Delhi • Singapore • Sydney • Toronto

Twayne's World Authors Series No. 874

Pierre Corneille Revisited
Claire L. Carlin

Copyright © 1998 by Twayne Publishers

Twayne Publishers
An Imprint of Simon & Schuster Macmillan
1633 Broadway
New York, NY 10019

Library of Congress Cataloging-in-Publication Data

Carlin, Claire L.
      Pierre Corneille revisited / Claire L. Carlin.
          p.   cm. — (Twayne's world authors series ; TWAS 874. French
      literature)
      Includes bibliographical references and index.
      ISBN 0-8057-4561-0 (alk. paper)
      1. Corneille, Pierre, 1606–1684—Criticism and interpretation.
   I. Title.   II. Series: Twayne's world authors series ; TWAS 874.
   III. Series: Twayne's world authors series. French literature.
   PQ1779.C37   1998
   842'.4—dc21   98-34788
                                                          CIP

This paper meets the requirements of ANSI/NISO Z3948-1992 (Permanence of Paper).

10 9 8 7 6 5 4 3 2 1

Printed in the United States of America

For my mother, Charlotte M. Carlin,
with love and gratitude.

Contents

Preface

The theater of Pierre Corneille has been part of the French literary canon since the seventeenth century. In France, a tiny portion of his dramatic output has been reverently preserved in the national secondary school and university curricula and touted as a high point of neoclassical culture. The reaction of young people in France is not always positive, however. In a survey cited in the *Journal Français d'Amérique* for 4–17 March 1994, French students chose Corneille as their least favorite author. My own informal discussions with people educated in France confirm this dislike; they are incredulous that a North American would choose to become a Corneille specialist. Fortunately, the reaction of students in North America is very positive, as they approach the plays without any obligation to see the author as an icon of their national culture.

Scholars have never tired of the theater of Corneille, as proven by over 300 years of critical debate. Cornelian theater has been a battleground, a dramatic site of conflict for competing critical stances. Our excitement stems partly from the enormous variety of subjects and genres treated by Corneille in over 30 plays, access to most of which has been denied to students. Such rich variety has lent itself to a number of radically different methods of interpretation. Aesthetic studies stress the construction of the plays, fascinating in their complexity. For other specialists Corneille's theater has been seen as a source of information about seventeenth-century political problems such as the end of feudalism and the rise of absolutism. Corneille's characters have been the subjects of psychoanalysis, of feminist critique and praise, and of poststructuralist, new historicist readings that highlight the difficulty of any definitive interpretation at all. This study will explore all of these approaches, especially those refined during the 25 years since the appearance of Claude Abraham's *Corneille* in the Twayne's World Authors Series. These recent critics convincingly justify the enthusiasm with which they plunge into this vast corpus.

Corneille has much to tell us about the seventeenth century and its conception of history, and the context in which he wrote cannot be neglected. Nevertheless, there is a more universal appeal to be found in these plays, for every one of them addresses the desire for recognition and the drive to excel. Corneille inherited from Renaissance humanism the need to place value on the individual; his heroes, male and female, attempt to be exceptional. Corneille's protagonists often achieve fantastic feats of heroism, but society's reception of these acts is what determines their success or failure in the eyes of the heroes and their audiences, on- and offstage. Fear accompanies desire; circumstances can defeat ambition. Audience interpretation is key, but it is unstable, lending a very modern, or postmodern, perspective to the work of this canonical author.

The passion to rise above the norm impels the Cornelian hero to act, a passion communicated to spectators and readers. It is an appreciation for and understanding of this passion I wish to communicate so that you might share in the enjoyment of the theater of Pierre Corneille.

Acknowledgments

Several colleagues have furnished invaluable editoral help in the preparation of this study. Many thanks to Harold Knutson, Mary Ellen Ross, Derek Turton, and B. D. Wonder for their careful reading of chapters of the manuscript. The University of Victoria provided an Internal Research Grant without which this work could not have been completed on time. The lion's share of my gratitude goes to my husband, Bruce Wonder, whose patience and support make writing possible.

Chronology

Each play is listed according to the date of its first performance. The date of the first publication is listed in parentheses after the title.

1606	Pierre Corneille born on 6 June in Rouen; eldest of six children of Pierre Corneille, a functionary of the French government, and Marthe Le Pesant.
1615–1622	Corneille is a student at the well-known Jesuit college of Rouen.
1624	He receives his license to practice law.
1628	His father purchases two modest government offices for him.
1629–1630	Corneille's first play, the comedy *Mélite ou les fausses lettres* (1633), is a great success in Paris during this theatrical season.
1630–1631	The tragicomedy *Clitandre ou l'innocence délivrée* (1632), Corneille's second play.
1631–1632	Corneille's third play and second comedy, *La Veuve ou le traître trahi* (1634).
1632	His *Mélanges poétiques* are published along with *Clitandre*.
1632–1633 [?]	His next two comedies, *La Galerie du Palais ou l'amie rivale* (1637) and *La Suivante* (1637).
1633–1634	*La Place Royale ou l'amoureux extravagant* (1637).
1634	Corneille's first important piece of drama theory is published with *La Veuve*.
1634–1635	*Médée* (1639), his first tragedy.
1635	*La Comédie des Tuileries* (1638), written by a team called the Five Authors, organized by Cardinal Richelieu, who work according to subjects proposed by their patron. This is their only project in which Corneille is known for certain to have participated.
1635–1636	*L'Illusion comique* (1639).

1637   *Le Cid* (1637), a tragicomedy, plays to packed houses. Letters of nobility are granted to Corneille's father. *La Querelle du Cid* begins with published critiques by the playwrights Mairet and Scudéry. Richelieu declares that the newly formed (1635) French Academy will judge the play's merit. *Les Sentiments de l'Académie française sur la tragi-comédie du Cid* appear in December. Corneille wants to reply, but Richelieu forbids it.

1638   Louis XIV is born.

1639   Corneille's father dies. Corneille becomes the guardian of his sister Marthe and his brother Thomas (b. 1625), who eventually became a successful dramatist in his own right.

1640   Corneille's first "classical" tragedy, *Horace* (1641).

1641   Corneille marries Marie de Lampérière, a young woman of the upper bourgeoisie.

1642   The tragedy *Cinna ou la clémence d'Auguste* (1643) is a great success. The first of Corneille's seven children, Marie, is born. Richelieu dies.

1642–1643   Premiere of *Polyeucte martyr* (1643), Corneille's first attempt at Christian tragedy. This completes the tetralogy of his four plays most famous today (*Le Cid, Horace, Cinna, Polyeucte*).

1643   Louis XIII dies. Regency of Anne of Austria, with Mazarin as prime minister.

1643–1644   The tragedy *La Mort de Pompée* (1644) and the comedy *Le Menteur* (1644).

1644   The first collection of Corneille's plays (eight) is published.

1644–1645   *La Suite du Menteur* (1645), Corneille's last true comedy, and *Rodogune, princesse des Parthes* (1647).

1645   Corneille collaborates in *Les Triomphes de Louis le Juste* (1649), a propaganda work.

1645–1646   Corneille's last Christian tragedy, *Théodore, vierge et martyre* (1646).

1646–1647   *Héraclius, empéreur d'Orient* (1647), a tragedy.

1647   Corneille is elected to the French Academy, on his third attempt.

1648   New edition of the collected theater (16 plays). Beginning of the Fronde, with the revolt of the Paris Parliament against Mazarin.

1649   Royal troops lay siege to Paris; a peace treaty is signed in March. *Les Triomphes de Louis le Juste* is published.

1649–1650   *Don Sanche d'Aragon,* Corneille's first heroic comedy (1650).

1650   The machine play, *Andromède* (1651). Several princes are arrested, as the Fronde gains new life among the nobility. Corneille is appointed to an important government office in Rouen. As a result, he sells the office he has held since 1628, only to have his new post taken from him after the Fronde is over. Thomas Corneille marries Pierre's sister-in-law. The two households live communally.

1651   The tragedy *Nicomède* (1651) reminds the public of Condé, the opponent of Mazarin. Translation of part of *L'Imitation de Jésus-Christ,* the fifteenth-century Latin poem.

1651–1652   After *Pertharite, roi des Lombards* (1653) is a failure, Corneille retires from the theater until 1658.

1652   Condé leads a renewed revolt of the nobility against the monarchy.

1653   The Fronde is over, with Mazarin's triumph.

1656   *L'Imitation* is published in its entirety, an enormous success. Corneille begins work on the 1660 edition of his theater, which will contain his theory of drama.

1658   While Molière's troop is in Rouen, Corneille and his brother Thomas pay court to the actress "Marquise" du Parc. Their poetry inspired by her is published in 1660.

1659   Corneille returns to the theater with *Oedipe* (1659), his *Oedipus,* written at the behest of the soon to be disgraced finance minister, Nicolas Fouquet.

1660   *La Conquête de la Toison d'or* (1661), Corneille's second, and last, machine play, is performed as part of the celebrations of the marriage of Louis XIV. The seventh edition of Corneille's theatrical works is published in an edition that includes the *Trois Discours* and the *Examens,* a critical commentary on each play.

1661   *La Toison d'or* is a hit in Paris, where it plays for an entire year. Mazarin dies. Louis XIV will govern without a chief minister. Fouquet is arrested.

1662   The tragedy *Sertorius* (1662). Corneille and his brother Thomas move from Rouen to Paris.

1663   *Sophonisbe* (1663). A quarrel erupts between Corneille and the Abbé d'Aubignac. A luxury edition of Corneille's theater is published. Louis XIV begins his annual payments to authors who celebrate his reign: Corneille receives 2,000 *livres* per year from 1663 until 1674.

1664   The tragedy *Othon* (1665). The ninth edition of Corneille's collected theater. Corneille's letters of nobility are revoked, along with all those accorded after 1630.

1665   Corneille's translation of the *Louanges de la Sainte Vierge.* Noble status is restored. Racine's second play, *Alexandre,* is a great success.

1666   The tragedy *Agésilas* (1666), a box office failure.

1667   The tragedy *Attila, roi des Huns* (1667). Corneille defends the morality of the theater in the preface.

1668   The first published comparison with Racine, by Corneille's supporter Saint-Evremond.

1669   Corneille's translation from the Latin of the *Office de la Sainte Vierge.* Racine's *Britannicus* (1670). The hostilities between Corneille and the young dramatist become heated. Racine's preface is highly critical of Corneille.

1670   Both Corneille's heroic comedy *Tite et Bérénice* (1671) and Racine's tragedy *Bérénice* (1671) premiere within a week of each other in November.

1671   The tragicomedy/ballet *Psyché* (1671), a collaboration of Molière, Quinault, and Corneille.

1672   Corneille's last heroic comedy, *Pulchérie* (1673).

1674   Corneille's last play, the tragedy *Suréna, général des Parthes* (1675).

1675   Corneille's pension is revoked, although four of his plays are performed for the Court.

1676   Five of Corneille's tragedies are performed for the king at Versailles. Racine's new preface to *Britannicus* is published, written without the invective against Corneille.

1678   Corneille asks that his royal pension be restored. He apparently receives no response.

1682   The last edition of his theater corrected by his own hand appears.

1683   Corneille's royal pension is finally restored.

1684   Pierre Corneille dies, 1 October.

1685   Racine welcomes Thomas Corneille into his brother's seat at the French Academy. Racine's speech recognizes Corneille's contribution to French letters. Corneille's nephew, Fontenelle, publishes the first version of his biography of his uncle.

Chapter One
A Life of Distinction

A Living Theater

The life of Pierre Corneille spans the seventeenth century. Born in 1606, he began writing plays in the 1620s, at a moment when the theater in France was on the threshold of an extraordinary expansion. Drama was to become the dominant literary genre of the golden age of French literature. In the Grand Siècle, or splendid century, as it is still known, Corneille was the first giant of the stage, with over 30 plays to his credit. By the time of his death in 1684, his place in the literary canon was firmly fixed, but his moments of glory had passed. A rather negative tone infuses a biography by his nephew Fontenelle, who tells us that although Corneille was the father of French theater, by the 1670s his fame had been justifiably overshadowed by the rise of his young rival, Jean Racine.[1]

Despite the eighteenth-century tendency to judge Corneille's corpus harshly, his works have been read and staged continually since his time. Generations of students and theatergoers have been exposed to Cornelian theater, but with emphasis on a mere four plays out of his vast oeuvre. The tetralogy (*Le Cid, Horace, Cinna ou la clémence d'Auguste, Polyeucte martyr*) covers only the years from 1637 to 1643. Although the impact of these tragedies was enormous, the decades since World War II have seen a revival of interest in the entirety of the Cornelian corpus. Literary critics, mining these riches, have inspired directors to explore texts that were long neglected.[2]

The fascination of Corneille's theater lies in basic psychology. It studies how human beings, ordinary and extraordinary, react to seemingly overwhelming challenges. In the tragedies that make up the majority of the corpus, the royal heroes are enmeshed in political dilemmas, but politics cannot be separated from family conflict and intimate relations. The problems confronted and explored remain relevant even in a twentieth-century Anglophone world. Imposing a global view on a large and complex set of works runs the risk of oversimplification, but a dominant theme can be heard from Corneille's earliest comedies until his final tragedy in 1674. The intense desire for distinction is a characteristic of all of his heroes and heroines. To become exceptional, out of the ordinary, is a driving force behind sublime acts of courage or brutality. The tragedy for these characters occurs when the mark of distinction is withheld, whether by society or by an intimate's refusal to accord the longed-for status. Corneille explores the various tensions that erupt as human aspiration meets human frailty in oneself and in others.

Corneille's theater can stand alone, well apart from the life of the playwright, whose intentions in writing each play we can only guess at. Nevertheless, most of us share a sometimes prurient curiosity about the lives of authors, as witnessed by the rise in popularity of literary biography in recent years.[3] Corneille's life is not one of high drama, but his personal preoccupations, pleasures, and traumas do shed some light on the themes developed in his works.

The Provincial Lawyer in Paris

Pierre Corneille was an ambitious man, but international success as a playwright could not have been predicted from his modest origins. Although his native Rouen, with its rich educational and cultural offerings, was France's third largest city at the time, Paris was the center of the French literary and political world; triumph in the capital was the only path to glory.[4] The geographical challenge was minor compared to the social one. The Corneille family was in the middle range of the bourgeoisie, climbing the social ladder but not well connected. As would have been typical for members of their class, Pierre's grandfather and father had purchased relatively minor offices in public works in the administration governed by the provincial parliament, while they also continued to add to their real estate holdings (Couton 1969, 5–6). Corneille's father obtained two public works offices for his eldest son in 1628, after Pierre was awarded his law degree.[5] The family's social fortunes were mounting but still quite modest. Therefore, the fact that Corneille was ennobled in 1637 thanks to his success in the theater is all the more striking. Indeed, Louis XIII's ennobling of an artist was unprecedented, and the extension of the letters of nobility to Corneille's father made the honor even more significant.[6] But what could achieved noble status mean in a society in which birth was the main source of social identity?

Pierre Corneille's social situation was painfully ambiguous. He was certainly not accepted as an aristocrat by the feudal nobility of the sword, but even the nobility of the robe, which had grown out of the class of lawyers and magistrates, did not see him as one of their own. Corneille treated nobility as a reward for contributing to the king's glory in a system of exchange: value added to the monarchy deserves recognition in this nontraditional, bourgeois view.[7] To compound the problem, Fontenelle tells us that his uncle was rather awkward socially (25). Corneille had been a stutterer as well, which would help to explain his lack of success in the Parisian salon world. Corneille was sought after by the young courtiers of Louis XIII and was the toast of Paris after his first play, the comedy *Mélite,* debuted in 1629 (Fumaroli, 23). But after his theatrical triumphs of the 1630s, Corneille avoided the Parisian nobility and the salons, expressing bitterness over his lack of social recognition in the capital (Couton 1969, 87–91). An example of Corneille's ambition and shaky social status occurred after his best-known play, *Le Cid,* captured the hearts of Parisians in 1637. Corneille's stunning success had inspired a literary quarrel, one of the most famous quarrels in a century full of heated literary controversies. Corneille's own declaration of his superiority was one of the elements to set off *La Querelle du Cid.* In a poem entitled "L'Excuse à Ariste," Corneille had declared, "It is I to whom I owe my fame, and no one else."[8] Milorad Margitic points out that this was not mere hubris: "By glorifying his personal merit, Corneille is publicly displaying his pride in being a bourgeois. Such behavior in itself is scandalous enough in a highly hierarchic society such as that of seventeenth-century France, where commoners are expected to show modesty appropriate to their humble origins and their low social status." But Corneille compounds the scandal by promoting accomplishment over birth as a source of social recognition.[9] Corneille's audacity combined with the professional jealousy of his rivals led to literary tracts for and against the play and almost to a beating. Corneille was humiliated by a nobleman who had the social and legal right to physically attack a nonaristocrat in order to punish what was seen as the playwright's vainglory.[10]

This was not the only humiliation Corneille would have to suffer in his dealings with Paris. His delicate relations with Cardinal Richelieu led first to praise, as the minister made Corneille one of his group of "Five Authors" who wrote collective plays using the cardinal's topics from 1635 to 1638. Richelieu also accorded a pension to Corneille, who, in turn, praised the cardinal in several poems and in the dedication to the tragedy *Horace* (1641). Richelieu was no doubt responsible for ennobling his protégé, and he even helped to arrange Corneille's marriage (*OC,*

1:1554–55). And yet Corneille was extremely bitter when the cardinal
insisted that the French Academy, founded by Richelieu in 1635, pass
judgment on *Le Cid* in order to put an end to the quarrel. Corneille fero-
ciously resented the academy's criticisms, but Richelieu's insistence that
the quarrel end and that Corneille not reply left the author bitter for
decades to come (*OC*, 1:1461-66).[11] Corneille's own entrance into the
academy came in 1647 only after three attempts (Couton 1969, 107).

With the death of Richelieu in 1642, Corneille found himself without
a royal pension. After the death of Louis XIII in 1643, the playwright's
courting of the new regime eventually led to the restoration of his
income (Couton 1969, 106). It is a sign of Corneille's bourgeois approach
to life that money was to him the primary symbol of success, more
important than his doubtful nobility. Indeed, his concern with financial
gain was a subject of mockery for his contemporaries, and theatrical
companies, booksellers, and even some of those to whom his plays were
dedicated noted his extremely shrewd business dealings (Couton 1969,
86). With a lawyer's approach to the business of theater, he prepared a
legal document to try to protect his literary property, a move unheard of
at the time (Fumaroli, 32–33). He held onto his administrative offices in
Normandy for 23 years, selling these very middle-class posts only in
1650, and then in the hope of obtaining a more prestigious administrative position (Couton 1969, 136). An assured income afforded him relative liberty, as shown by the dedications of his works to various sponsors.
His cessation of dedications after 1659 suggests even more firmly held
financial independence in his later years.

Political upheaval in France had always had a disastrous effect on the
theater, with its need for public participation. The expansion of the
genre during Richelieu's years in power was made possible by the relative political and social stability established by the cardinal after years of
internal turmoil caused by the sixteenth-century religious wars. Thanks
to Richelieu's active encouragement of an art form well suited to political propaganda, Louis XIII's Paris became the birthplace of French theater. Nonetheless, Richelieu's political and artistic legacy was mixed: the
feudal nobility was especially displeased with the cardinal's successful
moves toward a more centralized government, and the repercussions of
their resentment would be felt strongly during the late 1640s and
1650s, well after his death. The roots of Louis XIV's absolutism are
found in Richelieu's machinations: the eventual revolt of the nobility
followed by the monarchy's triumph set the stage for the Sun King and
made him determined to retain the upper hand. The years between

1642 and the beginning of Louis's personal reign in 1661 were turbulent ones for France and for Pierre Corneille.

Louis XIV's mother, Anne of Austria, became regent and appointed another Catholic cardinal, the Italian Giulio Mazarini, as her first minister. Anne and Mazarin, as he was known in France, were widely considered to be lovers, leading the already hostile French nobility to complain that corrupt foreigners were at the helm. The Paris Parliament was equally displeased with the couple, and an uprising in 1648 signaled the beginning of the Fronde, a civil war that lasted five years. The 1648–1649 theatrical season was canceled, but Corneille's name was still before the public since he had written extensive commentary for *Les Triomphes de Louis le Juste,* a propaganda tract for Mazarin. His pension was also made public at this time, and in 1650 Anne accorded him the title of *procureur des états* (the chief tax collector) for Normandy, a reward for his loyalty to the crown. The 1649–1650 theatrical season saw the performance of Corneille's musical machine play, *Andromède,* which he had written at the behest of Mazarin and which sought to demonstrate that the regime was in control and that happy times had returned. During the same season, Corneille's *Don Sanche d'Aragon* depicted a queen facing down the nobility in revolt (Couton 1969, 128–31). The public's hostility toward Anne and Mazarin was augmented by Mazarin's harsh treatment of the royal princes who were leading the revolt. The Prince de Condé was at the head of the disaffected aristocracy, and his imprisonment with threats of exile or even death from Mazarin moved the people against the cardinal. A coalition formed around Condé forced Mazarin into exile, whereupon Corneille, seemingly in response to these developments, produced *Nicomède* in 1651. A hero closely resembling Condé helped to make the play a smashing success. Corneille seemed to be at last on the side of the rebellious majority, but his former loyalty to the crown would not go unpunished. Corneille had sacrificed his other posts for half their value in order to obtain the office of *procureur,* but it was returned to its original holder, who then sued Corneille for his lost salary (Couton 1969, 134–36). Some bitterness on Corneille's part would be understandable after this affair. It was, however, only the beginning of a difficult period for the dramatist. He appeared to change sides once again, following public opinion that turned against Condé after the prince allied himself with France's enemies, Spain and Cromwell's England. Corneille's *Pertharite* in the 1651–1652 season shows a usurper who sees the error of his ways and returns his throne to the true monarch. *Pertharite* was the worst failure of Corneille's career, so abysmal a defeat that the playwright retired from the theater. Georges Couton speculates that the ethic of glory portrayed in the play simply did not fit the black mood of Paris at the end of the Fronde (1969, 137–39). In his letter to the reader upon the publication of *Pertharite,* Corneille explains with crankiness that he has become too old to be in fashion any longer and that he will leave the scene voluntarily before he is ousted against his will (*OC,* 2:715).

Corneille returned triumphant in 1659 with a new version of the Oedipus myth at the invitation of the powerful finance minister Fouquet (Couton 1969, 149). Fouquet was the most important patron of the arts since Richelieu, but the minister's arrest for treason in 1661 was the first of several shadows cast over the 1660s for Corneille; the venerated playwright was never to be sheltered from social humiliation. When one of his daughters was engaged to a minor nobleman in 1661, the aristocrat's family threatened not to attend this wedding with a social inferior (Couton 1980, xviii). In 1664 all letters of nobility issued since 1630 were automatically revoked, and although Corneille's noble status was restored the following year, this incident was one more indication of the precarious nature of his ascension on the social ladder. With Anne of Austria's death in 1666, it became apparent that the elderly playwright was no longer appreciated by the young court of Louis XIV, who preferred the work of his rival Jean Racine. Corneille could take comfort in the fact that he was awarded a retainer by the crown in 1663; the list of those receiving monetary bonuses was reviewed annually as a method of ensuring that writers continued to sing the praises of Louis XIV (Couton 1969, 159). The removal of Corneille's name from the list in 1675, the year after his last play, *Suréna,* was a blow hardly assuaged by its restoration in 1684, just before his death. Nevertheless, he did not give up the good fight. In 1676 he portrayed himself as a heroic warrior whose service to the king was just as valuable as that performed by his sons in the army (Viala, 203).

Had Corneille looked back to the beginning of the seventeenth century, he would have remembered that Alexandre Hardy was the dominant dramatist in France at the time. The social accomplishments of Corneille are illustrated by Hardy's inability to extract any social mobility at all from his career as a playwright. Corneille was the first Frenchman to achieve solid social and financial recognition from the theater (Fumaroli, 22–23). Despite the ambiguity of his noble status, his accomplishments can be considered worthy of one of his own heroes, who manage to transform even the most painful situations into moral victories.

Literary Combat

In 1660 the playwright looked back at his first play, the comedy *Mélite,* the hit of the 1629–1630 season in Paris. Corneille noted proudly that he had given the world a new type of comedy, original in its replacement of stock comic characters with cultivated young city dwellers whose elegant conversations about love and marriage replaced the buffooneries of traditional farce. The problem with the play from a distance of 30 years was its irregularity. In 1660 French theater had been imbued with the rules of composition that helped to form the neoclassical aesthetic for which seventeenth-century France is known (*OC,* 1:5 –8). Corneille tells us that he was ignorant of the rules of classical composition, and for good reason. It was only during the 1630s that these rules came to be established in French theater as a new generation of poets and critics began to produce dozens of plays and commentaries on the theater.

The political stability offered by Richelieu was accompanied by a move toward order in the arts, directed in large part by the cardinal himself (Couton 1969, 111). The chaos of the late sixteenth century was replaced by the rule of law in all aspects of French life, and theater as the most public of art forms was subject to particular surveillance. For Corneille, the imposition of rules adopted from Aristotle's *Poetics* represented a threat of constraint and rigidity against which he struggled throughout his career. The unities of time, place, and action, as well as the very French notion of verisimilitude, were treated very differently by theoreticians of drama as opposed to the working playwright, and Corneille always insisted on the need for flexibility in the practical interpretation of these rules.[12] His second play, *Clitandre* (first performed during the 1630–1631 season), forced him to confront the problem. An adventure-filled tragicomedy, *Clitandre*'s originality was as much a source of pride for Corneille as *Mélite*'s had been. Writing in 1632, Corneille admits that the plot is so complicated that it may be difficult for the spectator to follow the action, but at least events in the play are limited to 24 hours. He knows the rules now, he says, yet his attitude toward them remains belligerent: he may or may not choose to respect their strictures in the future. He will take the liberty of flouting the Ancients when he feels he can create pleasing effects, since progress in the arts as in the sciences is possible: Aristotle and Horace should not be given the last word on theatrical composition (*OC,* 1:94–96). At a time when these rules were still in the process of being integrated into French dramatic practice, Corneille's remarks were not revolutionary. Nonetheless, this early declaration captures the tone he would always maintain. Even as he came to accept the taste of the majority of critics and, eventually, spectators who supported the classical view, Corneille continued to tout his own originality and independence.

With the rebirth of tragedy in the 1630s, the influence of the theoreticians was solidified. Tragedy was the most noble genre and as such demanded stricter forms. Corneille's first tragedy, *Médée* (Medea), was performed during the 1634–1635 season. Even though *Médée* was his most "regular" play so far, in it Corneille manipulated the rules even as he incorporated them. In the dedication (1639), he makes explicit what for him would always be the fundamental rule of dramatic composition: to please the spectator. The rules for Corneille existed only in service to this fundamental goal (*OC,* 1:535–36). He would always seek success with the public first, then attempt to legitimize his work using his own interpretation of the Ancients.

Corneille's reputation for independence was seen by some as simple vanity, an accusation augmented by his proud remarks in the "Excuse à Ariste" poem at the time of the *Querelle du Cid* in 1637. The number and vituperative tone of the documents on both sides of this quarrel are striking (see Gasté for a collection of a number of these tracts). Despite the dislike inspired by Corneille's haughty attitude, however, the quarrel was not mainly personal: it concerned serious issues of classical doctrine. *Le Cid* was a tragicomedy, a designation changed to tragedy by Corneille in 1648. The critics asked how the most popular play of the decade could show so little respect for the unities of time, place, and action. How could a subject so morally unacceptable as a young woman agreeing to marry the murderer of her father be allowed to triumph on the French stage? Moreover, Corneille's rival Georges de Scudéry accused him of plagiarism, since Corneille had modeled his play on a Spanish original (Gasté, 103–11). The irregularities of *Le Cid* were many, and Corneille's basic defense was the play's popularity. His reply was to ask how a work that brought crowds into the theater could be considered fundamentally defective. The French Academy cleared Corneille of plagiarism but condemned his other infractions, leaving the author with the simmering anger against all his critics that we see expressed in his correspondence of the time (*OC,* 1:804–8). Corneille would bide his time at Richelieu's order, but in publishing an edition of his complete works in 1648, the playwright justified his practice as he had been doing since the preface of *Clitandre* in 1632 and as he would continue to do.

It was during his retirement from the theater from 1651 to 1659 that Corneille had the leisure to develop fully his considerations on dramatic theory. The *Trois Discours* (Three Discourses), a new edition of his theater, and analyses of all his previous plays were published in 1660, just after Corneille had reentered the theatrical world with his *Oedipe* (Oedipus). These documents are remarkable not only for the virtuosity with which Corneille addresses the problems associated with the classical rules but also for their tone.[13] Corneille becomes the hero of his own version of the story of the development of classicism in France, proving his critics wrong by returning to the texts of Aristotle and Horace and interpreting them in a very personal and original manner. The drive for distinction that I consider characteristic of the Cornelian hero can be seen clearly in the *Discours*. As in the plays, distinction can be achieved only through performance of exceptional feats, the quality of which must be judged by spectators or, in the case of the theoretical writings, readers. In the Cornelian dramatic universe, one is exceptional only insofar as a public labels one's conduct exceptional. Corneille the theoretician, like Corneille the playwright and like the Cornelian hero, presses active involvement on his audience and asks for their approbation. In the *Discours,* Corneille's heroic performance leads him first to dissect the writings of the Ancients, then to redefine and reconstruct them according to the needs of his theater. While insisting that he follows Aristotle, Horace, and their disciples closely, he transforms their writings in such a way as to justify every choice made in the construction of his plays, using them as authorities. Yet it is Corneille who emerges as the definitive authority. His contemporaries are shown to be rigid and unnecessarily limiting in their interpretation of the Ancients. Corneille claims to be the only theoretician who truly understands them (Carlin 1990, 55–70).

No doubt the powerful accumulation of his ideas on theatrical composition helped Corneille realize that he still had a contribution to make to the French stage. The trauma of *Pertharite*'s failure had passed, and Corneille had confirmed for himself the value of his own aesthetic. In a recent book on Cornelian theater, the French scholar Georges Forestier posits the notion of the sublime as its central principle.[14] The perfection of tragedy in Corneille's sense relies on the artistic perfection of violence, according to Forestier; the sublime implies beauty and grandeur based on exceptional, often shocking conduct, necessarily extreme, and capable of provoking admiration in the spectator, whatever the character's moral qualities (275). This convincing perspective will be examined further as the individual plays are discussed, but it should be noted that Forestier's views on tragedy can be extended with minor adjustment to the entirety of Corneille's corpus, including his theoretical writings. One of the basic rules of the classical aesthetic, that of verisimilitude or plausibility (*vraisemblance* with its corollary *bienséance,* or decorum), stressed the necessity to avoid shocking the audience. That which conforms to the rule of verisimilitude conforms to preexistent public opinion. Even the authority of history was insufficient to justify the portrayal or even the discussion of morally unacceptable acts onstage such as the possibility that Chimène, the heroine of *Le Cid,* might marry the man who killed her father. As Forestier points out, the Cornelian approach to tragedy could not have been further from the theory of verisimilitude held by the majority of theoreticians (277). Corneille was an extremist, on the cutting edge of his profession. He paid the price for his daring in heavy criticism, but he also reaped the rewards that come from capturing the imagination of the public.

Corneille's return to the theater resulted in 10 more plays, almost one-third of his total theatrical output. The years between 1659 and 1674 contained both successes and failures for the aging playwright. A glorious moment was the appearance of a luxurious in-folio edition of his theater in 1663, a format normally reserved for the Greek and Latin classics. More important, however, was the irritant in the late 1660s of the emergence of Jean Racine as a serious rival. Comparative analysis of the theater of Corneille and Racine has drawn critics since Saint-Evremond initiated the comparison in 1666; it continues to this day. Saint-Evremond developed his attack on Racine in 1668 by praising Corneille's authentic depiction of the heroes of antiquity, as opposed to Racine's inability to capture Greco-Roman virtue and his fixation on the tender expression of uncontrollable love (*OC,* 3:1578–81). Corneille quite obviously criticized Racine without naming him in his reply to Saint-Evremond (*OC,* 3:725–26), and this was only the beginning of attacks and counterattacks on the part of Corneille and his young challenger. Racine's first preface to *Britannicus* (1670) was particularly aggressive in its negative evaluation of Cornelian tragedy. The rivalry became even more intense in late 1670 when Racine's *Bérénice* debuted just one week prior to Corneille's *Tite et Bérénice.* Racine won this contest easily, and Corneille's defeat was confirmed in 1671 when his next play, *Pulchérie,* was turned down by the two most important theatrical troops in Paris, Molière's and the Hôtel de Bourgogne. When a declining com-

pany, the Marais, took on *Pulchérie* in 1672, it was a great success, but
this success did not erase the humiliation of being replaced by Racine as
the dominant author of tragedy in France.

The apogee of Corneille's fame had passed, but he remained proud of
the last segment of his theater and defended it spiritedly in a 1676 poem
addressed to Louis XIV, who had had five of Corneille's plays performed
at Versailles during that year (*OC,* 3:1313). Corneille's biographer
Georges Couton calls the last 10 years of Corneille's life "the empty
years" (1969, 192).[15] While it is true that Corneille experienced a sad
lack of recognition from the literary establishment during that time,
there was renewed interest in his tragedies in the 1680s, after Racine
had stopped producing for the theater. The elderly Corneille continued
to write poetry and letters and even revise his plays as late as 1682. His
last two years were a period of physical and mental decline, but his work
would live on for his critics and partisans alike.

In yet another literary quarrel raging during the seventeenth century,
the quarrel between the "Ancients" and the "Moderns," Corneille was
resolutely in the camp of the Moderns. His stated opinion of 1632 that
improvement on Aristotle's theories was possible never changed. His
daring allowed him to experiment with more theatrical genres than
most dramatists of the century. His invention of a new sort of modern
French comedy in the 1630s was followed by particularly Cornelian
brands of tragicomedy and tragedy, to say nothing of his musical
machine plays and completely new forms of theater such as the "heroic
comedy" he created in the 1650s. Corneille's theater survived the acer-
bic remarks of Voltaire in the eighteenth century and the almost complete disappearance for two centuries of both his youthful comedies and
the late tragedies and heroic comedies. Versatility and audacity characterize the oeuvre of this man of distinction.

The Wounded Lover

Corneille is known more for his dynamic heroes than for the portrait of
lovers in his theater. Indeed, the stereotypical contrast with Racine that
has been handed down to us since the seventeenth century emphasizes
the latter's more successful, more modern depiction of amorous passion. To oversimplify the contrast, while Racine's lovers are dominated
by an uncontrollable love, Corneille's couples are often able to disci-
pline their feelings with attention to other interests, be they familial or
political. Nevertheless, love plays an enormous part in Cornelian the-

ater. Indeed, it was his first love at 16 that inspired Corneille to become a playwright.

Couton has discovered the name (Catherine Hue) and probable cause of Corneille's disappointment in his first relationship; although they were both members of the bourgeoisie, Pierre was Catherine's social inferior, and marriage was out of the question (Couton 1980, xiii–xv). Corneille states clearly in "L'Excuse à Ariste" that trying to express this love was his impetus for learning to write first poetry then plays (OC, 1:780–81). Fontenelle confirms the story, adding that Catherine was known as "Mélite" in Rouen after the success of Corneille's first play (22). The sweet sentiments of the young man's love poetry gave way to more complicated emotions when he began writing for the theater. In all five of Corneille's comedies from 1629 to 1634, a certain harshness infuses stories of young couples in search of love. The primary obstacle to their union is not the strict father of Roman and Italian classical comedy but rather the lovers' own ambivalent feelings and inability to fix upon a single love object. Financial considerations also enter into the plots of most of these comic plays, suggesting a social realism that combines with emotional realism to create an almost bitter atmosphere at times.

Another event in Corneille's personal life may have contributed to his concern with the way in which social status affected relationships. In love again in 1641 and wishing to marry Marie de Lampérière, he was once more rejected on the grounds of social and economic inferiority. It was only thanks to Richelieu's intervention that Marie's father was forced to accept Corneille as a son-in-law (Couton 1980, xvii–xviii). Almost nothing is known about the Corneilles' married life. The couple did produce seven children, most of whom survived to adulthood, and the household took in Pierre's two youngest siblings, Thomas and Marthe, as well (Couton 1969, 85). Corneille's closest domestic relationship was with Thomas, who followed in his elder brother's footsteps as a successful dramatist.[16] They often traveled to Paris to oversee the production of their plays and profit from the diversion of the capital, moving there together in 1662.

Corneille was inevitably involved with the politics of Parisian theatrical companies, including Molière's. A company retained exclusive rights to a play until it was published, causing tension between playwrights and actors, and Molière and Corneille found themselves at loggerheads on more than one occasion, to the extent that they exchanged insults in print (Couton 1969, 157–58). Corneille was at ease with actors, and flirting with actresses was a favorite game for this man who performed so awkwardly in Parisian salons (Couton 1969, 89). One flirtation in particular has reached us consecrated in verse. The object of Corneille's adoration was Thérèse du Parc, known as "Marquise," an actress Corneille would have met in 1658 when Molière's company was in Rouen. Corneille apparently convinced Du Parc and her husband to join a rival company in Paris, and this may have been the origin of the dispute between Molière and Corneille. Corneille was sufficiently smitten by the 25-year-old Du Parc to write and publish love poetry dedicated to her in 1660. Written while he was in his fifties, this interlude represented a true midlife crisis for the playwright, whose amorous advances were not returned (Couton 1969, 148). There was a positive result to this adventure: yet another disappointment in love had an immediate effect on the expression of love in the plays performed when Corneille came out of retirement in 1659. Corneille's last published poem to Marquise appeared in 1677, although it was apparently written between 1664 and 1668 (*OC,* 3:1698–99). "Je suis vieux, belle Iris" (I am old, beautiful Iris) is a charming plea for understanding; do not place me in the same category as all the other admirers you mock, begs the text (*OC,* 3:1315). The aging playwright had the opportunity to renew his acquaintance with Marquise in 1667 when she starred in *Attila,* but the birth of her daughter by Jean Racine in 1667 or 1668 must have been a blow to Corneille's normally healthy ego (*OC,* 3:1699–1700).

Corneille's last recorded amorous adventure took place in 1671, when Molière and Corneille collaborated on the tragicomedy and ballet *Psyché* for a command performance at Versailles. Corneille wrote the majority of the work's charming poetry, apparently inspired by his passion for Molière's wife, Armande, who played the lead role (Couton 1969, 178). At the age of 65, Corneille may have been considered less of a love poet than Racine, but sentiment was never absent from his work.

The delicate sensibility demonstrated in all 10 of Corneille's last plays and his poetry of the time help to illustrate that literary influences had always combined with events in his personal emotional life to produce a nuanced language of love. This was already visible in the early comedies. Despite Corneille's justifiable insistence on their originality, these complex works resonate with the influence of two related literary movements of the time, the pastoral (in novel and theater) and *précieux* poetry, both characterized by the delicate exploration of the sentiments surrounding budding love.[17] In the 1650s, Corneille, along with the rest of the French literary world, was exposed to the movement known as *la préciosité*. Linguistically, *la préciosité* shared with the "precious" poetry of the beginning of the century an emphasis on refinement in the choice of images, a distancing from explicit discussion of the body, and the repetition of certain poetic conceits such as love as a burning flame or the eyes of the beloved as pools in which to lose oneself. *La préciosité* brought a social dimension to the discussion of male-female relations that intrigued Corneille greatly.[18] It was during the 1650s that he became linked with Michel de Pure, whose novel *La Prétieuse* discusses the humiliating treatment of women in the marriage market, where they are objects of economic exchange. Without suggesting that Corneille espoused the novel's radical view that women be liberated from the constraints of marriage, the solution of platonic love outside marriage discussed in De Pure's novel and in the novels of Madeleine de Scudéry did seem to appeal to the playwright, especially given his harsh experience of the economic realities associated with marriage (Couton 1969, 146). Platonic love for unmarried couples is proposed as an ideal in several of his late plays, such as *Agésilas* (1665–1666), *Othon* (1666–1667), *Tite et Bérénice* (1670–1671), and *Pulchérie* (1671–1672). Particularly touching is the portrait in *Pulchérie* of an elderly man in love, tortured by jealousy, who represses resentment in favor of a pure, undemanding adoration of the object of his desire. Fontenelle claims that this depiction is autobiographical (25).

The theme of marriage as a sacrifice to politics occurs in these plays as well as in Corneille's last play, *Suréna* (1674–1675). The possibility of platonic love makes the sacrifice of a loveless marriage bearable for several of Corneille's heroes and heroines during this period. A new ethic appears in Cornelian theater after 1659. There is more emphasis on personal happiness for the royal protagonists of these tragedies than can be seen in his plays before the "retirement" of the 1650s. The many possible reasons for this shift will be discussed when we examine these plays, but changes in public sensibility, in political life, the rivalry with Racine, and the aging process all represent possible partial explanations of a new direction for Corneille.

Decline and disappointment haunted Corneille's final years. Not only did he face the dismal failure of certain of his plays (*Agésilas* and *Tite et Bérénice* were particularly badly received), he also met with personal tragedy. Two of his sons died (in 1665 and 1674), and his close relationship with his brother Thomas seems to have ended on a sour note. It was only at the end of Corneille's life that the split occurred, sometime between 1681 and 1683 (Couton 1969, 195). Although we do not know what caused the break, we do know that Corneille's last months were spent in a sad isolation. Even fraternal love wounded him in the end.

Although the final phase of Corneille's career was clouded by the loss of prestige and of close relations, one of the major themes of his work at this time suggests the sustaining support of his religious faith. The theme of sacrifice is present from the early comedies on, but in the last 10 plays, it moves to the forefront in his treatment of the problem of marriage as a political tool, devastating to individual desire. The willingness of characters to experience personal sacrifice without material compensation is a distinguishing characteristic in the contrast between Corneille and Racine. Racinian protagonists are never capable of the kind of sublimation we see in Corneille's plays. The influence of Catholicism in Corneille's work is clear, and his interpretation of religious themes is very different from that of his younger rival.

The Triumph of Faith

Corneille was educated at Rouen's Jesuit college, and these formidable educators had a lifelong effect on their pupil, who went so far as to dedicate the 1660 edition of his theater to them. The Society of Jesus had made dramatic inroads into the field of education since the founding of the order by Loyola in 1556, but the Jesuit curriculum proved to be increasingly controversial in seventeenth-century France, mainly because of disputes over doctrine with their most ferocious Catholic enemies, the Jansenists.[19] Corneille's positions when arguing with the Jansenists and other critics of the morality of the theater as well as his differences with Racine over the conception of tragedy can be seen as the result of his Jesuit formation.

Classical humanism played an important role in the Jesuit program: Latin language, rhetoric, philosophy, and literature absorbed the majority of study time, with the rest given over to theology (Couton 1969, 7–9). Marc Fumaroli has illustrated the profound influence on Corneille of the theatricality of their instructional methods. The study of Latin rhetoric included recitations and dialogues; poetics and logic were instruments for schooling the rhetorician's creative imagination, with emphasis on ornate style and the ability to touch the listener's emotions (Fumaroli 1990, 85–103). In plays written for student actors, the young men were encouraged to experience the passions they portrayed onstage as a means to imbue their performance with verbal energy. The shock of strong emotion, of the experience of the sublime, although within the parameters of a strict decorum, was considered a wholesome activity. Corneille learned from the Jesuits that eloquence is the human mirror of the divine Word and that human love is a reflection of the divine order (Fumaroli 1990, 53, 138). Indeed, from the Jesuit perspective, no passion is in itself condemnable since all passions are essentially a manifestation of divine Love in the soul of the sinner (Fumaroli 1990, 110).

Corneille would have studied Aristotle's *Poetics* from the Jesuit point of view: the hero need not fall from grace if he has worked to merit divine support (Fumaroli 1990, 72–73). This aesthetic is visible in the plays of the greatest Jesuit dramatist, Father Bernardino Stefonio (1562–1620), a direct model for Corneille, according to Fumaroli (1990, 140). His successor, Father Galluzzi, developed a Jesuit conception of Greek tragedy wherein heroes are not victims of fate. Rather, they are admired for the exercise of their liberty in the face of temptation or persecution. Tyrants who victimize the virtuous need not be punished onstage, as divine justice will operate after death where necessary (Fumaroli 1990, 150–51). This is exactly the view taken by Corneille in the *Discours de l'utilité et des parties du poème dramatique* (Discourse on the Usefulness and Parts of the Dramatic Poem) in 1660, a position that was controversial in the context of the debate about the morality of the theater (*OC*, 3:122; Carlin 1990, 56). Corneille's fundamental stance on the question of whether theater should have as its first goal the pleasure of the spectator or moral instruction was clear. Repeatedly in his theoretical writings from 1645 on, Corneille insisted that providing pleasure is the dramatist's paramount goal; moral lessons automatically follow when the play is well conceived (*OC*, 2:95–98, 3:119). One of Corneille's close Jesuit contacts, Father Delidel (to whom Corneille wrote an ode in 1668), insisted that souls can only be converted to Christianity by an attractive appeal. Being touched by grace is pleasurable, in Delidel's description (Fumaroli 1990, 116).

The Jesuit pedagogical practices that so heavily influenced Corneille were still in use in the 1660s, when both Corneille's *Discours* and the Jansenist theologian Pierre Nicole's *Traité de la comédie* (*On Theater,* 1667) were published. Nicole's treatise, along with the less eloquent tracts by the Prince de Conti and Varet in 1666, made the clash of views on the question of the morality of the theater very explicit (see *OC*, 3:1540–41). Nicole's primary example of the problem was the theater of Pierre Corneille. In Cornelian theater (as in Jesuit instructional plays), strong emotion is portrayed, along with the capacity of the protagonists to control or repress such emotion for higher moral ends. The value placed on human liberty and the favorable evaluation of our willpower run counter to the Jansenist insistence on human frailty. The notions that grace can be earned and that achieving it can be a pleasurable process were reprehensible in Nicole's vision of Christianity. Jansenist theology rested on the doctrine of predestination, the belief that grace could not be earned but was instead a gift from God, independent of any human will or action. From the Jansenist perspective, it was extremely presumptuous of a human being, tainted by the original sin of Eve and Adam, to suppose that she or he could achieve any lasting moral victories at all. Corneille's specific transgressions included substituting pagan morality for Christian in his Roman history plays. Corneille's heroes are full of pride hidden under a cloak of Roman virtue and the aristocratic code of honor. His heroes' vanity is especially shocking when religious subjects are depicted onstage: the martyrdom of saints in *Polyeucte martyr* (1642–1643) and *Théodore vierge et martyre* (Theodora, Virgin and Martyr, 1645–1646) is a dangerous topic because Corneille's saints are more heroic than humble. The distance from the Jesuit stance is strongly marked since religious subjects were an essential part of their schoolroom drama. Nicole acknowledges that Corneille's theater was known for its exemplary moral models, which is precisely why he targets it. A condemnation of Cornelian theater meant that all plays were sinful by definition.

Corneille replied to Nicole in the preface of *Attila* in 1667, stating that he would silence the critics of the theater by showing his willingness to submit his work to the authorities, both ecclesiastical and secular, for evaluation of its moral worth. Would his enemies do the same? he asked. After all, a certain group critical of the theater is responsible for the translation of comedies of the Ancient Roman playwright Terence wherein young girls are pregnant out of wedlock, and merchants are selling prostitutes; his plays contain no such improprieties. Moreover, when Corneille portrays love, it is always associated with suffering and is depicted in order to excite pity rather than to encourage amorous adventures. He gives *Le Cid,* his most famous play, as an example: the lovers suffer and are never contented (*OC,* 3:642). These are effective digs at the Jansenists because in 1667 the sect was embroiled in a dispute with both the pope and Louis XIV over its radical position on human versus divine authority, seen as threatening to both sorts of power. The translation of Terence by Le Maistre de Sacy is blamed on the entire sect and seen rather unfairly as emblematic of their hypocrisy (*OC,* 3:1541). The question of love onstage is more delicate. Corneille specifically criticizes "the tenderness of satisfied love" in tragedy. This last remark is pointedly directed at Racine, who portrays lovers in the throes of uncontrollable, always destructive passion. Corneille strikes at his Jansenist enemies along with his rival because Racine's Jansenist background shows up in his theater in a way that Corneille finds potentially morally damaging for susceptible spectators. Satisfied or not, Racinian passion was not tamable, whereas for Corneille, the responsibility that accompanies free will could not be avoided with the excuse of fundamental human weakness.

Racine broke with the Jansenists during his theatrical career, a necessary move given the sect's condemnation of the entire genre. He would renew ties with his former masters on his retirement from the theater, after a mere nine plays, confirming the impression that the influence of Jansenism was always present in his work. In *Morales du grand siècle,* Paul Bénichou proves that a Jansenist sensibility, combined with the reaction of his generation to the absolutism of Louis XIV, infuses Racine's work and helps to explain the contrast with Corneille.[20] Corneille's defense against the Jansenist critique of his work is confined to the brief remarks preceding *Attila,* suggesting that perhaps he was not free of self-questioning in the face of Jansenist theology.

Fontenelle tells us that during the 1660s and until the end of his life, Corneille often consulted Jesuit casuists in order to assure himself that his own pride was not an obstacle to his salvation (25). Indeed, this concern was the impetus for his translation from the Latin of *L'Imitation de Jésus-Christ,* Thomas a Kempis's 1472 meditation on the life of Christ, as Corneille explains in the dedication to Pope Alexander VII (*OC,* 2:789). *L'Imitation* appeared between 1651 and 1656, during Corneille's retirement from the theater, but he had obviously begun the work before the disaster of *Pertharite. L'Imitation* became a best-seller during that troubled time for the country, enhancing Corneille's reputation (Couton 1969, 142)—and increasing his need to worry about his own vainglory. At least one Jesuit theologian had warned against the moral pitfall of worldly success, especially when obtained in God's name (Fumaroli 1990, 74–75). Nonetheless, Corneille's faith continued to express itself in poems and translations, resulting in an output of over 40,000 lines, almost equal to his entire theatrical corpus.[21] His devout Jesuit Catholicism expressed itself in terms of humility only occasionally.

Corneille had much to be proud of. He absorbed every aspect of his century's rich culture, marking it with his personal vision. Fumaroli sees in his writings a meeting of two major inspirations, the Latin intellectual culture of the Jesuits and the French courtly ethic of heroism and love (1990, 31–32, 119). Add to that his concern with contemporary political issues and one has a summary not only of his theater but also of his poetry. All three trends were the subjects of poems by Corneille throughout his life. Pierre Corneille is an obvious representative of the neoclassical culture of seventeenth-century France in all its complexity, as a more detailed study of his works will show.

Triumph through Tragedy

The basic structure of Cornelian theater remains intact throughout his corpus, evolving and full of nuances. The search for distinction on the part of his protagonists can be seen from the early comedies on, but the terms of judgment applied to the hero seeking approbation change markedly with *Le Cid* in 1637. *Le Cid* is still Corneille's most studied work, and as John Lyons puts it, this play "will haunt all subsequent Cornelian tragedy."[22] In *Le Cid,* the heroes have to deal with a radical shift in values, and "the values of the society are determined by changes in the political and social situation, by changes in objective reality" within the world of the play (Lyons 1996, 9). Tragedy occurs for the characters as "men and women are caught in the changes in the social values on which they base their actions and their relationships," relationships that are damaged because of "the human difficulty in adapting to rapid historical change. . . . The structure of Cornelian tragedy is deeply temporal and pits any rigid commitment to a timeless ethos against the corrosive power of social, political, and legal change" (Lyons 1996, 10).

Corneille lived through enormous changes in political, social, and aesthetic standards and found himself on several occasions judged according to new values, a dilemma facing many of his heroes. The tragedy of distinction denied threatened Corneille's career with regularity, but Pierre Corneille never ceased to struggle to achieve the recognition he rightly deserved.

Chapter Two

The Playwright's Apprenticeship, 1629–1635

Comic Structure in Cornelian Theater

When Corneille first published his collected plays in 1644, he began the process of stripping his early works of the very elements that made them original when they were performed in the 1630s. The 1648 and especially the 1660 editions remove familiar speech along with sensual and sexual references, replacing them with the elevated diction and modesty characteristic of classical theater. Corneille was right in 1660 to tout his innovations in comic theater, but his simultaneous censorship of these creations of his youth was unfortunate.[1] Although heavily influenced by the pastorals and tragicomedies popular in the 1620s, Cornelian comedy introduces a note of realism completely absent from these prevalent theatrical genres.

The pastoral no doubt represents the strongest influence on these plays; its popularity had grown steadily ever since Honoré d'Urfé began publishing his five-volume novel, *L'Astrée,* in 1605.[2] Corneille's originality lies primarily in his characters' use of language, which differs from the set pieces of the pastoral. The pastoral's lyrical passages full of flowery rhetoric are not terribly dramatic, containing no real exchange, no dialogue between characters, no material life; the characters are "shepherds" and "shepherdesses" whose rural existence centers not on sheep but on the search for love in a courtly tradition modified by an idyllic fantasy setting. Using thematic elements borrowed from tragicomedy and lowly farce, Corneille's characters discuss the situations in which they find themselves; they speak of money, they allude to their bodies, they sometimes act violently, yet the atmosphere of the pastoral often returns in their breathless examination of love. All of Corneille's plays have five acts and are written in the 12-syllable alexandrines typical of French classical theater, but he experimented widely within formal boundaries. With the variety of tone we find in his comic verse, the playwright invented an original dramatic language. He reinvigorated comedy, which was a moribund genre before Corneille infused it with new life.

Corneille combined several sources in his renewal of comic theater. Besides the pastoral, tragicomedy, and farce, I would add the classical or "New Comedy" inherited from Greco-Roman antiquity, to which he refers in the 1660 *Examen* of *Mélite* (*OC*, 1:6). In my view, the same basic structure persists throughout his theater, and its roots can be found in classical comedy.[3]

In Northrup Frye's landmark study *The Anatomy of Criticism,* four seasonal archetypes are associated with the genres of comedy, irony, tragedy, and romance. The late Canadian critic links comedy with a *mythos* of springtime renewal: society is reborn when a young couple marries after having overcome all obstacles to their union. The principal impediment in comedy is a blocking character, usually a "heavy father" figure. Either the avarice of a parent wishing to marry off a daughter for financial gain or the inappropriate desire of an elderly man to marry a young woman poses a threat to society, whose rebirth depends on the formation of an ideal youthful couple.[4]

In Cornelian comedy, as in the pastoral, the blocking character often comes from within the ranks of youth, complicating Frye's basic comic schema. Potential members of an ideal couple prove themselves to be flawed in some way, by greed or fear or desire so strong that it manifests itself in behavior destructive to the collective good. As in classical comedy, these characters are sometimes reintegrated into society at the end of the play, but sometimes they are expelled as scapegoats whose removal facilitates social cohesion. In either case, society's needs are examined as Corneille experiments with various twists on the traditional ending of a comedy. Questions of money, age, and unsatisfied emotional demands often tint the idealized final scenes with cruelty, but at least one couple always emerges to assure social renewal.[5]

Some of the best-known Corneille critics have found these comedies not terribly gay in tone or have even found them sombre; Octave Nadal, Serge Doubrovsky, Jacques Scherer, and André Stegmann have all downplayed the humor in these plays, viewing them from the perspective of the tragedies.[6] Although I too will develop structural parallels between Corneille's comedies and his tragedies, I insist that his comedies can indeed provoke laughter. The youthful blocking characters are comical in the very intensity of their desire. They are tricksters whose schemes are often extravagant, actors whose role playing is often daring, or sometimes they are simply victims of their own delusions of grandeur. They

are performers, and the spectator (on- and offstage) must judge the quality of the illusion they attempt to project. Is the performance convincing,
and more important, does it serve the aims of the collectivity? In Cornelian comedies and tragedies, approval from society is the only visible
measure of success for the protagonist, and this is the foundation of its
comic structure. A new society crystallizes around the hero at the
moment of resolution, which is a moment of discovery or anagnorisis, the
moment when we recognize that a new society is possible (Frye, 163).

In his *Psychocritique du genre comique,* Charles Mauron develops a definition of comedy that complements Frye's.[7] Whereas Frye uses Jungian
archetypes as his starting point, Freud is Mauron's inspiration for the
evaluation of spectator reaction to comedy as opposed to tragedy. In
tragedy, the individual spectator identifies with the suffering of the
tragic hero, entering into an intimate relationship with him or her.
When watching a comedy, we function as part of a group, evaluating
the potential scapegoat's conduct and condemning it with our laughter
when it merits ridicule. As a character's behavior becomes more socially
destructive and thus deserving of mockery, his or her chances of being
expelled from society grow (Mauron 1954, 8–15, 26–27).

The notion of performance takes center stage in this very theatrical
definition of comedy. Corneille's comic protagonists are creators of illusions that can be labeled either negative or positive in terms of their
social impact; negative and positive illusions often compete within the
same play. Frye likens this conflict to a lawsuit in which the spectator is
a jury member who must judge whose creation is more "real," the plain-
tiff's or the defendant's (166). In a more theatrical vein, the projection of
illusion requires that the character perform as actor, director, and
dramatist in a play of his or her invention.[8] Necessarily providing a star
turn for him- or herself, the profoundly theatrical comic hero embodies
the drive for recognition that will characterize the Cornelian hero in
general. Frye tells us that "the resolution of comedy comes . . . from the
audience's side of the stage" (164). Our role as a combination jury and
group of drama critics is crucial. When the resolution comes, it is
through our recognition not only of a social rebirth but also of the quality of the hero's performance. As Frye states, audience response in comedy may seem like a moral judgment, but there is also a large social and
aesthetic component: the defeated illusion seems simply absurd or
improbable in the end (167).

I would emphasize that our judgment also has obvious psychological
dimensions. This is not to say that we can examine the psychology of the

comic character, who is not after all an individual with a well-developed subjectivity. The character's language and actions, however, form part of a structure that affects spectators in a way that can be analyzed in aesthetic, social, and psychological terms. Corneille makes a move toward the individualization of his characters that will not be fully pursued in comedy until Molière arrives on the scene (Conesa, 127). The progress Corneille does make toward personalized, emotive discourse enriches the spectator's experience considerably as it adds to the complexity of Cornelian comic structure.

Although my own global vision of Cornelian theater was formed by his five early comedies, my first contact with Corneille followed the normal course of high school or undergraduate studies: *Le Cid* occupies first place in the canon, with the other three tragedies of the tetralogy close behind. The richness of the comedies and their potential as a source of insight for Corneille's oeuvre are a wonderful surprise for nonspecialists. Fortunately, Corneille scholars have rediscovered this gold mine since World War II, but especially in the past 20 years, producing eight books devoted solely to the comedies, in addition to numerous articles and references to the comedies in general studies of Corneille. Plot summaries of these plays can begin to suggest why this enthusiasm exists, and why I believe that the search for distinction on the part of Corneille's protagonists is a good point of departure for analyzing the entire corpus.

The Early Comedies

Mélite

In *Mélite ou les fausses lettres* (Mélite or the False Letters, 1629–1630 season), Éraste wishes to introduce Mélite, the beautiful and charming object of his affections, to Tircis, a practical-minded friend who believes one should marry only for money. Tircis is extremely critical of Éraste's doglike devotion, but on seeing Mélite, the skeptic finds himself instantaneously smitten. Mélite claims to scorn love just as Tircis did, but she is to undergo the same magical conversion experienced by Tircis. A perfect balance is created as their love at first sight contrasts with the one-sided relationship Éraste continues to cultivate despite his rejection by Mélite. Excluded and embittered, Éraste is left to plot his revenge on the lovers.

The ruse Éraste devises involves a gullible braggart, Philandre. When Éraste presents Philandre with love letters supposedly addressed to him by Mélite, Philandre easily accepts the idea that she has fallen madly in

love with him. He immediately breaks with his fiancée, Cloris (sister of
Tircis), for the unknown but fascinating Mélite. Philandre ignores what
he believes to be Mélite's request to keep the letters secret, and he
boasts of his conquest to Tircis, who thinks he has been betrayed. Tircis
challenges the usurper to a duel.

Since Philandre's love is not strong enough for him to consider risking death, he makes a cowardly retreat. In the meantime, the (false)
news of Tircis's suicide makes Mélite faint from shock. Her death is
reported to Éraste, who loses his mind, mistaking Mélite's old, ugly
nanny for the ghost of Mélite.[9] When Éraste hears that Mélite is alive,
he comes to his senses, whereupon he is forgiven his treachery, which
had, after all, been inspired by an entirely noble passion. Éraste is
awarded Cloris's hand in marriage, so the only young lover permanently
excluded from the happy ending is Philandre. His "love" for Mélite is
totally self-centered, a mere figment of his egotistical imagination; the
sort of reciprocity created by the Tircis-Mélite union could never be realized between Philandre and Mélite. Tircis suggests that Philandre take
the old nanny, who ends the play on a note of farce by recalling her
youth. The happy ending is reinforced as the exclusion of those who are
unable to experience true love makes the world of the lovers more idylli-
cally perfect.[10]

Mélite's hand is the prize sought by all three male characters, and he
who wins it will have proved his superiority over the others. Éraste's
folly is comical, but it can also be read as a sign of his search for glory,
since he imagines that he is fighting all the demons of hell on Mélite's
behalf (5.2.1615–94). A talented creator of illusions, he is trapped in a
dreamworld by remorse and freed from it once his penance is done.
When he becomes a boon to society rather than a destructive force, he is
reintegrated into the group.

La Veuve

Corneille's next venture was *Clitandre,* a tragicomedy we will examine
after considering the first five comedies. The series of comedies continues with *La Veuve ou le traître trahi* (The Widow or the Traitor Betrayed),
first performed during the 1631–1632 season. The title suggests that
betrayal remains a staple of these comic plays. The widow is Clarice,
whose fiancé is Philiste. But she is also the love object of Alcidon, who
pretends to be in love with Philiste's sister, Doris, in order to disguise his
feelings for Clarice. Doris, however, is not fooled and plans to marry Flo-

range, as her mother wishes. Alcidon declares his need to avenge this insult and convinces his friend Célidan to kidnap Clarice for him. Philiste, knowing nothing of Alcidon's true feelings, tries to help his friend by breaking his sister's engagement to Florange. Célidan then expects Alcidon to free Clarice and to accept Doris. Another elderly nanny figure appears: Clarice's nurse has been in cahoots with Alcidon. A suspicious Célidan forces the old woman to admit the plot; he returns Clarice to Philiste and is given Doris's hand as his reward.

Once again, possession of a woman is the sign of distinction, although Alcidon's audacious plot is inspired not by his desire to possess Clarice but by his wounded pride. Alcidon will be expelled from the happy society at the end of the play because his drive for recognition is destructive for the collectivity.

La Galerie du Palais

The title of *La Galerie du Palais ou l'amie rivale* (1632–1633) refers to a popular Paris marketplace; *l'amie rivale* is yet another false friend, this time a woman. Hippolyte is the rival who betrays her friend Célidée. Célidée is in love with Lysandre but says that she will dutifully accept her father's choice of her husband; luckily, Lysandre is his choice. But the course of true love must meet some obstacles in drama, so in a love chain reminiscent of the pastoral, Célidée finds herself attracted to a newcomer, Dorimant, who prefers Hippolyte, while Hippolyte only has eyes for Lysandre.

A complex set of relations is established in the play as Célidée makes Lysandre, and eventually herself, suffer—with Hippolyte's encouragement, of course. Célidée is extremely cruel to Lysandre in a test of his love, but he remains faithful. In a bid to restore Célidée's love, Lysandre tries to make her jealous by turning toward Hippolyte. Célidée is furious and convinces Dorimant to challenge Lysandre to a duel by saying that Lysandre is trying to win Hippolyte away from him.

Lysandre violently expresses his resentment of Célidée but will not cease to love her. Thanks to Hippolyte's ruse, however, Célidée believes that both men are pursuing her friend, while the men think that each is trying to steal the other's lover. The duel begins among this confusion, but Célidée arrives to stop it, and she and Lysandre are reunited, more in love than ever after this test of their feelings. Hippolyte is willing to accept Dorimant, though she insists on admitting the truth now: she loves only Lysandre. Two couples are united, despite the taint that hangs over the Dorimant-Hippolyte match. The union of Hippolyte's mother and Célidée's father is even suggested, although they are deemed too old to enjoy the delights of marriage—and besides, as the last line says, that would seem too much like the ending of a comedy. The complex exploration of doubt and cruelty in the development of young love makes this play memorable.

From the perspective of Corneille's basic comic structure, Hippolyte's aggressive entry into the contest of love is noteworthy. She is the first of many female characters who will aim for glory with just as much energy as the male heroes.

La Suivante

La Suivante (1632–1633) has an even more ascerbic ambiance at moments, although bits of farce intrude. The variety of tones characteristic of these comedies, with their mixture of literary influences, becomes quite evident here. The title is difficult to translate: the *suivante* is a sort of lady-in-waiting or exulted maidservant to a woman of the leisure class, either the nobility or the upper-level bourgeoisie. In this play, Amarante is of noble birth like her mistress, Daphnis, but the *suivante* is poor; thus she occupies an ambiguous social category. Amarante's resentment in trying to compete with the wealthy and privileged Daphnis is not surprising: Théante has been courting Amarante, but Daphnis is more attractive to his ambition. Théante hopes that his friend Florame can distract Amarante, but Florame too has his sights on Daphnis. Amarante's vanity in claiming that she can conquer Florame thus appears ridiculous, if not pathetic, until she reveals her awareness of the attraction of Daphnis's fortune. Both women set their caps for Florame, but their true sentiments are only clear in monologues. All four protagonists use role playing in an attempt to manipulate others into the desired position. They constantly repeat the falsehood that they are ready to sacrifice their love selflessly for the benefit of others, a noteworthy theme since noble sacrifice is a leitmotif of Cornelian tragedy.

Another character is introduced in the second act. Géraste, Daphnis's father, wants to marry a much younger woman, Florame's sister, Florise, whom we never see: she remains an object of exchange. Géraste would like to be loved for himself but knows that money and power are the ultimate guarantors of his union. Géraste makes clear the tension already seen in the young couples: idealism about love is tempered by social reality.

In the contest between Daphnis and Amarante, Amarante has the advantage of being more lucid than her mistress. She sees the mutual love of Daphnis and Florame but continues to believe she can win Florame for herself through deception. When Clarimond emerges as yet another suitor for Daphnis, Amarante convinces Géraste and Clarimond that Daphnis loves the newcomer. Trying to be a generous father, Géraste gives his permission for this marriage. But when he finds that the Daphnis-Florame match is a condition for his marriage to Florise, Géraste tells Daphnis that she can no longer marry the man she loves. Confusion reigns because of Amarante's ruse.

The denouement will of course lead to a double marriage (Daphnis-Florame and Géraste-Florise). Géraste's "unnatural" desires are not satisfied at the expense of his daughter's happiness; instead they are complementted by the good luck of her preference. Serendipity (or the comic life force) saves him from becoming the heavy father figure of classical comedy. This unconventional ending is made more so by Amarante's final monologue: she is bitter and hopes that Géraste will pay for his tampering with the natural order of the world. But Corneille maintains his comic schema as he develops it: Amarante and Théante are appropriately the only losers. (The blameless Clarimond is an episodic character who disappears after act 3.) Each is punished for a clever performance that runs counter to the interests of society. Their relative poverty and Théante's cowardice when faced with the possibility of a duel make them unfit for the reward of marriage.

La Place Royale

Parents disappear from *La Place Royale ou l'amoureux extravagant*. It was first performed during the 1633–1634 season, and once again, the title refers to a trendy location in Paris in an apparent effort to attract spectators.[11] The "extravagant lover" of the subtitle is Alidor, who adores Angélique. Angélique in turn loves Alidor devotedly, but her friend Phylis argues that a woman must protect herself by keeping several men guessing as to her preference. Despite her defensive aims, the strategy Phylis pursues is risky. She is told by her suitors Cléandre and Lysis that they do not want what anyone can have; solitude threatens to end Phylis's carefree social games. But she insists that emotional distance will allow her to accept happily any husband accorded to her by her absent parents. Phylis pleads with Angélique to practice a bit of flirting not only for self-protection but also to give some hope to

Phylis's brother, Doraste, whose love for Angélique has made him miserable.

Cléandre also loves Angélique but courts Phylis in order not to offend his friend Alidor. (This situation echoes that of Alcidon and Philiste in *La Veuve*.) Alidor reveals to Cléandre that not only is he not offended, he will help Cléandre in his quest for Angélique. Alidor wants his freedom back; Angélique loves him too much, and the emotional intensity of their relationship has become unbearable to him. In act 1, scene 4, he explores his dilemma: marriage will completely end his freedom while at the same time lead to probable boredom with the inevitable diminution of his love for her. Yet he cannot simply walk away from Angélique. While he wants to end all contact with her, he also wants to control her fate by ensuring that he can hand Angélique over to his surrogate, Cléandre.

As a first step in disentangling himself from Angélique, Alidor allows a letter from him to another woman to circulate. When Angélique confronts him with the evidence of his unfaithfulness, he insults her, suggesting that she look in the mirror to see how unattractive she is. Angélique is furious and washes her hands of Alidor, though she admits she is still in love with him. Phylis encourages Doraste to ask Angélique's parents for her hand, which he receives. Cléandre is enraged—for Alidor's sake, he says—and challenges Doraste to a duel.

Alidor does not want a duel to take place. He wants to be able to give Angélique to Cléandre, using deception. Alone at the end of act 3, scene 4, Alidor suffers from the loss of Angélique, expressing a sort of masochistic enjoyment at the thought of winning her again in order to assure Cléandre's success. He questions his own sanity but proceeds to recapture Angélique's heart by claiming that he was only testing her love. Alidor threatens suicide if she marries Doraste, an affront to his honor. The only solution, he insists, is to elope.

While Angélique entertains grave doubts about their scheme, Alidor is very pleased with himself. Phylis spies on him and learns that Alidor and Cléandre plan to kidnap Angélique during the night. Alidor hesitates for a moment but intends to hand her over to Cléandre as if she were a sack of gold—valuable, but really little more than a piece of property to dispose of. Angélique is framed as the enemy by Alidor at the beginning of act 4: "I want to be the master" in a combat against Cupid, he declares (4.1.994). But later he waffles again, torn between love for Angélique and his desire for an elusive liberty. "Am I still Alidor?" he asks himself, in the throes of a crisis of alienation (4.5.1075).

He wants to retain sovereign power over himself, seeing the repression of his love as a heroic gesture.

Unfortunately for Alidor's plan, Phylis is mistakenly taken rather than Angélique. When Angélique appears, Alidor supposes that she has been unfaithful, since she is supposed to be with Cléandre. Realizing what actually happened, he says that he will try to flee with Angélique again the next day. Alidor leaves at a run when he sees Doraste approaching. Act 4 ends with Angélique's confession to Doraste that she will never marry him, but when Doraste reveals Alidor's plot, she retreats in shame. She will end up in a convent, having lost all of her illusions about love.

In act 5, scene 1, Cléandre returns with Phylis, whose tears have inspired a rather sadistic love in him. She continues to be sarcastic and playful but agrees to marry him if her parents wish it. Cléandre would like to have a clear explanation of her feelings, but she will continue to disguise them, perhaps even to herself.

Now that it is too late, Alidor is ready to devote himself to Angélique. Doraste, Cléandre, and Phylis all encourage Angélique to take him back, but she refuses. His exaggerated behavior runs counter to the stability and calm she now craves and that she will find in the convent. The play ends with a monologue from Alidor, who claims to be very pleased indeed with the way things have turned out. He can stop loving and start truly living, he says, because he will live only for himself. Love's games and disguises can continue, but his liberty will remain intact, thanks to Angélique, whose dangerous charms will be safely locked away. He won't even need to feel jealous with God as her betrothed (5.8.1562–1601).

The Comedies and the Critics

Not surprisingly given its complexity, *La Place Royale* has inspired more commentary than any of the other early comedies. Alidor has been seen as a precursor to the hero of Cornelian tragedy, most notably by Doubrovsky, who says that when Alidor tries to surmount a deeply felt love, he enters into a complex battle to establish a heroic identity. Alidor may lose this battle, but Doubrovsky insists on the fascinating complexity of his character (1963, 68–72). Nadal also believes that Alidor exhibits characteristics of the Cornelian hero, although his flight from Angélique puts heroic status in doubt (113–14). Constant Venesoen's book on the comedies reminds us that the play's subtitle is "the extravagant lover" and that the seventeenth-century definition of *extravagant* highlights folly and inappropriate behavior.[12] Venesoen insists that Alidor is a comic, even farcical character in his exaggerated resistance to love and that he continues the pattern set out by Éraste in *Mélite,* Alcidon in *La Veuve,* and Théante in *La Suivante:* his tricks, lies, and bad faith move him away from the ranks of happy young lovers. Only his occasional lucidity distinguishes him from Corneille's other comic tricksters, because he articulates the fear that lies at the bottom of his desire to escape from Angélique's love. Misogyny motivates his desire for liberty, according to Venesoen, making his quest risible rather than admirable (46–48).

Alidor has inspired so much scholarly interest thanks in part to his psychological complexity. Han Verhoeff's Freudian study uses Mauron's work on the psychology of individual writers in order to reveal what he sees as a repeated motif in the comedies. Corneille's male protagonists, with Alidor prominent among them, display a fear of women and marriage, in Verhoeff's interesting but reductive view. He takes up the same theme in a 1982 book on Cornelian tragedy.[13] In her book on the comedies, Cynthia B. Kerr also examines the characters' psychology. They are seen as impulsive, irrational, egotistical, and manipulative.[14] They are ruled by their passions, especially violent love, and the tensions and confusion it provokes lead to comical situations (Kerr, 1, 10–12). Relationships are characterized by hypocrisy and naïveté, as the characters try to mask their deceptive practices in a struggle for dominance, not realizing that they too may be the victims of another's ruse (19–23). Irony is strong as broken engagements and promises lead to social instability (110). Kerr concludes by insisting that these portraits of love in all its unreasonableness are not pessimistic; despite the irony and cynicism of the plays, the basic message she reads in them is that one should be aware of the chaos that usually accompanies passionate relationships, but love should be pursued even so (133–35).

Kerr's interpretation is largely convincing, and her discussion of the struggle for dominance reinforces my view of the characters' search for distinction, but one element of her conclusion is flawed. She states that the behavior of the characters is not judged and that no moral questions are raised in Cornelian comedy (133). There is always a suggestion of reward or punishment meted out to the protagonists at the end of the comedies, however. While it is true that unfaithful lovers and tricksters are integrated into the happy ending, only a "conversion" to socially constructive behavior like Éraste's at the end of *Mélite* or Hippolyte's at

the end of *La Galerie du Palais* will result in marriage. For the protagonist to triumph at the end of these plays, a performance that the group
can approve even after all masks have been removed and all plots uncovered is required. Kerr cites the example of Florame in *La Suivante* as a
morally bankrupt character who uses Amarante to reach Daphnis but
who is rewarded in the end despite his deception. Florame in fact reinforces my hypothesis that psychological, social, and aesthetic considerations form the basis of a particularly Cornelian didacticism. Florame is
the best match socially and economically for Daphnis. Moreover, he is
both a talented actor and a seductive personality. The unfortunate end
of a character like Angélique in *La Place Royale* can be seen in aesthetic,
social, and psychological terms as the result of her refusal to engage in
the role playing and adaptability that prove successful for Phylis, while
Alidor's antisocial tendencies make him unsuited for integration into a
couple.

Kerr is correct to mention a certain cynicism in the comedies and to
say that the Cornelian comic universe is neither immoral nor amoral,
and that it has its own morality, outside conventional notions of good
and evil. Corneille presents, in Kerr's view, a "realism in love" that she
aligns with Machiavelian political realism (133). I frame the problem
differently. Corneille is creating a theater new in its demands on the
audience, forcing the spectator to evaluate the characters' performances
in terms of social utility and aesthetic quality (see Carlin 1990).
Corneille has for generations been seen as the father of modern French
drama because, as Conesa says, his characters *do* rather than simply *tell*
(236). Their engagement in the action implies our own; I return to the
idea of the basic comic structure of his theater because it allows the
dynamics of this engagement to become clear.

Other critics who have found bases for interpreting the entire oeuvre
in the comedies include Théodore Litman, Robert Garapon, and G. J.
Mallinson.[15] Litman disagrees with Kerr's negative evaluation of the
moral qualities of these characters. He finds in them a progressive
capacity for self-examination leading to self-knowledge (11). As psychological and moral considerations deepen, Litman sees the roots of Cornelian tragedy in these plays, which he does not consider at all comical
in their confrontation of grave moral problems (11, 265). Although Litman deforms their comic nature, his discussion of the characters' need
for admiration from peers is interesting. They lie to themselves and others as they try to create a brilliant facade in order to hide faults; they
hope that the mask will transform the inner self. The process of image

construction is shown to be faulty when aspirations do not result in a convincing performance; then the character appears ridiculous (258–68). The quest for distinction is examined here in terms first put forward by Jean Starobinski: the need to impress, to overwhelm the other (*éblouir* in French), is an expression of power, and the use of power is a central theme in Cornelian comedy and tragedy.[16]

Robert Garapon takes up the theme of power by concluding that all of Corneille's characters fight against tyranny and usurpation of their independence (1982, 107); the desire for distinction thus appears in yet another analysis. But desire can be destructive, according to Garapon. He divides the comic characters into two groups: those who love "with discernment," whose inclinations are based on reason, and those in the throes of an uncontrollable, irrational desire. The first group thrives, while the second ends up losing freedom and their equilibrium (89). Liberty is thus linked with the proper use of reason, a situation that applies equally to the tragedies in Garapon's clever analysis. Both Garapon and Litman propose global readings of Corneille's theater that have the advantage of seeing the comedies on their own terms rather than simply as precursors to the tragedies, although structural similarites are undeniable.

Among the most stimulating studies of Cornelian comedy is G. J. Mallinson's 1984 book, *The Comedies of Corneille: Experiments in the Comic.* Like Conesa, Mallinson discusses classical comedy, tragicomedy, pastoral, and farce, seeing elements of all of them in Corneille's early plays (1984, 9–24). Their only structural constant is the happy ending: a *comédie* of any sort is "the play which sees the joyful resolution of all conflicts, establishes order and suggests a lasting sense of harmony, even justice" (25). In my view, the problem of social order and harmony remains central not only to Corneille's comedies but to the many dramatic genres he sampled throughout his career. The fertile theatrical activity of the 1630s, especially in comedy, was a tremendous boon to Corneille's future work as a playwright.

While Mallinson stresses the importance of examining each of Corneille's comedies separately, his analysis of *Mélite* serves as a model for the other four plays. The keys to *Mélite,* according to Mallinson, are the emphasis on role playing, the gradual move from blindness to insight, the irony that ends the play on a note of frustration and bitterness for blocking characters, and, once again, the notion of order restored—though not without a price paid by those who threaten it (1984, 41–53). The spectator can laugh at moments (for example, at

Éraste's folly or Philandre's vanity [127, 131]), but Corneille manipulates the traditional happy ending: "The formal patterns of comedy, through Corneille's refusal to fulfill them totally, are thrown into relief" (53). Corneille is the first dramatist to highlight the lack of logic inherent in the conventional harmony at the end of a comedy (54). His questioning of this convention has implications for his conception of dramatic genre and opens the door to his experiments in tragedy, tragicomedy, and other hybrid genres of his own invention such as heroic comedy.

The devices used in *Mélite* are repeated in the other comedies, but with a deeper exploration of their effects, especially comic irony. The implications of role playing multiply with each play, culminating in *La Place Royale*. Mallinson joins Venesoen and Verhoeff when he labels *La Place Royale* "the comedy of fear" (1984, 134). Alidor reaches an interesting new psychological plane, as he *pretends* to be inconstant in his love for Angélique when his love and his fear of its hold on him are actually constant elements of his make-up. By "giving" Angélique to Cléandre, he can experience his love from a safe distance (140–43). His self-deception is fascinating, as he tries to win Angélique back by "acting" as though he still loves her. He plays the role he longs for yet fears to fulfill (143–45). The comic order and good humor of the opening fade, as all of the characters contribute to the unhappy ending: "Tensions apparent already in the *dénouements* of the last two comedies are here brought finally to the surface, and Corneille presents characters who are simply unable to bend to the exigencies of convention" (162). From my perspective, the ending of all the comedies can be considered "happy" in that social stability in the form of at least one marriage is imposed, brought about by the repression of aberrant behavior. The comic life force is less idealized than at the end of the most romantic sort of comedy, but social renewal does take place.[17] Human aspiration is given free reign in problematic protagonists like Philandre, Alcidon, Théante, and Alidor—perhaps a manifestation of the *libre arbitre* or free will so essential to Corneille's Jesuit schoolmasters. Since these social misfits misuse their potential, turning it against society's best interests, the illusions they create are not durable and they cannot participate in the projection of society's renaissance, a rebirth more convincing for the refusal to idealize many of the young couples completely.

Playing with convention is indeed at the heart of Corneille's endeavor as a dramatist. As he manipulates audience expectations, he creates the pleasure of surprise, which in tragic theater is associated with the notion

of the sublime. It is noteworthy that Mallinson focuses on the denouements of the comedies, just as Georges Forestier does in studying the
tragedies. Mallinson is correct to say that Corneille "adapts comic techniques for the investigation of tragic dilemmas" (1984, 219). Mallinson
sees the Cornelian tragic hero, like the comic, as a performer attempting
to come to terms with political or moral codes, or with his own self-
image. Complex motives, mixtures of strength and weariness, conviction and doubt, plague Corneille's protagonists, according to Mallinson
(220). Forestier's perspective remains in the aesthetic realm: he is more
interested in exploring the construction of Cornelian tragedy from the
ending of the story backwards, since he believes that all French classical
tragedy was constructed in this way (14–16).

The implications of Forestier's thesis will be explored later. The relevant issue here is that while Forestier emphasizes the aesthetic, and
Mallinson's approach tends to combine linguistic and psychological concerns, they share my preoccupation with the basic structures visible in
Cornelian theater. They are certainly not the only scholars to concentrate on the tantalizing problem of structure in Corneille from a number
of methodological perspectives. For example, Marie-Odile Sweetser in
La Dramaturgie de Corneille finds two formulas present throughout: the
typical Cornelian plot includes a rivalry between protagonists and an
extraordinary situation resolved by completely unexpected means.
Antithesis and paradox are the dominant stylistic figures employed by
Corneille, and they reflect these recurring plot structures.[18] The merit of
this system is that it does indeed apply to the totality of the corpus, and
the analysis of individual plays can be developed with finesse from this
starting point. Another basic comic structure, and one that harmonizes
well with my own thesis, is proposed by Milorad Margitic, who insists
on the comic protagonists' feelings of superiority to others, a view they
must protect by using one of two defense mechanisms, or basic myths:
they either become Rebels Against Love or Slaves of Love.[19] This outline
can indeed be found throughout the corpus. Serge Doubrovsky sees the
Cornelian hero engaged in a battle for mastery over his peers, a battle
that extends to the love object; psychology meets politics, with inspiration from Hegel. Doubrovsky concentrates on the tragedies but finds
the roots for this structure in the comedies (1963, 33–83).

Many of the above-mentioned critics place Corneille's comedies in
the cultural and social context from which they emerged, although this
is not the focus of their analyses. Among those who place more emphasis on events of the early seventeenth century, several commentators

besides those mentioned at the beginning of this chapter have worked on the pastoral elements in Cornelian comedy. Marc Fumaroli calls *Mélite* an "urban pastoral" and sees examples of the pastoral structure not only in the early comedies but also in some of Corneille's latest works, including his last play, *Suréna,* which Fumaroli calls a "pastoral tragedy." The characteristics of pastoral Fumaroli sees in Corneille's urban plays include the chain of love (one character loves another who rejects him in favor of another love object who in turns pursues another woman); a rejected lover whose plots against his or her rival almost end in tragic results; a sudden reversal (a change of mind or bit of good news) leading to not just one but often two marriages; and the idealization of love, preferred to social duty (1990, 36). These characteristics are indeed present in *Mélite* and in many Corneille plays, including all six early comedies (the ones examined above and *L'Illusion comique*). Thus Fumaroli's suggestion of a basic structure in Cornelian comedy joins the trend in Corneille criticism that seeks to find a stable thematic or structural foundation for an extremely varied oeuvre. Alain Couprie also stresses the continuing resonance of pastoral elements in the entire Corneille canon.[20]

Another literary trend of the late sixteenth and early seventeenth centuries often mentioned in connection with Corneille's plays of the 1630s is the baroque. A fascinating but slippery notion, it furnishes yet another set of characteristics that may apply to Cornelian theater as a whole. The twists and turns of the plots in a confusing and unstable world, the inconstancy of the young lovers, the tension created by their self-contradiction, the difficulty of distinguishing appearance from reality, and especially their ostentatious behavior as showy actors are all characteristics of the baroque as defined by Jean Rousset in his masterful 1954 study.[21] Seeing baroque elements in Cornelian comedy and in his theater in general reinforces my thesis about its comic structure, as the search for distinction is well illustrated by characters who are impelled to perform. Indeed, the notion of theatricality as the unifying principle of the corpus has been used by several scholars whose intriguing work on the tragedies we will consider in chapter 3.

The baroque offers yet another road into tragedy by way of its very problematic status as a literary concept. Rousset acknowledges that a tension exists within the idea of the baroque because it is seen both as a limited historical period and as a set of stylistic traits. He argues that the baroque sensibility permeates almost the entirety of the seventeenth century, contaminating the classical aesthetic of order and containment that dominates the era (and most especially tragic theater) from the 1640s on (1954, 8–9). But as Timothy Hampton has shown, even Rousset's flexible treatment of the baroque is not without problems:

> [T]his aestheticizing depiction of the Baroque seems to elide all consideration of historical, political, and social concerns. It places the Baroque in history only to the extent that it frames it by two specific years [1580 to 1670] and claims that the Baroque provides "an entire period" with themes in which it can "recognize" itself. Yet it is this very scene of recognition that provides the ground for a reconsideration of the Baroque. For the scene of recognition that Rousset evokes—the scene in which a given historical moment confronts its own representations—is anything but innocent. . . . The encounter between a subject and a text in which she or he is to find self-recognition constitutes that moment at which subjectivity is defined and circumscribed by the discourses of power, whether political or aesthetic. It is through recognition that people become the subjects of political and social systems.[22]

The text that controls its reader, the play that exerts its power over the spectator, is a topic implicit in my theory of Cornelian comic structure. The consumers of these works are pushed into an active role as judges of the aesthetic and social worth of the character's performance. An ironic tension develops as the audience is *forced* to become active, or as we tend to say nowadays, empowered. The psychic distance maintained by the spectator of comedy in Mauron's terms remains intact throughout the corpus. The evaluation of a perfomance's worth and its stakes for society change when history becomes the subject of Corneille's theater with *Le Cid* in 1637, but the entry into tragedy does not erase the underlying structure built in the comedies. The spectator is part of a group who decides whether the hero's drive for distinction serves the collectivity and merits applause—or not.

Ultimately the concept of comic structure as I define it represents the critical perspective most able to subsume a variety of other approaches. The idea of a basic comic structure shares with the other "structural" views already described the desire to find a framework that is not reductive, yet the other theories tend to fall into thematic categories that I find rather limiting. Using comic structure as a point of departure, aesthetic, linguistic, semiotic, psychocritical, sociological, and historical methods can be more fruitfully considered across the boundaries of dramatic genre.

Corneille's three other plays of the period before *Le Cid* are a tragicomedy, his first tragedy, and a comedy he called "a strange monster" because of the way it plays with the concept of genre. Corneille's experiments take him into new territory, but he remains faithful to the basic edifice he created for the comedies.

Experiments in Genre

Entertainment for the Eyes: *Clitandre*

Corneille's tragicomedy *Clitandre ou l'innocence délivrée* (Clitandre or Innocence Preserved) was his second play, performed in the 1630–1631 season. Its plot is so complicated that he admits in the preface that the spectator seeing it for the first time may emerge from the theater a bit confused (*OC,* 1:95), but the audience of a tragicomedy at the time expected a multiplicity of events.[23] Corneille wanted to show that he could follow the Aristotelian rules then coming into vogue, but by the standards of the 1640s, this play would seem hopelessly out of date. He insisted in 1632 that *Clitandre* showed that he understood in particular the unity of time, but that he had improved upon the practice of the Ancients. Corneille proclaims the originality of his visual effects: onstage action replaces the messengers so prevalent in the theater of antiquity. The notion that the arts and sciences had not yet reached the pinnacle of perfection and that Corneille would aid in their ascent would be a recurring theme of his future theoretical writings. Nevertheless, the number of incidents crammed into 24 hours and several locations makes *Clitandre* anything but "regular," to say nothing of a rape attempt and a king who almost commits a gross injustice. Respect for *bienséance,* or decorum, so important when the rules of classical composition are in place, is thoroughly violated here.

We begin with an extended love triangle. Caliste and Dorise love the dashing Rosidor, spurning the attentions of Clitandre and Pymante, respectively. Rosidor prefers Caliste, but his position as the king's favorite is not enough to win her hand since Clitandre has the prince and the queen in his corner. Dorise pretends not to mind Caliste's triumph over her, but jealousy eats away until she finds a sword in the woods and decides to use it to attack Caliste. Dorise tricks Caliste into entering the forest by telling her that Rosidor has been unfaithful and that they will surprise him with his new lover. Meanwhile, Pymante has decided to get rid of Rosidor, his only obstacle to winning Dorise. Pymante lures Rosidor into the forest by sending him a note, supposedly from Clitandre. Pymante and two allies disguise themselves as peasants and ambush Rosidor.

Both of these clandestine meetings are set for dawn. Rosidor comes across Dorise, about to kill Caliste, while he is fighting off the "peasants." He loses his sword, so he grabs the one Dorise is planning to use on Caliste. Rodisor kills two of his attackers and sends Pymante fleeing. Dorise escapes as well, leaving Caliste to faint in Rosidor's arms. Rosidor unmasks his assailants and finding Clitandre's servants, blames Clitandre, who will be jailed and condemned to death by the king. There is little hope for Clitandre as his protector, the prince, has left for the hunt.

As Caliste and the wounded Rosidor make their way back to the palace, Dorise finds the servants' clothing and disguises herself. Pymante, also still in disguise, discovers her and realizing that she has witnessed his crime, leads her into the cave where he has left his sword. He eventually recognizes Dorise by a hairpin she is still wearing and reveals himself to her. When she continues to reject him in favor of Rosidor, he assures her that his rival is dead and restrains her with the apparent intention of raping her. Furious, Dorise attacks Pymante with the hairpin, gouging out one of his eyes. She escapes, but he pursues her, sword in hand. They run into the prince, whose horse has been killed out from under him during a lightning storm.

The prince saves Dorise, who recounts all the incidents that have taken place in the woods. A friend of Clitandre's arrives to warn the prince of the threat menacing his favorite. The prince realizes that Pymante is responsible for the attack on Rosidor and arrives in time to save Clitandre. Clitandre is pardoned, Caliste and Rosidor are engaged, and Dorise is given amnesty thanks to her assistance to the prince in fighting Pymante. The prince proposes that Clitandre marry Dorise, but Clitandre refuses. Nonetheless, the king insists that they will form a second happy couple by the time Rosidor recovers from his injuries.

Some critics have seen in *Clitandre* the same subject as in the comedies (love complicated by jealousy and deception), given a more serious bent by the king's error in judgment and the intervention of the royal family in arranging the marriages.[24] The possibility of death could move the play into the realm of tragedy, according to Corneille's defintion of the genre in the *Discours* (*OC*, 3:123–34), and indeed, in the 1660 edition of *Clitandre*, he changed the designation to the more noble genre, tragedy, making many other modifications to "correct" the play when viewed from the perspective of the classical aesthetic. But its many adventures and conventional happy outcome make the 1632 edition typical of the many tragicomedies produced prior to 1640. Another sign that *Clitandre* should be classified as a romantic (tragi)comedy is the role of providence in bringing about the denouement. The prince's opportune rescue of Dorise signals that nothing is inevitable and that a sorry fate, even if deserved, may be interrupted. This intervention of providence is a hallmark of comedy, in Frye's view: the threat of a tragic destiny is always comfortingly averted (170). This sort of providential ending can be found throughout Corneille's theater, serving as another indication of its comic structure.

Corneille may have been inspired by a real-life tragedy whose events he transformed into a more positive story in *Clitandre,* suggests David Clarke.[25] In the preface (*OC,* 1:96), Corneille obliquely alludes to a possible correlation with the execution of the Maréchal de Marillac, which took place in March 1632, the same month in which *Clitandre* was published. The play is dedicated to the Duc de Longueville, an enemy of Richelieu who bitterly resented what was seen as Marillac's unjust death (Clarke, 119–20). But as Clarke notes, Corneille was normally interested in high principles rather than local truths, and *Clitandre* can also be read as a demonstration of God's providential design for a Christian social order, served by both the king and his people, whose spiritual destiny can be linked to service to the crown. The hero in this sense is not self-sufficient but functions as part of divine order (Clarke, 37, 123–31). This view is corroborated by Susan Read Baker, for whom "*Clitandre* can be read, like all of Corneille's theater, as a meditation upon stability and change," wherein human events serve as a backdrop for divinely ordained moral values.[26] Nonetheless, human agency remains paramount in Cornelian drama, even when it appears to receive divine assistance. Free will in the service of God and humanity is seconded by Providence, in the Jesuit tradition in which Corneille had been educated. The audience must also exercise its will and pass judgment on the protagonists. Providence's support of the protagonists is a strong indicator that our approbation should be granted.

Another element of Jesuit tradition that has been found in *Clitandre* is the use of allegory, suggested in Clarke's interpretation of the play as a model for the Christian social order. Clarke rightly insists, however, that Corneille avoided heavy-handed allegory, since successful theater cannot stray too far into either the allegorical or rhetorical modes (83–87). I can only agree with this statement, which runs directly counter to Germain Poirier's intriguing but ultimately unconvincing interpretation of the play.[27] In it, Clitandre represents the Jesuits, protected by Christ (the prince) and the Virgin Mary (the queen). Grace (Caliste) and the Defender of Grace (Rosidor) help Liberty (Dorise) to follow her true path to Reason rather than that of (Protestant) Evil (Pymante) (Poirier 1990, 55–70). Poirier provides etymologies for all of the names in order to prove his point, but Corneille never mentions the possibility of the play being an allegory. This reading severely limits the potential impact of the work, especially given its parallels with other Corneille plays.

Jacques Truchet notes that Corneille was predisposed to grandiose monsters like Pymante.[28] He is the scapegoat on whose defeat the happy ending can be constructed, and as is always the case, the scapegoat or blocking character tries to impose his vision on others. The heroes who serve society will pursue the same goal in much of Corneille's oeuvre, but their illusions win the audience over as Pymante's purely egotistical performance cannot. Indeed, Pymante is quite a performer, searching for distinction with his extreme gestures of violence. Baker considers both Pymante and Dorise to be actors, creating their own drama in their attempts to deceive others. The power of pure theatricality is demonstrated in *Clitandre,* according to Baker, as the ruses of the characters encourage the spectator to reflect upon the text as fiction, upon the links between aesthetics and epistemology (34–36). This analysis complements my own view about the responsibility for aesthetic and social judgment that Corneille forces spectators to take. Questions about epistemology (the nature and limits of knowledge itself) are implicitly addressed in the plays and the theoretical writings, in an entertaining manner. The dedication of *Médée,* published in 1639, is the first clear statement by Corneille about the primacy of pleasure over instruction for the audience (*OC,* 1:535). It is indeed a pleasurable play, and one that seeks to provoke a strong reaction.

Corneille's Medea

Médée is Corneille's first tragedy, performed for the 1634–1635 season. Corneille's Jason is a cad, confessing to his friend Pollux that he is ready to abandon Médée in order to fulfill his destiny as a seducer of princesses; certain of the comic characters come to mind. Jason plans to marry Créuse, daughter of King Créon, who has given refuge to Jason and Médée as they flee from their criminal past. When with Médée, Jason will claim that he has no choice but to accept the hand of Créuse while his wife is sent into exile. He must protect his and Médée's sons.

When Médée makes her impressive entrance in act 1, scene 4, she declares that a creative form of revenge will be hers, "a masterpiece of carnage." Her confidant, Nérine, urges Médée to disguise her vitriolic energy, but Médée refuses. She will face all enemies alone and unafraid: she is sword and flame, earth and sky, heaven and hell incarnate.

Créon further enflames her desire for revenge. He insults Médée, ordering her to leave within a day. She justifies her past murders, all committed for the love of Jason; her duty and honor were sacrificed to him. Créon, however, sees Médée as the only guilty party. She has become both a political liability and an obstacle to his daughter's happiness.

Médée is not Créon's only problem. The elderly king of Athens, Égée, also wishes to marry Créuse. Égée is jailed after after an attempt to kidnap Créuse, but Médée frees him in order to guarantee herself a safe haven. The theme of the elderly lover as seen in Géraste of *La Suivante* resurfaces here, not for the last time in Corneille's theater, as both Égée himself and Créuse mock his devotion to the young princess who rejects him.[29] She has chosen Jason, claiming both blind love and political necessity: Jason would not be divided between Corinth and another kingdom.

Créuse has set her heart on both Médée's husband and her magnificent golden gown. Jason tries to convince Médée that the dress should serve to thank Créon for sparing her life and taking in her sons. Médée reminds Jason that she has always placed her love for him over duty; she is furious at his unfaithfulness. In order to exact her revenge more effectively, eventually she takes Nérine's advice and begins playacting: she claims to understand Jason's desire to reign but insists on keeping her sons. She remains calm in the face of Jason's refusal and his egotistical insistence that she should continue to love him even as he rejects her.

Alone with Nérine at the end of act 3, Médée realizes that her sons represent her best weapon against Jason. In her magic grotto, she prepares the poison that will make her gown lethal to Créon and Créuse. As Médée becomes increasingly calm, her jealousy grows and her demeanor becomes even more threatening. Créon refuses to heed warnings about Médée's power—after all, she is only a woman. He tests the dress on a criminal to no effect. Créuse burns with desire to wear it; the burning becomes literal. Médée's magic, benevolent in freeing Égée, shows its malevolence as she enjoys her revenge. As Créon tries to save his daughter, the agony of Créon and Créuse fills the first four scenes of act 5. Créuse asks Jason to avenge them; he considers killing his sons as part of his attack on Médée but hesitates—as she will not.

Médée appears on a balcony to inform him that his children are already dead. She sarcastically tells him to go court his mistress. When

the enraged Jason tries to break down the door of the building, Médée
flies away in a chariot pulled by two dragons, mocking him all the
while. The play ends with Jason's impotent lament and suicide.

Neither Jason's onstage suicide nor the noisy deaths of Créon and
Créuse conform to the proprieties of *bienséance,* as Corneille himself
noted in 1660 (*OC,* 1:540). He goes on to explain that the audience
would not feel pity for them in any case, given their unjust treatment of
Médée, who wins all of our sympathy. These statements of 1660 can be
linked with his 1639 comments on the pleasure the spectator would
derive from the play, despite the fact that it depicts the triumph of vice
and contains no characters who are morally pure (*OC,* 1:535; in the first
Discours in 1660 Corneille again asserts his right to leave vice unpunished [*OC,* 3:121–22]). The morality of a play lies not in the choice of
subject but in the quality of imitation: an ugly action accurately portrayed is all the audience needs in order to draw for themselves the
proper moral lesson (*OC,* 1:535–36). As David Clarke notes, the knowledge of a "higher moral significance" beyond local propriety is in itself a
source of pleasure for the spectator of a Corneille play (62). In the tradition of Plutarch's humanistic didacticism, drama in Corneille's view
helps one learn to exercise moral judgment; pleasure is heightened by
moral understanding (*OC,* 1:535; Clarke, 63, 78). Clarke highlights
Corneille's humanist refusal to separate emotion and intellect. Passion is
rectified by reason; move spectators' passions and they will make the
effort to understand higher moral truth—which is a pleasurable experience (Clarke, 79). The idea that passion can be rectified by reason is one
of the main differences between Corneille and Racine, whose Jansenist
leanings led to the opposite portrayal of the passions as always uncontrollable. Extreme pity and terror in a one-to-one identification of the
spectator with the tragic hero/victim place Racine's spectator solidly in
the realm of tragedy if we define tragedy as does Charles Mauron in *Psychocritique du genre comique.* The comic structure remains intact in
Corneille's first tragedy, with the emphasis on the spectator as judge.

Reminders of comedy surface as well in the mixture of tones; Jason's
flippancy as he prepares to abandon Médée, Créuse's obsession with a
dress, and Égée's plight as a lovesick elderly king all help to diminish an
aura of tragedy, despite three rather gruesome deaths. And then there is
the magic: Médée frees Égée with a wave of her magic wand, and
Jason's suicide is preceded by the spectacular effect of the chariot drawn
by dragons. All of these elements contribute to a lessening of the horror
of Médée's murder of her children. Corneille insists that we should be on

her side, and we are: we see her illusory hope that Jason still loves her in act 2, scene 1; we see her grandeur in comparison with the petty concern of Créuse with the dress as well as Jason's base political scheming. In his edition of the play, André de Leyssac says that it is her duty to right wrongs.[30] Her creativity in vengeance turns out to be a service to society, as she rids the scene of corruption. Médée's performance merits our approbation, which we accord her despite her crimes. Marie-Odile Sweetser notes that Médée is not the incarnation of Evil that some critics have seen in her.[31] She refuses guilt in her transgressions—just as Corneille does in remaining faithful to the principles of his art, which sins against the rules of classical composition (Sweetser 1995, 123).

Marc Fumaroli also sees a correspondence between Médée and Corneille. In the 1639 preface, Corneille calls the play *méchante* (bad, evil) (*OC,* 1:535); Fumaroli considers the play a sort of allegory of the theater. Médée herself is *méchante,* and the play does not live up to the expectations of those who think immoral subjects should never be portrayed onstage. There is a complicity between Médée's magic and Corneille's will to manipulate spectators through powerful words (Fumaroli 1990, 500–504). In an allegorical reading of *Clitandre* more flexible than Poirier's, Baker sees the tragicomedy as a reflection on and of the writer's creativity (28–34). Similarly, Fumaroli finds Corneille reflecting on his art from within *Médée.*

Médée provides the pleasure of grand spectacle as she destroys conventional patriarchal authority, but this authority reasserts itself in Corneille's oeuvre—although the tensions created by the need to suppress this anarchic force do not fade away completely, as Mitchell Greenberg's interpretations of Corneille show. Greenberg finds a series of binary oppositions in the play: Médée represents the female, nature, matter, and chaos as opposed to male culture, ideal form, and the order of patriarchy.[32] The patriarchal desire for posterity is shown in Jason's need to keep his children and to deny their link to Médée; the Law or legal system, represented by Créon, reinforces the suppression of the rebellious woman (Greenberg 1986, 29–30). She chose Jason over her father, over the Law, and is now being rejected and demonized for her transgressions. When her magical, natural powers are taken up again, it becomes clear that male culture's belief that it can suppress the feminine is only a delusion: she is the Phallic Woman, unbridled power recognizing no law (21–23).

Greenberg notes that Jason has a larger role in Corneille's play than in either of his models, Euripides and Seneca. Jason participates in his own downfall and shares in the guilt for society's destruction. But within the play, only Médée is blamed. She becomes the scapegoat, and yet without her, Jason is impotent. Jason's scandalous suicide means that culture, order, and community are destroyed with Médée's departure; she represents an integral albeit threatening part of civilization whose repression is as dangerous as allowing her to inhabit patriarchal society (Greenberg 1986, 27–34). The threat of the feminine continues in the tragedies to come, according to Greenberg, but when Corneille leaves the world of myth for history, the repression of woman's chaotic nature is more successful (36).

I agree that the entry into history leads to tragedy as individual aspirations are absorbed into a more fixed social structure. André Stegmann speaks of dramatic tension emanating from the relationship between the individual and society, a tension he sees building from *Horace* (1639–1640) on.[33] This tension already exists in the early comedies, and it is certainly present in *Médée*. Society suffers while Médée emerges triumphant; as Fumaroli states, Corneille has separated morality from art. Vice can be spectacular, entertaining, and it does not need to be punished on his stage. But Médée's expulsion from society was not her choice. Forced into a destructive performance, she creates an illusion harmful to the collectivity onstage, but not to the audience who sympathizes with her. Corneille makes a sorceress and murderess admirably heroic with his own black magic. Fumaroli correctly sees a parallel with the "white magic" of Corneille's next play, which is more explicitly an allegory of the theater (1990, 504).

Corneille's Comic Illusion

L'Illusion comique returns Corneille to comedy while simultaneously allowing him to play with tragicomedy and tragedy once again.[34] In the dedication, he calls the play "a strange monster"; he also deems it "bizarre and extravagant" and insists that he has created something totally new (*OC,* 1:613, 1:1428). The play is indeed original, and it was greatly appreciated by the public in 1635–1636 when it was first performed, remaining popular in 1660 when the other comedies were seen as outmoded. Still performed frequently, *L'Illusion comique* is great fun, despite opening with a father in distress.

Pridament sent his son away in disgrace years ago and has not seen him since. Feeling guilty and longing to renew the tie, he seeks help from a magician, Alcandre. Alcandre assures Pridament that his son has done well; the touch of a magic wand conjures up a collection of magnificent clothing, appropriate for the wealthiest, most distinguished aristocrat. Clindor's social condition has changed, says Alcandre, and he now has the right to dress as a nobleman.[35] Alcandre agrees to produce the ghost or image of Clindor and his companions but warns Pridament not to leave the cave on pain of death once the illusion is operating.

Acts 2 through 4 depict Clindor's adventures, with an even greater mixture of tones than we see in the earlier comedies. Clindor is employed by Matamore, a variation on the *miles gloriosus,* or military man, hiding his cowardice with bravado, a stock character since Plautus. Matamore provides very amusing verbal play because his declarations of fabulous exploits are comically exaggerated and entertainingly creative.[36] After claiming to have single-handedly conquered a few foreign kingdoms with a mere glance, breath, or mention of his own name, Matamore's thoughts turn to love (2.1.231–45). He is adored by all women to the extent that 1,000 used to die each day for love of him, to say nothing of the goddesses who crowded at his feet. He has taken care of this inconvenience by ordering Jupiter, on threat of losing his position as ruler of the gods, to make him handsome only when he wants to be (2.2.259–308). The contrast between Matamore's other-worldly fantasies and the reality of his insecurity is intensified by the physical comedy of farce during his last appearances. Not only does he have to endure threats of bodily harm from his valet, Clindor, he beats a hasty retreat in act 4, scene 4, for fear of attack from the servants of Géronte, the "heavy father" figure. Matamore has hidden in Géronte's attic for four days (living on nectar and ambrosia) in order to avoid the beating, but hunger drives him into the open. His lines at moments of tension in the plot highlight the diversity of registers that keeps spectators off balance. For example, the verbal virtuosity of Matamore's first appearance is abruptly interrupted by his fear at the sight of Adraste, a competitor for the affections of the play's heroine, Isabelle. The clever Clindor plays along with his master, while behind his back Clindor also courts Isabelle. The gaiety of the situation is altered in act 2, scene 1 by Adraste's threats to Isabelle: either she will accept his marriage proposal or be forced to do so by her father. The lighter atmosphere returns in scene 2, as Isabelle pretends to accept Matamore's hallucination, but a more serious tone invades the expression of her love for Clindor in scene 5. He is nothing but a valet, but she will sacrifice all of Adraste's riches in favor of Clindor.

Despite a classical comic plot leavened by Matamore, the tone shifts more strikingly when Clindor kills Adraste in a duel in act 3. As Clindor waits in prison to be executed, the spectator knows that we are now in the world of tragicomedy, whose adventures can be life-threatening but where hope always remains. Isabelle's servant, Lyse, had betrayed Clindor and Isabelle to Adraste out of jealousy, augmented by Clindor's toying with her affections. But in act 4 she takes the initiative to save him by seducing the jailer. Two couples are formed as Clindor, Isabelle, Lyse, and the jailer leave for a new life together at the end of act 4. The story is not over, however. Alcandre will conjure up new "phantoms" two years older and living in luxury.

There are two versions of act 5, although both contain "tragic" action. Both begin in a garden with Lyse and Isabelle, magnificently clothed, awaiting the arrival of Clindor. Clindor, seemingly true to the character traits he displayed in flirting with Lyse, has come to seduce yet another woman, Princess Rosine. But his wife ambushes him and showers him with invective. Isabelle also suggests how dangerous it is to commit adultery with the wife of his protector. Clindor claims he cannot help himself; although he still loves Isabelle, Rosine is irresistible. After this admission, Isabelle attempts suicide, probably with Clindor's sword. This shocking act "cures" Clindor, who declares his undying love to his wife.

During this touching scene, Rosine arrives. Clindor tells her that their liaison is over, but in the folly of passion, she threatens to denounce him to her husband. At this moment, the prince's servants arrive, and both Clindor and Rosine are killed. Isabelle will be taken to the prince, who has long been in love with her. With the 1660 edition of his theater, Corneille modified this ending by having Isabelle faint and expire on top of the body of her husband.

The curtain falls in Alcandre's cave. Pridament is of course extremely upset to see his son dead, but the magician has one last surprise in the play's final scene. The curtain reopens to reveal Clindor and his friends counting their money: they have become actors. Pridament is at first scandalized, but Alcandre explains that things have changed for the new generation and that the theater is now a very honorable and lucrative profession, appreciated by everyone from commoners to the king. The best minds of the nation are devoting themselves to the theater! Pridament is of course converted, convinced now of the brilliance, the usefulness, and the attraction of the theater (5.6.1811).

With this last scene, Corneille adds an important twist to the notion of the play within the play, which had been a popular baroque device since at least 1628.[37] This comedy, in which Corneille uses every possible commonplace of French theater of the 1630s, is really about the theater; its title refers to the *theatrical* illusion.[38] Prospero's "All the world's a stage" in Shakespeare's *The Tempest* and the concept of the *theatrum mundi* were not new notions in France. But here the comments on the benefits of going to the theater and allowing oneself to be transported to the world of illusion show a self-consciousness about his art that Corneille's contemporaries did not express explicitly within the confines of a play. As Robert Nelson points out, the reactions we see from Pridament at the end of every act are "dramaturgy dramatized." Alcandre in his cave/theater verifies at these moments that he has aroused Pridament's surprise and curiosity, staples of Cornelian theater.[39] "Corneille's subject is not the theatricality of life but the theatricality of theater," states Nelson (1958, 56).

Role playing takes on a new importance in this context as all four founding members of Clindor's theatrical troop show their talents prior to act 5. Clindor, a member of the bourgeoisie, plays the role of valet while claiming to be a nobleman, "le Sieur de la Montagne." He tells Lyse that he prefers her to Isabelle, but since she has no money, he will keep courting the mistress. Ralph Albanese sees this as proof of his penchant for being onstage: Clindor's "real" identity consists of a series of roles, and becoming a professional actor is the only way he can be reintegrated into the social order. He must "theatricalize" his nonconformity (Albanese, 139–40). Isabelle enters into and out of Matamore's fantasy world with ease. Lyse seduces the jailer in order to save Clindor and pretends with Isabelle and with the jailer that Clindor had never been a love interest for her. The jailer demonstrates his enjoyment of acting in a rather cruel game right before freeing Clindor; he informs the prisoner that he has been granted the privilege of being executed at night so as to avoid the shame of public hanging.

The case of Matamore is all the more interesting because his status as an actor has to be questioned. As Albanese says, he is imprisoned in his mask, a dreamer full of folly (138–39). The *fanfaron* character is really a distortion of an actor, according to Mallinson (1984, 186). He notes the originality of having Clindor (and, I would add, Isabelle) accept Matamore on his own terms. The spectator joins the lucid characters in entering momentarily into Matamore's world thanks to his impressive control over language (Mallinson 1984, 165–69). The power of the dramatic (or comic) illusion is thus underlined from yet another angle.

The value of theater lies in its many lessons: versatility and adaptability are necessary in order for characters to survive in Corneille's dramatic universe, as in the "real" world. The transformative power of the creative imagination is shown, as Alcandre's illusion produces life from death, familial reconciliation, and social salvation. Harmony and order reign at the end of the play, as at the end of any classical comedy, suggesting the attractiveness of comedy's basic structures. Learning occurs thanks to *L'Illusion comique,* but it is instruction by means of pleasure: "My reward is in pleasing you," Alcandre tells Pridament (5.6.1820). The practical effect of the comic illusion is not only that Pridament can regain his son—he has also learned about an important source of happiness and new knowledge: the theater, useful not on moral grounds but rather in the aesthetic realm so essential to the quality of life. I can only partially agree with Nelson when he says that Corneille keeps the ethical separate from the aesthetic, however (1958, 57–60). While Corneille insists strongly in his theoretical writings that his first goal is the pleasure rather than the instruction of the spectator, he gives this pleasure an ethical dimension when the structures of both the plays and the *Discours* force us into the role of judge (Carlin 1990). The success of the hero's performance, like the dramatist's, is for us to determine.

An important message was communicated by *L'Illusion comique* just at the time when Corneille was about to attain lasting fame with one of the most widely discussed and controversial plays of the century. Alcandre the writer/director is a glorious figure at the height of his profession. Clindor too has achieved distinction thanks to the theater, as will Corneille—in an extraordinary fashion, thanks to *Le Cid* and the quarrel surrounding it. Striving for superiority will remain a major theme of Corneille's oeuvre.

Chapter Three
The Tetralogy

The Hero Performs

The triumph of the comic illusion is the triumph of a hero who convinces his audience, on- and offstage, that he has served them well. Alcandre, the magician of *L'Illusion comique,* and Corneille, the playwright, have entertained the spectators of their work, and in giving them pleasure, have taught them about the value of public servants, who in the early plays are dramatists, actors, and the young couples who project the hope of social renewal. A top-notch performance benefits society; observers have the duty to determine which spectacles should be applauded. Paul Bénichou explores the special role played by the spectator of Cornelian tragedy as judge of the hero's capacity to lead, to protect, and to impress his audience (26–27). As Starobinski says, the individual hero may deploy an overwhelming energy, but it counts for nothing without the validating echo of universal admiration (68). In *Le Cid, Horace, Cinna,* and *Polyeucte,* themes such as honor and virtue form the basis of the hero's performance, replacing the willfully harmful inventiveness of the tricksters seen in the early comedies and in *Clitandre.*[1] The blocking character/scapegoat does not disappear in the tetralogy but undergoes interesting alterations. Trouble still brews within the ranks of the young couples portrayed, although these plays resemble Frye's romantic comedy rather than the ironic comedy Corneille produced prior to *L'Illusion comique.*

As the young couples are formed, female characters continue to play an important role. But they are not able or willing to serve society as the male heroes do, and therefore, the label *hero* does not really apply to the female protagonists. The male heroes of these four plays deploy their energy and creativity for the good of the community, with great glory for themselves as a result. The fundamental comic structure of Cornelian theater remains in place, forcing the spectator to become actively involved in judgment of the heroes; these dramas continue after more than 300 years to hold our interest because they render this basic structure much more ambiguous than it had been in his previous works. Corneille had many successes after the tetralogy, but these four plays are considered his most "typically Cornelian" and most brilliant works. They are bound together by the victory of a hero applauded by the society surrounding him, but victories are attained at a heavy personal price. A fascinating aura of unresolved conflict haunts the hero, and the renaissance of the society that is served by him is troubled as well.[2]

Le Cid

Still Corneille's most popular play, Le Cid has had at least eight new editions since 1970.[3] Set in medieval Spain, the story is based on a legend dramatized in 1618 as Las Mocedades del Cid by the Spanish playwright Guillèn de Castro. As Corneille's play begins, we learn that the count, Don Gomès, has chosen Don Rodrigue as his daughter Chimène's future husband. Chimène is delighted, but premonitions of danger haunt her. Also troubled is the Infanta (the king's daughter), who considers herself the matchmaker between Chimène and Rodrigue, suppressing her own love for Rodrigue as inappropriate for a princess.

Chimène soon finds that her fears were justified. Rodrigue's father, Don Diègue, an elderly former military chief, has been chosen by the king to instruct the prince. Don Gomès, the current leader of the army, is so angry at the slight to his prowess that he slaps Don Diègue. The old warrior is unable to avenge the affront to his honor, so he calls on his son Rodrigue. In his famous stances, a set piece in a different verse rhythm from the rest of the play, Rodrigue expresses his torment. He realizes that his relationship with Chimène will be unalterably damaged, and yet he has no choice but to maintain his father's and his own honor. He ends the first act on an affirmative note. He will hesitate no longer and will die in combat, his blood not tainted by dishonor.

The count has in the meantime been asked by the king's representative to apologize to Don Diègue and accept the king's will. The count refuses, pointing out the king's dependence on his military skill. Many scholars (notably Bénichou) have seen in this dispute the conflict between the aristocracy and the centralizing monarchy in France under Richelieu, who had banned the duels so frequent among the nobility. The danger of duels to the security of the state is proven when young Rodrigue miraculously kills the count.

As Chimène awaits news of the duel, she explores the double bind in which she finds herself. She would like to forbid Rodrigue from dueling

with her father, but she knows that society would reject him as a dishon-
orable coward if he did not fight. The Infanta, meanwhile, sees hope for
her own love because if Chimène is obliged to break with Rodrigue and
if he wins the duel, he will be worthy of her. The Infanta's hopes are
kept alive by Rodrigue's victory and Chimène's actions following it.
Chimène eloquently demands that Rodrigue be executed for killing her
father, setting up for herself the same tension Rodrigue had to face
between love on the one hand, and duty and honor on the other. This
tension continues throughout the play, although these concepts are
inseparable from one another: Chimène and Rodrigue agree that neither
could love someone without honor. Chimène envisages suicide after
obtaining Rodrigue's death, and despite the insistence of her companion
Elvire, of the Infanta, and of the king that she should abandon her quest
to have Rodrigue punished, she persists—with Rodrigue's approval.

In act 3, scene 4, during another "duel" considered scandalous by
Corneille's critics during the subsequent *Querelle du Cid,* Rodrigue hides
in Chimène's home in order to speak with her. He offers her his sword so
that she can exact her own vengeance on him, preserving her honor in
the only pure manner, he says (3.4.955–60). Chimène rejects the gory
proposal, admitting her love and refusing ever to kill him herself. Both
are concerned with their *gloire.* This term carried more meaning at the
time than "glory" suggests: *gloire* connotes a well-developed self-image
indissociable from one's reputation in society. As Bénichou says, the
noble's desire concentrates on pride, which grows in a steady movement
from self-contemplation to the desire literally to make a spectacle of
oneself, which is the very definition of *gloire* (25). Rodrigue predicts dishonor for Chimène if it becomes known that she loves the murderer of
her father. In refuting his argument, Chimène redefines *gloire:*

> It will, if I spare you, collect more praise;
> I *want* dark slander's strident voice to raise
> My honor to the skies, and mourn my woe,
> Knowing that I love yet still pursue my foe.
> (3.4.969–72)[4]

Chimène claims to be just as much of a hero as her lover, but in fact she
does not declare her love publicly until the final scene of the play. On
the contrary, she denies any feeling for Rodrigue when faced with
increasing pressure from the king to accept him as her husband. The

king goes so far as to announce Rodrigue's (false) death in order to force
a confession of love from Chimène, to no avail. Social pressure works
doubly on Chimène. Despite her daring vision in the above quotation,
scandal threatens if she proclaims her love (and the French Academy did
indeed find her emotions scandalous when they evaluated the play).[5]
Moreover, her pursuit of revenge for her father's death is increasingly
criticized within the play as socially destructive because Rodrigue has
replaced her father as the protector of the state. He defeats the attacking Moors between acts 3 and 4, leaving him invulnerable to Chimène's
demands for justice.

In introducing the battle with the Moors, Corneille was criticized
(notably by Scudéry and the academy) for breaking the unity of action.
He had overloaded the play with an implausible number of extraordinary events in 24 hours in an attempt to respect the unity of time. The
unity of place was also very loosely followed as the scenes inside
Chimène's house suggest a change in decor. Corneille always rejected a
strict interpretation of the unities, to which few playwrights adhered
completely in the 1630s. When in the 1660s Racine used the limits
imposed by the unities to create an intense, stifling atmosphere,
Corneille continued to insist on flexibility. His plays remain filled with
events while Racine's simpler plots distill emotional conflicts. Political
life stays in the background in Racinian tragedy, whereas for Corneille it
is an essential ingredient, never divorced from the love story, always
altering it inexorably.

After act 3, Rodrigue is the Cid, named by the Moors as their lord.
Although his new relationship with the monarchy makes him immune
to punishment for the death of the count, he nonetheless continues to
suffer from his loss of Chimène. His father had castigated his concern for
a mere woman, worth nothing in comparison to honor and reputation.
But Rodrigue belongs to a new generation. He is a courtly lover, a
knight who would serve his lady, and not just a simple warrior. The pastoral influence seen in the comedies does not disappear when Corneille
begins to address political questions, but it certainly takes on a new resonance.

Rodrigue continues to display the traits of a perfect courtly lover in
act 5, scene 1, during his second private meeting with Chimène. The
king is determined to silence her by permitting her chosen champion to
duel with Rodrigue; she must marry the victor. Rodrigue plans to let
himself be killed by Don Sanche so that Chimène may be avenged.
Chimène, however, is so horrified both at the thought of Rodrigue's

death and at the idea that she will become Don Sanche's wife that she encourages Rodrigue to win the duel and win her hand, though she expresses shame at her weakness.

It is only when she believes Rodrigue to be dead that Chimène can give free rein to her sentiments. In act 5, scene 5, Don Sanche arrives with Rodrigue's sword, but before he can explain that Rodrigue has required him to present the sword to her, she lashes out, refusing to fulfill her promise to marry him and declaring to the king her intention to enter a convent in order to mourn both the count and Rodrigue. In the last scene of the play, everyone expects Chimène to accept Rodrigue as her husband. Everyone, that is, except Rodrigue, who understands that Chimène can never forget her duty to her father without destroying her identity, her *gloire*. He encourages her once again to take his life with her own hands. Once again she refuses, and she refuses marriage as well. But the possibility of marrying Rodrigue in the future is left open, both by the king's insistence and by Chimène herself in an ambiguous final statement.

Chimène's apparent acquiescence drew heavy criticism in *Les Sentiments de l'Académie Française sur la tragi-comédie du Cid* (*OC*, 1:810–11), to which Corneille was forbidden to respond. Although Corneille changed the genre designation of the play from tragicomedy to tragedy in the 1648 edition of his works, it is in the 1660 edition that the alterations are major, especially with regard to Chimène's role. Her last speech becomes more respectful of the king in refusing the marriage while at the same time leaving much less room to suppose that she will some day accept it.[6] The decorum of classical tragedy replaces the verve and open-ended quality of the original version.

The ambiguous ending is one of the principal reasons for the varied interpretations this play has inspired. Dozens of articles, chapters, and monographs have been devoted to *Le Cid*. When one asks whether the play is a tragedy, the answer often depends on how much emphasis is given to the sociopolitical as opposed to the personal. Couton downplays any tragic import when he stresses Corneille's profound Christian humanist optimism learned from the Jesuits. *Le Cid* is for him a celebration of man's impressive abilities to overcome obstacles.[7] Michel Prigent, who also concentrates on the political in Cornelian theater, agrees that the hero triumphs here, although in his view heroic victories will not continue as the corpus develops.[8] Doubrovsky sees an exalted Rodrigue, who has learned self-mastery by converting sensual love into "heroic" love; in the end, Chimène is saved from her cowardice and sentimentalism by his heroism. Doubrovsky believes that the marriage will take place and that if love based solely on sentiment has disappeared, this is a necessary sacrifice that allows Rodrigue to accede to heroic status in the political order (1963, 99–132).

These critics have accentuated the optimism they find in the last scene of the play, but those who do not read the play in primarily sociopolitical terms see a less positive ending. Nadal is on the same track as Doubrovsky when he says that Chimène is reduced to impotence by Rodrigue's domination of her (Nadal, 139), but his analysis finds no attenuating optimism in Rodrigue's triumph. Love is the enemy of heroism, and Chimène will not share in a "heroic" love. Rodrigue will remain guilty for her, and he understands this, according to Nadal (171–77). Évelyne Méron considers Corneille to be the poet of pain, of loss, of solitude, of failure, of dissatisfaction, and of eternal misunderstanding between lovers.[9] Milorad Margitic's *Essai sur la mythologie du "Cid"* is one of the few book-length studies of the play. Using the theory of myth developed by Roland Barthes, Margitic sees the characters as mythmakers who are in the process of constructing identities for themselves.[10] The characters desire a heroism that will defy the ravages of time, but Don Diègue and the count serve as examples of the impossibility of achieving an eternal heroic state (Margitic 1976, 34). Lofty ideals disguise the fact that personal interest governs all of the characters' moves, but society participates in Rodrigue's efforts at self-deification (75–83, 121). The unfortunate result of his exalted status is self-mutilation and desolation as he moves away from intimate contact with his father and with Chimène (97–117). This reading gives my notion of performance for the public good a particularly negative twist, one that the text fully supports.

Those critics who highlight the female characters also find a tragic dimension in *Le Cid*. The Infanta, whose role some have considered superfluous, serves to enhance Rodrigue's worth in the eyes of the spectator, and she provides another example of a female character's virtuous suppression of desire in favor of *gloire*. She seeks to enhance her self-image, confirmed by the recognition of others, although in the Infanta's sheltered world the only audience is her governess, Léonor. Whereas Rodrigue has nothing to hide in his quest for *gloire*, both Chimène and the Infanta feel it necessary to disguise their love for him in public even as they proclaim in private that this love dishonors them not at all. The heroines subscribe to the same ethic as the male characters, but society makes it much more difficult for them to uphold it. The role of the

Infanta also helps make the many structural symmetries in the play more visible. Many scholars have noted the oppositions set up between Chimène and Rodrigue, the two fathers, Chimène and the Infanta, the Infanta and Sanche (both passive rivals of the main couple), Sanche and Rodrigue, Rodrigue and the count, the new monarchy versus the feudal aristocracy, and Rodrigue and his father.[11]

Corneille's fascination with symmetry is given a new weight with Greenberg's *Corneille, Classicism and the Ruses of Symmetry*. In a play where we witness the beginnings of the absolute monarchy, Chimène is the disruptive element that prevents these well-balanced tensions from resulting in a final harmony. "The figure of Chimène introduces into this world of masculine devolution the unsettling, decentering, 'unnatural' force of desire that is recalcitrant to political accommodations, to any 'raison d'État' " (Greenberg 1986, 46). Rodrigue and Chimène seem so alike in their shared values, says Greenberg, but the men in the play are linked by a system based on the exclusion of the feminine (49).[12] Han Verhoeff considers Chimène to be completely isolated at the end, and symmetries are broken as the Infanta joins the ranks of the male characters and everyone on stage participates in castigating Chimène for her pursuit of punishment for Rodrigue (1982, 71–72). In Barbara Woshinsky's interpretation, "the separation of words from events and the substitution of words for deeds, intrinsic to Chimène's language, are basic premises of Corneille's rhetorical vision."[13] But *res* and *verba,* things and words, must eventually reconnect, as they do for Rodrigue—and as cannot happen for Corneille's female characters, who lack access to the sword as a concrete, physical means of realizing their claims to heroic behavior (Woshinsky, 32).[14]

I will end this very partial review of critical works inspired by *Le Cid* with an example that furnishes a striking illustration of the multiplicity of meanings generated by the play. In a 1984 conference paper published in 1988, Doubrovsky looks back at his 1963 analysis and finds it incomplete, even wrong in some places.[15] He replaces his former emphasis on the defeat of Chimène with a more critical view of Rodrigue's role, discovered due to a change in methodology. The Hegelian master-slave dialectic that informed Doubrovsky's *Corneille et la dialectique du héros* is replaced with a (Lacanian) psychoanalytic approach reminiscent of Greenberg's in 1986. Both critics find the personal and the political inseparable, and both see Chimène as a threat to patriarchy, but Doubrovsky emphasizes Rodrigue's *joy* at putting her in a position of inferiority during their first meeting. The proffering of the sword is a symbolic rape and graphic representation of Chimène's weakness, which must be exploited because woman is the first and the only real enemy of the hero (Doubrovsky 1988, 21–28). To love is to risk contamination by the repressed feminine in oneself, and at the end of act 3, scene 4, Rodrigue is defeated just as Chimène is by the admission of love (35). The state will not tolerate a division of loyalty in its hero/servants, but Rodrigue is "revirilized" by the fight with the Moors. The patriarchy forces Rodrigue to become completely masculine, thus (as Margitic says), part of his nature is quashed when he accedes to his identity as a hero (Doubrovsky 1988, 41). The tragedy becomes a tragicomedy—for him, but not for Chimène (35–38). The mutual recognition of weakness in love in act 3 is a moment of anagnorisis as Aristotle defined it, the act of recognition that reverses the direction of plot lines (40–41). Against his will, Rodrigue plunges into tragedy along with Chimène, until another reversal propels him out of the morass of sentiment.

The idea of recognition is central to my thesis about the Cornelian hero's need for social approbation. Terence Cave examines the complexities of Aristotelian recognition in his book *Recognitions: A Study in Poetics*. Anagnorisis in Aristotle's *Poetics* is the move from ignorance to knowledge on the part of characters or spectators (33). Chimène and Rodrigue recognize new, negative identities for themselves when they come together. Illusions of the heroic repression of love abound in act 3, scene 4, but as Doubrovsky says, they are both defeated at the end of the scene by the admission of their frailty as lovers. "Oh mortal griefs!" cries Chimène; "How vainly we implore!" responds Rodrigue (3.4.991). Can what has been recognized be successfully repressed? Certainly not for Chimène, with no outlet in action. Rodrigue dazzles his public, and his last words signal his satisfaction with the outcome:

> To win Chimène, and serve my sovereign, too,
> What can you order that I cannot do?
> Though I must bear with being so far from her,
> I now can hope, and I am happy, Sir.
>
> (5.7.1833–36)

Chimène renounces her vengeance, but her parting words are: "Must I for his deeds be the salary, / Soiling eternally my own good name, / My hands dipped in my father's blood and shame?" (5.7.1810–12). Tragedy is to be found in the role of Chimène, triumph in Rodrigue's successful repression of sorrow and recognition as society's savior by spectators on- and offstage. Chimène and her father are the scapegoats of this play, with the potential for her eventual integration into a society that rejects her father's feudal values. Classification of *Le Cid* as definitively either tragedy or tragicomedy is impossible, and this ambiguity in theatrical genre is generated by Corneille's manipulation of a fundamentally comic structure in which the audience serves as judge.

Horace

Horace, first performed in 1640, is considered the first French classical tragedy since it manages to follow the unities of time, place, and action more closely than previous tragic plays. From the first scene, the atmosphere is more somber as lengthy replies make for a rhythm entirely different from *Le Cid*'s varied speech patterns.[16] The tragic dilemma is once again intensified by the reactions of the female characters to a painful situation that leaves little room for a positive resolution. *Horace* is the story of the founding of Rome's greatness in its defeat of the rival city of Alba. Although male-female relations are essential, the political dimension of the play becomes much more significant than in *Le Cid*.

Sabine, Horace's wife, opens the tragedy lamenting her torn identity. An Alban, she has married into a Roman family, and a war between the cities devastates her. She plans to side with the losers, a very un-Roman attitude, which seems to contrast with that of Horace's sister, Camille. Camille is engaged to Sabine's brother, Curiace, but she has appeared joyous at the announcement of a definitive battle. Camille's joy is short-lived, however. It was inspired by an oracle that predicted her imminent union with Curiace. Nightmares have erased her optimism with the realization that she will never be permitted to marry a man who is either the victor or the slave of Rome. Camille's devotion to Curiace is complete, and, like Sabine, she abhors the effect of politics on her personal life. Thus, when Curiace appears, she wrongly assumes that he has renounced Alba in favor of their love. A temporary truce has been declared while three warriors are chosen to represent each side. Total war will be avoided and the losers will be subjects rather than slaves, according to the new agreement.

Camille and Curiace imagine a bright future, but of course their hope is soon dashed. Horace and his two brothers have been selected to fight the three Curiatii. Curiace is proud to have been chosen but expresses his friendship and sorrow at the situation to Horace. Horace, however, is

stern: "Alba has named you; I know you not" (2.3.502). Curiace finds
Horace's idea of heroic virtue barbarous, but for Horace their painful
dilemma furnishes an opportunity for greater glory. No regret, no weakness can be allowed; Horace claims to feel only joy. He tells Camille that
whatever the outcome, there must be no mourning, only celebration of
the victors.

Camille expects Curiace to refuse the honor bestowed on him, in def-
erence to her love. Although touched by her pleas, he is determined to
do his duty. The next attack against Curiace's resolve comes from his sister. Sabine asks the men to kill her in order to dissolve the ties that bind
them and provide more legitimacy to their fight. Even Horace is shaken
by her entreaty, to the point that he asks his father to sequester the
women during the combat; Sabine has threatened to throw herself
between her two families. She tries to convince herself to honor the victors, but she realizes that she will always think of the victims and will
therefore be unable to live up to Horace's standards of virtue. In *Horace,*
women are dangerous, as Greenberg and Verhoeff both indicate throughout their analyses of the play.

Sabine and Camille are arguing over which of them is suffering more
when they learn that the two armies have stopped the battle, unable to
bear the sight of family members fighting each other. The gods are consulted, but no relief is given. More suspense is generated by the announcement that Curiace and his brothers have killed two of the Horatii and that
Horace himself has escaped. His father is devastated by the dishonor his
son has brought on the family, but soon Horace's departure is revealed as a
strategy for victory. He was able to take on the combatants one at a time
and thus to win the day for Rome. His proud father goes to comfort
Sabine, telling Camille that she has lost little in comparison to her sister-
in-law; she can easily replace Curiace with a Roman fiancé.

Of course, Camille refuses Roman virtue, which she names brutality
in the long monologue of act 4, scene 4. She confronts Horace with her
loathing in the next scene and tells him that she hopes his glory will be
sullied by some act of cowardice. She even goes so far as to express
repeatedly her hatred of Rome, which infuriates Horace to the point
that he kills her—offstage, in accordance with classical propriety (*la
bienséance*). The murder of his sister accomplishes her goal: she is united
with Curiace, and Horace's glory is indeed tainted. Horace justifies his
act, but Sabine's plea that he kill her too once again touches him. She
will mourn her brothers and by Horace's rules deserves to die; she
desires death as the only possible remedy for her suffering.

The elder Horace agrees that his daughter merited death, but not by her brother's hand. Horace's excessive pride and ambition were punished by the gods when he demeaned himself, according to his father. Earthly judgment arrives in the person of the king, Tulle, who listens to the case for and against Horace. Horace's primary accuser is Valère, another of Camille's suitors, who tells the king that since Horace has proven himself to be a menace to the liberty of Romans, he should pay with his own life.[17] Horace is ready to die not to expiate his sister's murder but because his reputation can only continue to degenerate from this point on. He asks the king's permission to sacrifice himself to his *gloire* (5.2.1593–94).

Both husband and wife repeatedly express a death wish in act 5. Sabine would like to die in Horace's place, seeing no room for her Alban identity in the new Roman order of things. But she will live, a disturbing element seemingly not integrated into the newly constituted Rome. As for Horace, the elder Horace explains (in the longest speech of the play) that his son should not be put to death since his crime was inspired by love for Rome. The political dimension of the tragedy is underscored by the elder Horace's admonition to his son that only the king and the elite surrounding him can guarantee a hero's honor. Public opinion in its instability should be discounted, and service to the monarchy as well as to his father should be his reason for living. But Horace cannot ignore public opinion, recognizing that the title of hero depends on the approbation of the entire community. Horace expresses his awareness that the people of Rome will never be satisfied with just one miraculous act, and his desire to die is a means of avoiding the injustice of their impossibly high expectations (5.2.1555–72). Since Horace does not believe he can maintain heroic status, he chooses death. Tulle refuses Horace permission to kill himself, however, because the hero is the military support of the new state. The king knows that without Horace he would have no throne.

The Roman State has been born, but at what price? John Lyons has studied the links between history and tragedy in the play: there are no moral lessons but rather the story of the founding of Rome (and, by implication, of France, its heir) (1996, 40). The play reveals the fratricides necessary to establish the city, then the empire. First Romulus murdered Remus (an event alluded to twice in the play), then Horace killed the Curiatii. When he went on to attack his sister, was this act merely an extension of those battles essential to the protection of the state, as both Doubrovsky (1963, 152) and Stegmann (1968, 2:584) suggest? Corneille criticized the death of Camille in the 1660 *Examen* as a break in the unity of action, since a second subject (danger for the individual) is introduced into a play about threats to the state (*OC,* 1:841). But Lyons sees Camille's demise as essential to the tragedy not because there is no difference between two "heroic" acts but rather because the position in which Horace is placed illustrates how acts get interpreted after the fact (1996, 41–44). We are led to agree with Valère's interpretation of the battle: Horace's flight after his brothers were killed was a conscious strategy to win and not an act of cowardice. But is the historical assumption necessarily "true"? In the ideological context of the coming Roman Empire, any other interpretation would be unacceptable (Lyons 1996, 46). The scandal of his sister's death is also assimilated into official history (48).

The heroic Horace, also a scapegoat, is reintegrated into the community, but the fit is uncomfortable because codes of conduct are changing before our eyes in the tragedy. Horace may have saved the state, but his values are fundamentally archaic, according to Lyons (1996, 47–49). Curiace, Sabine, and Camille are not ready for the new world order, but neither is Horace. Just like his sister, he places domestic concerns ahead of the state by seeking private justice against her. The time when the family could dispense its own justice and coexist with other self-regulating clans has passed in the play (as it has in France of the 1630s, I would add). Moreover, his claim that he was defending the state by killing her implies that he has the right to kill in the state's name (Lyons 1996, 55). He becomes dangerous, as Valère says (5.2.1487–1510). "Rome's survival will come at the price of an inner scar" (Lyons 1996, 70)—or several scars, as Albans like Sabine continue to exist, their former identity repressed, within Rome.

Does the spectator identify with the scarred hero's suffering, and does the play thereby fulfill Mauron's definition of tragedy? In a classic 1952 study, Louis Herland sympathizes with Horace's solitude. Horace is in a state of despair, in Herland's view, because he loved both Curiace and Camille, and he desires death because he is afraid to examine the destructive side of his heroism.[18] (John Lyons believes that Horace has in effect already committed suicide in killing Curiace, whom he sees as another "self" [1996, 50]). Despite Horace's tragic lassitude, Herland concludes that his pride remains intact and that he is indifferent to judgment by the public or the king (203–4). This view contrasts with André Stegmann's reading of the play. Stegmann shares my preoccupation with the problem of the exceptional individual seeking recognition from the collectivity and sees Horace in a state of exaltation thanks to his public service—even after Camille's death (1968, 2:582). Horace realizes that some see him as a monster, but he accepts his fate with pride in his accomplishments in strengthening Rome. He considers the murder a reasonable, just act, as justifiable as killing the Curiatii. He knows, however, that he cannot change the public evaluation of Camille's death (2:583–84). But to what "public" is Horace playing? Doubrovsky points out that Horace needs the recognition of "slaves" (the masses) as well as "masters" (the aristocracy) because without both groups behind him, the hero cannot achieve his goal of preserving his reputation for eternity. The public has to continue to be impressed, and the only way to do this is with the installation of a new system, a new state, recognized by the entirety of society (Doubrovsky 1963, 175–83).

Tulle incarnates the state and ends the play on a note of harmony by dispensing a brand of justice acceptable to all social classes. Camille receives her due as, in the last words of the play, the king announces that she will be entombed with Curiace. Two recent interpretations of Camille's burial differ sharply. Greenberg sees her entombment as a sign of the repression of any challenge to Roman law (1986, 87). Harriet Stone disagrees, believing that Tulle commemorates her revolt and preserves her place in history.[19] Camille's burial could easily have been kept hidden and thereby devalued (Stone 1996, 48). Instead, "Tulle consolidates his power without erasing from memory how that power came into being" (54–55); "Camille's final entombment does not supplant the more dominant closure provided through the play's representation of the king's authority and the idea of Rome as a unique and totalizing power" (57). Joined to the commemoration of Horace's acts, the closing reference to her shows the value of what has been excluded (57–58).

The duty, honor, and *gloire* espoused by Chimène interest neither Camille nor Sabine, who do not share the ethic of the male characters. This debate between the genders is often framed by critics as a conflict between public and private values in the play, but as Hélène Merlin has shown, the notions of "public" and "private" were not the same in the seventeenth century as they are today.[20] In *Horace,* the political dispute gets bound up in family ties, just as in *Le Cid,* the private quarrel between Don Diègue and the count is about their place in public (Merlin, 251). Chimène is asked to pass from her private complaint against Rodrigue to consideration of the public good, but she wants to link private goals with public ones, as Corneille's male heroes are able to do

(Merlin, 260–61). Chimène's attempt fails because, in supporting her
father, she supports the fading feudal system with its insistence that
individual nobles are as important as the king. Merlin notes that in
every Cornelian tragedy, the hero interiorizes public concerns and supports their value in his very public heroic acts of sacrifice (262–63).
Corneille's heroes are asked to communicate and dedicate their power to
the public (90–107, 380). This analysis contributes to my own view of
their service to society. In *Horace*, Curiace hesitates to make the heroic
sacrifice and is lost, while Horace gains glory. Sabine and Camille refuse
to give their approval to heroic acts of sacrifice, but they do have their
own power to wield. They use it differently from each other and from
the male characters, with varying impact.

   Once again, Corneille ends a play by leaving questions of interpretation wide open. The comic schema remains in place, but innovations
have been introduced to the basic Cornelian dramatic structure. Nadal
devotes an entire chapter to Camille and her violent, total love, which
affirms the right to private happiness divorced from the interests of the
state, in a move rare in Corneille's theater (180–83). Camille is the mirror image of her brother, his true adversary (Doubrovsky 1963, 154).
They both serve their cause gladly, ready to sacrifice their lives and
receive recognition from the king and the society surrounding him.
They share a heroic drive for distinction, but Camille's refusal to place
the collective good above her individual interests denies her access to
gloire, which requires subordination of the personal to the political. In
comedy, the rebirth of society comes from the formation of a healthy
young couple, but the entry into historical subjects means social renaissance only though the development of the state. The hero who serves
the state must pay for his glorious reputation with the sacrifice of his
affective life. The hero of Cornelian tragedy lives and performs on a public stage.

Cinna

After the depiction in *Horace* of the early days of Roman regional hege-
mony, in *Cinna ou la clémence d'Auguste* (1642) the Roman Empire is in
place. Georges Couton follows a long critical tradition when he explains
that Corneille and his fellow dramatists were using the history of Rome
to explore seventeenth-century political questions. In *Cinna,* the
attempt to assassinate a tyrannical ruler was a reflection of Richelieu's
problems with the rebellious aristocracy, according to Couton (*OC,*

1:1582–91). Of course, this is not the only possible reading of the play. As is always the case with Corneille, interpretations grounded in the seventeenth-century context can exist alongside analyses that use twentieth-century critical theories, illuminating the text from different perspectives.

The conspiracy in *Cinna* is led by a woman, Augustus Caesar's "adopted" daughter, Émilie, who has been orphaned by the ruler's political execution of her father. The exposition furnished by Émilie's opening monologue lays out the dilemma clearly: her hatred of Auguste is intense and she plans revenge for her father's death, to be carried out by her fiancé, Cinna. She worries that her plot will lead to Cinna's death, but the desire for retribution wins out. Cinna and Maxime, the other leader of the revolt against Auguste, are suddenly called before the emperor. Émilie briefly panics and wants Cinna to flee, but as the first act ends, she regains her composure, wishing to die alongside her lover.

To the surprise of Cinna and Maxime, Auguste is still unaware of their conspiracy. He wants to consult them about his future as emperor: will he be happier if he abdicates? Cinna responds with irony not evident to Auguste. If Auguste renounces power, does he not implicitly condemn the tyranny of his reign? Surely he must stay on the throne, says Cinna. Maxime encourages Auguste to step down, however. Auguste decides to follow Cinna's advice and remain emperor. He rewards both courtiers, Maxime with the post of governor of Sicily, and Cinna with Émilie's hand in marriage. Auguste's trust of the three conspirators gives a pathetic aura to his role at this point.

After the interview, Cinna castigates Maxime for suggesting an easy way out. Cinna knows that Émilie requires vengeance, not the voluntary departure of Auguste. We discover Maxime's motivation at the beginning of act 3. Maxime is in love with Émilie and in encouraging Auguste to abdicate, he intends to thwart Cinna's chance to serve her. Why should he and his friends risk death for Cinna's greater glory? Maxime lets his servant, Euphorbe, convince him to betray Cinna. At this point, Cinna is suffering mightily from the dishonor of his role playing with Auguste. He sees no solution to his dilemma because if Auguste is not attacked, Émilie will not be avenged. Indeed, she is incensed when he suggests that Auguste is no longer a tyrant. She has no interest in showing mercy to her intended victim and will kill him herself if Cinna is no longer willing to assist her. Cinna replies that he will do her bidding, but he will kill himself after attacking Auguste, in order to preserve his sense of honor.

With the conspirators in turmoil at the beginning of act 4, Euphorbe
reveals the conspiracy to Auguste, with Maxime's blessing. Euphorbe
claims that Maxime has thrown himself into the Tiber in remorse.
Auguste feels anger at Cinna along with guilt at his own past crimes and
resolves to kill himself after condemning Cinna. "Die," he repeats to
himself five times in 10 lines (4.2.1170–79). Auguste's wife, Livie,
intervenes, however, advising him to show clemency to Cinna and to
stay on the throne. Livie's advice seems at first like a political ploy. Since
extermination of perceived enemies has not worked to put down revolt,
why not try a new strategy? "Look for the most useful way out," she
says, rather than provoking more resentment from an unhappy public
(4.3.1210–1215). Livie ends the scene alone, addressing the spectator
and emphasizing the grandeur that Auguste will be able to attain if he
decides to pardon his enemies: he will be "a true Monarch" instead of a
tyrant (4.3.1265–66). Livie suggests the magical, transformative, but
paradoxical potential of pardon as punishment.

Before the denouement, however, there are more anguished encoun-
ters among the plotters. Maxime, alive and well, reveals his love to Émilie and asks her to flee with him. Furious at his betrayal of Cinna, she
decides to give herself up to Auguste. Maxime intends to kill Euphorbe
and then himself in order to regain his tarnished honor, but none of the
three plotters will have to die.

Act 5 contains Auguste's judgments upon them. Cinna and Émilie,
proud of their treason, debate the honor of inspiring the revolt and ask to
be put to death. Maxime arrives to share the guilt; this last straw brings
Auguste to a firm decision. "Je suis maître de moi, comme de l'univers" (I
am master of myself, as of the universe; 5.3.1696), he boldly declares.
Auguste pardons everyone, including Euphorbe. The effect of these acts
of clemency is the "conversion" of his enemies. Even Émilie repents her
hatred, and Livie observes that Auguste has learned the art of gaining his
subjects' true allegiance. It was "Octave," not yet emperor, who committed crimes in the struggle for power, not "Auguste," the virtuous sovereign whose sins were absolved from the moment the gods permitted him
to accede to the throne (5.2.1605–16).

This passage suppports David Clarke's interpretation of the play as a
portrayal of the divine right of Christian kings (219–31); Jacques
Ehrmann comes to the same conclusion by a very different route in his
anthropological reading inspired by Claude Lévi-Strauss's structuralism.
In a network of exchange, says Ehrmann, the characters are concerned
with acquisition and methods of payment, a cycle that is broken by

Auguste's gesture of clemency.[21] The symmetrical structures seen in previous works take on added importance here. As Gordon Pocock notes, *Cinna* builds up a pattern that holds more meaning than plot or characterization.[22] Pocock and Susan Tiefenbrun both explore the play's patterns in detail, although their interpretations lead to conclusions that differ from those reached by Clarke, Ehrmann, and Couton.[23]

Corneille himself points to the importance of structure for the play. We leave Livie in act 4, scene 3, after her advice to Auguste, and are suddenly in Émilie's chambers once again. Corneille was criticized, and criticizes himself in the *Examen,* for not respecting the unity of place and the related rule, the *liaison des scènes,* which states that one scene should follow logically from the preceding one, preferably with the carryover of at least one character. Corneille excuses himself by saying that, of course, Émilie and Auguste could not be in the same room before act 5, and in any case, the whole play takes place in Auguste's palace, thereby preserving the unity of place fairly closely for the 1640s (*OC,* 1:911). Another explanation for the contrast between scenes is that it reinforces the spectator's impression that reversals are constantly occurring throughout the play. Tiefenbrun notes in her semiotic reading the enormous irony that shows up in the way the scenes are arranged, as Émilie stresses the duty of love to serve hate, and we see hate lead to forgiveness by Auguste, which in turn leads to the conversion of the conspirators. Binary patterns of reversal illustrate the characters' confused search for identity, as Émilie wavers between extreme self-confidence and indecisiveness, while Cinna sees switches in position all around him, in public opinion, in Émilie's wishes, in Auguste's politics, and he questions his own paradoxical idea of *gloire* born of regicide (Tiefenbrun, 181–85). Cinna hypocritically defends the monarchy in act 2, scene 1, while Maxime is hypocritically truthful in telling Auguste to step down. The conspirators are puzzled by Auguste's talk of abdication in act 2: they wonder if long-term reversal of character is possible (Tiefenbrun, 188). The very title of the play is ironic: why begin with the unheroic Cinna when Auguste's clemency is the key event? (193). As Tiefenbrun concludes, "*Cinna* is a play about not knowing—not knowing oneself, and not knowing others for what they really are" (194). In my view, *Cinna* is a play about recognition, about finally being able to recognize the exceptional qualities of leadership that will save this society from the confused circle of exchanges and reversals in which it is mired.

Tiefenbrun believes that a state of ignorance may remain at the end of the play, for the spectator cannot be sure that "all this miraculous magnanimity and conversion are not just more of the same duplicity, a political ploy, and a logical extension of the ironic context whose reversal model presupposes unreliable narration" (204). The play ends happily, she admits, but ambiguously (205). Pocock reads the patterns of reversal differently when he emphasizes that "man, by changing himself, can change the moral universe" (59). "The emphasis is on Auguste and his trumphant *recognition* as a worthy ruler after 'cette action' "(Pocock, 61; my emphasis). Auguste takes responsibility for the future and ends the play by linking his moral exertion with its effect on the public. In the last two lines he says that the conspirators must declare publicly that "Auguste knows everything, and wants to forget everything" (5.3.1779–80). Human striving thus creates and expands the moral universe (Pocock, 62)—but this effort would be for nothing without the participation of the audience, who validates the success of the expansion.

Pocock sees human will governing Providence in *Cinna* (59). In Corneille's next play, the possibility of such an interpretation of the role of divine Providence was a source of scandal.

Polyeucte martyr

Polyeucte was almost as controversial as *Le Cid,* for the influence of those who did not believe that religion should appear on the stage was growing when it was first perfomed in 1642. By the time of Pierre Nicole's *Traité de la comédie* in 1667, *Polyeucte* had become for that segment of the population the symbol of all that was wrong with French theater.[24] The martyred hero here is not a humble Christian but rather embodies the drive for distinction that is typical of the Cornelian protagonist. As Ronald Tobin demonstrates, the hero seeks martyrdom, a voluntary act on his part, and he expresses his desire for *gloire* on earth and in heaven using the same vocabulary as Corneille's secular heroes.[25] The heroic quest begun by Rodrigue culminates in this last play of the tetralogy. After the conquest of foreign invaders in *Le Cid,* then of intimate rivals in *Horace* and *Cinna,* the history of the foundation of the modern Western state had almost been completed. The story of the Roman world depicted in *Horace* and *Cinna* left the spectator of Cornelian tragedy at the apogee of the power and prestige of the empire. Missing from the tale was the Christianization of the West; *Polyeucte* would illustrate that step.

Besides the hero's desire for distinction, another theme present in all of Corneille's previous work is the feminine as a threat to patriarchy. The hero's fear of women, thoroughly explored by Han Verhoeff for both the comedies and the tetralogy, is made explicit in this play. But the heroine, Pauline, expresses her own fears as well. Fear is a recurring motif in *Polyeucte* from the first scene.

Polyeucte and his friend Néarque open the play, but Pauline is evoked in the very first lines: how can Polyeucte possibly be troubled by a frightened woman's dream? Polyeucte feels the pull of his wife's love and concern for his safety, but for Néarque she is the instrument of the devil, preventing Polyeucte from pursuing Christian baptism. Must all earthly love be abandoned if one gives oneself to God? asks Polyeucte (1.1.69). Néarque responds that God must come first, despite the diffi-culty of being a Christian in a Roman province (Armenia) where perse-cution can be expected. Tension between opposing tendencies character-izes the play: the first scene establishes the conflict between male courage and ambition and the contamination of it by the female dream world, full of sentiment, diluting the drive to virtue. In scene 2, Polyeucte agrees with Néarque on the need to flee Pauline's dangerous tears.

The conflict between human love and divine love is also a recurring theme. Since the Middle Ages, religious vocabulary had been used in courtly love literature. In *Polyeucte,* the terms are reversed, as this termi-nology is reappropriated to express the intensity of religious devotion felt by Polyeucte and Néarque. Already in the first scene, the burning flame of love, holy fervor (*sainte ardeur*), and perfect love for God are contrasted with Polyeucte's feelings for Pauline. The introduction of Sévère, the ideal courtly lover who is also ready to die for the object of his worship, further complicates the use of these terms.

Sévère is present at first only in Pauline's memory and in the dream she describes in detail in act 1, scene 3. Pauline had married Polyeucte at the command of her father, Félix. The Roman governor of Armenia, Félix sought a political alliance with Polyeucte's prominent Armenian family. Pauline's love for Sévère, a Roman soldier with no fortune, was sacrificed to her father's ambition. In her dream, Polyeucte, whom she has come to love, is sacrificed to Sévère, believed to be dead. In fact, Sévère has now become a "political divinity" since his triumphs with the Roman army. The image of sacrifice that haunts Pauline will be realized. The persecution of Christians creates an atmosphere of intense fear in Pauline's dream: she fears their radicalism, she fears the changes in her husband, she fears that Sévère will try to punish Polyeucte for marrying her, she fears her father who in the dream joins in the attack on

Polyeucte, and she fears her own feelings for Sévère. Her panic upon learning that he is approaching the city is understandable.

Félix blames Pauline in act 1, scene 4 for obeying him by marrying Polyeucte. Félix is sure that Sévère is returning for Pauline and that her marriage will spur him to take revenge. Pauline tries to reassure him: Sévère is a *généreux:* his heroism is accompanied by exemplary moral virtue.[26] But Pauline refuses to see him, aware that her own virtue will be severely tested with the onslaught of Sévère's charms. Félix insists that his daughter must satisfy Sévère's desires any way she can. Félix's base motives are thus contrasted with the fine qualities demonstrated by both Sévère and Polyeucte.[27]

Félix insists that Pauline see Sévère, a sight she wishes to avoid because she fears Sévère's penetrating gaze. She sees herself as a virtuous combatant who will fight against Sévère and her feelings for him, but also as a victim of her father's orders (1.4.353–64). Félix's blindness when evaluating the character of Sévère, Polyeucte, and Pauline risks the victimization of all three, but Polyeucte's clear vision will save them in the end, when Sévère's earthly virtue is not enough. Another strong semantic field has been established by the end of act 1. The vocabulary of sight is used repeatedly by all of the characters. For Polyeucte, clear vision means following the light of Christianity; those blind to it will be denied salvation.

Sévère opens act 2 by further developing the theme of sacrifice. The official sacrifice to the Roman gods is really in his mind a tribute to Pauline, a divinity to whom he will offer himself. Sévère hopes that the sacrifice he made in giving her up will be rewarded now, but when he learns of her marriage, the great warrior is stricken. Pauline fears battle between Sévère and Polyeucte, but each man recognizes the other as a *généreux.* Love contributes greatly to their identity: Sévère's devotion to Pauline has been replaced in Polyeucte's heart by devotion to God. When Polyeucte is arrested for destroying statues of Roman gods, his solution to his de facto abandonment of Pauline is to *give* her to Sévère, in act 4, scene 4, in recognition of Sévère's superior qualities.[28] Polyeucte is willing to sacrifice his wife in order to prepare himself for the sacrifice of his life. The recognition Polyeucte seeks can only come from a divine source. His ambition makes Sévère's earthly concerns seem unimportant in comparison. Polyeucte, like Christ, will illuminate a blind world to God's grace (2.6.712).

Pauline resists Polyeucte's plans for martyrdom with all her strength. The further he escapes from her influence, the more her love for him grows, from a combination of motivations: jealousy of his God, fear of losing him after all she has sacrificed, the glorious duty of suppressing her feelings for Sévère—all inspire her reactions at different moments. A combination of *gloire* and fear is expressed by Polyeucte as well, but his only fear remains the effect of Pauline's entreaties on his resolve to die. Persecution by Félix is seen as a step toward the martyrdom he desires; as late as act 4, scene 3, Polyeucte considers Pauline his only enemy. But by act 5, scene 3, Polyeucte is able to harden his position: "Live with Sévère, or die with me," he tells her (5.3.1609); "I no longer know you if you are not a Christian" (5.3.1612). Her pleas to Félix to serve him only irritate Polyeucte. He pushes Félix to follow through on his threats and is taken to the executioner's block, Pauline in his wake. In a typically Cornelian ironic antithesis, the pagan laws that bring about Polyeucte's death lead to eternal life (see Tobin, 593).

When she returns to confront her father in act 5, scene 5, Polyeucte's blood has served as baptismal water for her. Her eyes are finally open, she says, and Christian grace has converted her (5.5.1726–27). Her virtue and the understanding of Christianity that she expressed previously (3.3.646–53) prepare the spectator for her conversion, and as Nadal remarks, once Polyeucte is gone, her obsession with human love disappears as well (207).[29] Félix's conversion is not as easily justified, although his emotional confusion in act 3, scene 5 suggests that he was ready to receive the clear message of religious doctrine. Félix also pretends to have converted in act 5, scene 2 in order to buy time before deciding on Polyeucte's punishment. His gross hypocrisy and unstable value system throughout the play are attacked by Sévère in the final scene: Félix created his own dilemma when he refused to believe that Sévère wanted to save Polyeucte. Unable to understand heroism, Félix is blind to its operation until the fake conversion is replaced by a real one, thanks to Polyeucte's martyrdom. Grace arrives as a gift from the heavenly hero whose sacrifice, like Christ's, transforms human concerns into more noble and glorious sentiments. Even Sévère's future conversion is hinted at (5.6.1797).

Tobin reminds us of the etymology of the verb "to sacrifice": *sacre/facere*—to make divine or holy that which was profane (596). Only a larger-than-life hero could channel all the desire and fear expressed in the play into the making of a new order, the Christian order on which French civilization was founded. Sévère announces the end of the persecution of Christians as he affirms Félix's power as governor. Thus the play ends with a political message as well as a religious one: a patriarchal hierarchy headed by God the father, followed by the emperor (father of his people), followed by Félix, is firmly in place.[30] Social harmony, recuperating all dissident elements, is founded on Polyeucte's martyrdom, an act combining the values of the Cornelian hero in all his ostentatious glory with Christian faith and sacrifice.

Heroism and sainthood blend without conflict in *Polyeucte* according to many modern scholars, although some, like the seventeenth-century critics of religious theater, find the very idea of the Christian hero faulty and unconvincing.[31] The synthesis of the heroic and the divine in the play is eloquently described by Thomas Pavel, who says that *Polyeucte* is successful as drama, holding our interest because the sacrament of baptism transforms the hero almost before our eyes.[32] Polyeucte is changed, touched by grace, revitalized, and in act 2, scene 6, we see the contrast between the newly baptized hero and Néarque, who counsels moderation rather than an attack on the pagan gods in the temple. Polyeucte exhibits the same extreme zeal that we saw in Rodrigue, Horace, and Auguste, once they had decided to respond heroically to a challenge and to serve their society by performing extraordinary deeds, only here the inspiration is religious. Polyeucte clearly gives all the credit to God: "I owe everything to his Grace, and nothing to my weakness" (2.6.681). Polyeucte explains to Pauline that grace can operate with lightning speed and that God touches human hearts when they are least expecting it (4.3.1276); thus the conversions of Pauline and Félix gain even more plausibility (Pavel, 88). In the rapid action of the denouement, they do not have time to consider the implications of their conversion, to deliberate, to hesitate, but rather than being unbelievable, this speed illustrates the awesome operation of grace (89).

There is no doubt that Polyeucte is rare among Christian saints and martyrs. Couton cites the famous seventeenth-century theologian Bossuet to show that orthodoxy did not permit aggressive, violent acts from martyrs, except in exceptional cases (*OC,* 1:1646). All of Corneille's heroes in the tetralogy are exceptional, above the norm of humanity. Pavel notes that the Christian humanist project in place since the Renaissance is in itself a heroic effort since the ideals of ancient Rome and of the Counter Reformation had little to do with the empirical reality of a society often in political and ideological turmoil (155). Pavel goes so far as to say that Christian humanism and classicism were in profound disharmony with the social milieu in which they prospered philosophically (153). Corneille's texts of the tetralogy, and especially *Polyeucte,* express an ideal, the ideal of a hero/savior who brings harmony to the world. The realization of this ideal in the real world may have been impossible, but the audience could nonetheless derive an enormous amount of pleasure from observing it in action. These are plays of wish fulfillment in the Freudian sense, the wish fulfillment that Charles Mauron sees as the basic life force expressed in comic theater. The unresolved tensions that can be read in *Le Cid, Horace,* and less so in *Cinna,* disappear completely in the magical force field of Christianity in *Polyeucte.* Corneille experimented with his comic structure while maintaining it intact throughout the tetralogy. The dividing line that separates these plays from those that follow signals the growth of the tragic dimension of his work.

Reading Lessons

The endings of the plays in the tetralogy have led many critics to question their status as tragedies. Indeed, *Le Cid* was initially designated a tragicomedy, and Corneille made the change to tragedy only in the 1648 edition of his collected theater, at a time when tragedy was recognized as the more distinguished genre. The question of theatrical genre is an interesting one in the 1630s and 1640s, when the rules of classical composition were coming to be fully accepted. Among the first definitions of tragedy was Jean Mairet's in the preface to his pastoral tragicomedy *La Sylvanire* in 1631. Mairet says that tragedy needs to depict the fragility of human life and that the tragic ending must portray kings and princes reduced to despair (482). Several other dramatists and theorists of the period agree with his assessment, among them the influential Jean Chapelain, at the head of the French Academy from its founding in 1635.[33] Corneille, however, would offer a rather different definition when he published his *Discours* in 1660. The notion of a life-threatening peril is essential to Corneille's conception of tragedy, and he agrees that the characters must be noble, preferably royal (*OC,* 3:123–24). Where he differs from Chapelain, Mairet, and the others is in the requirements for the ending of a tragedy. The notion of despair is nowhere to be found in Corneille's description of tragic action. The dignity of tragedy requires a threat to the state or the expression of a passion more noble and "male" than romantic love, for example, ambition or vengeance. Romantic love should be present; it pleases the spectators and can inspire the more serious dilemmas necessary in tragedy, but love must always take second place to them.[34] There is no mention of an unhappy or despairing ending for the heroes, and no tragic flaw in their character is held to be necessary. Corneille's practice reinforces this reading of his position: tragedy can end on a positive note. Other theoreticians and playwrights were in explicit agreement with Corneille on this point, and the publication of several treatises just before or after 1660 suggests Corneille's dominance of theatrical trends since the 1630s, as well as the influence of his *Discours*.[35]

Of course, not everyone agreed with Corneille, as the triumph of Racinian tragedy in the late 1660s would show. Critics like André Dacier and René Rapin, along with Jean Racine, refuted Corneille's thesis and proposed a tragic vision resembling that of Mairet and Chapelain, specifically with regard to their conception of the tragic hero whose faults would lead to disaster.[36] Conflicting views on the nature of tragedy were brought to a head in the seventeenth century, primarily because of the success of Corneille's tetralogy and its innovative approach to the genre.

The controversy over the definitions of tragedy (a type of play) and the tragic (the tone and attitude usually communicated by a tragedy) continues to this day among scholars specializing in the theater of Corneille. While most cite the necessity of examining the whole Cornelian corpus, the tetralogy is the most frequent starting point for this sort of discussion. The most influential interpretation in the early part of this century was Gustave Lanson's view that the heroes are guided solely by their reason and will and not by their passions. Lanson finds that once decisions are taken, the hero remains unshakable, and this firmness is his most remarkable, most Cornelian characteristic.[37] This position was overturned in 1948 by the publication of Bénichou's *Morales du grand siècle* and Octave Nadal's *Le Sentiment de l'amour dans l'oeuvre de Pierre Corneille*. Both of these critics share a perspective that insists on the combination of reason and passion, not seen as opposites but as complementary elements, helping the hero to project an idealized image of himself to others. Thus, the hero's desire for glory is both a passion and an ideal. Bénichou emphasizes the passion of pride in aristocratic rank, while Nadal constantly returns to the hero's ability to construct a heroic identity thanks to faith in himself. In 1966, Jacques Maurens published a study whose provocative title is *La Tragédie sans tragique: Le Néo-stoïcisme dans l'oeuvre de Pierre Corneille*.[38] Maurens also emphasizes the absence of interior conflict in the heroes of the tetralogy (or *grandes tragédies*, as they are also known). Their free will coincides with God's will, so that their grand gestures are rewarded by divine Providence (Maurens, 242–50).

As Maurens advances into the corpus, his analysis becomes more problematic. All critics have had to come to grips with Corneille's seeming turn away from optimism after the tetralogy. Serge Doubrovsky's *Corneille et la dialectique du héros* (1963) finds an evolution from self-assurance to failure in his analysis of Cornelian heroism. In a model based on Hegel's master-slave dialectic, Doubrovsky sees the hero on a quest for mastery, which requires an object of domination. A progression is evident in the tetralogy, as the hero vanquishes others in *Le Cid,* himself in *Horace,* power in *Cinna,* and finally God in *Polyeucte.* But what conquest can rival the victory over God? An inevitable decline sets in after the optimism of the tetralogy, according to Doubrovsky (1963, 259–61)—although the reader should not assume that a failed hero means a failed play. Corneille experimented with variations on the theme of the drive for distinction. Marie-Odile Sweetser asks whether there is not a tragic dimension in the impossible attempt to transcend the human condition (1977, 48). Robert McBride emphasizes the hesitation, doubt, and even despair expressed by the heroes of the tetralogy, all of which increase in the tragedies of the 1660s and 1670s.[39] Indeed, when the hero cannot independently resolve the dilemma before him, the tragic potential is felt, no matter what the outcome of the play. In the 1980s, the tragic in Cornelian theater continued to be highlighted by scholars. Michel Prigent sees a tragic worldview in Cornelian tragedy because the heroic act must be eternalized in time in order to have the enduring effect sought by the hero, a quasi-impossibility given that the state served by the hero will eventually crush him (26–28).

In the tetralogy, however, the hero has not yet felt the full weight of history. He appears to emerge triumphant, as Rodrigue in *Le Cid* conquers the Moors, Horace aids in the founding of Rome, Auguste in *Cinna* consolidates the Roman Empire, and Polyeucte helps bring Christianity to the Roman provinces. Corneille tells a mostly optimistic story of the birth of the European Christian state. Nonetheless, unresolved tensions remain in these plays, opening them to interpretation and keeping critics intrigued still today. As John Lyons says, tragedy in Corneille's theater is the tragedy of adapting to rapid historical change (1996, 10). The tetralogy opens the discussion of such change on a largely positive note, and although the problems to come are hinted at, they are swept under the carpet, repressed but not entirely dissipated.

The threatening elements of these plays center on what Mitchell Greenberg has called "female trouble" in his analysis of *Horace* (1986, 66). Indeed, the female characters express desires and fears that remain

unaddressed in the final scenes. Harriet Stone goes over this same
ground when she states that "woman's performance precludes
metaphorical closure and the ordering of history into a paradigm of
male power."[40] The notion of performance can once again be tied into
psychological, social, and moral concerns, despite the reluctance of some
critics to take the "perfomative" aspects of Cornelian theater beyond the
aesthetic realm.

   Nonetheless, interesting perspectives on the corpus are to be found in
the work of specialists who concentrate on theatricality, such as Mary Jo
Muratore, J. D. Hubert, and Georges Forestier. Muratore's 1990 mono-
graph insists on the advantages to be gained from concentrating on the
form of the Cornelian play. Metadrama, the examination of the process
of creation itself, is a favorite topic for Corneille, in Muratore's view.[41]
The Cornelian hero is the character whose performance is not upstaged
or equaled, who imposes order on an orderless reality. He dominates the
other characters, and their emulation of his behavior signals his success,
based solely on the virtuosity of his performance, with no suggestion of
moral rectitude as a guiding principle (Muratore 1990, 7). Although I
agree that Corneille continually illustrates the sovereignty of the creative artist (Muratore 1990, 20), in fact there is a moral dimension to
the hero's triumph, as the preceding analysis of the tetralogy has
demonstrated. Hubert's notion of the attainment of plenitude through
role playing opens the door to an interpretation that goes beyond the
aesthetic, even though plenitude is essentially an aesthetic concept.[42] As
it signals the definitive harmony of the individual and the universe, the
microcosm and the macrocosm, Hubert's idea of plenitude suggests to
me a moral and social dimension, since the effect on the spectator is to
inspire admiration for the performing hero, and this admiration always
has a moral component in Corneille's theater. Hubert links plenitude
with the sublime, the point of departure for Georges Forestier's recent
study of the tragedies, as has already been noted.

   The role of the spectator is essential to my notion of the comic structure of Cornelian theater, wherein approval from society defines the
hero. The importance of the judging audience is essential to any "theatrical" reading of the oeuvre. Timothy Reiss points out that the spectator is not merely a recipient of entertaining or moral effects from drama
but is an integral part of the theatrical ritual.[43] The hero's sense of identity, of success, comes from his capacity to convince others of his greatness, to convert them to his worldview, to bowl them over (*éblouir,* as
Starobinski says). The hero seeks the admiration of his audience, a con-

cept made explicit by Corneille in the 1660 *Examen* of his 1650 play, *Nicomède:* it is the hero's virtue that inspires admiration (*OC,* 2:643).

Jacques Scherer stresses in *La Dramaturgie classique en France* that tragedy and comedy during the seventeenth century have a similar dramatic structure (11–12). Cornelian tragedy and comedy share the structure I have labeled comic, a structure that corresponds to the definition of comedy we find in Frye and Mauron, but Corneille writes both tragedies and comedies using these same elements. Frye describes the movement of comedy as "the movement from one kind of society to another" (163). Such transformations can be wrenching: we are once again reminded that Lyons defines Cornelian tragedy in terms of the corrosive power of social, political, and legal upheaval (Lyons 1996, 9–10). In comedy, a new but vaguely defined society is projected optimistically into the future (Frye, 168); change is not felt to be threatening. In Frye's fifth phase of comedy, close to romance, tragedy hovers, but it is not so much avoided as contained: confusion gives way to order (182). In these four plays, we are still outside the territory of tragedy, still clearly in the domain of the archetypal comic structure, rather than in the *mythoi* of romance or tragedy. Comedy's most essential characteristic, in Frye's view, is anagnorisis, that is, recognition or discovery (192). In Corneille's tetralogy, this discovery occurs not from the perspective of the hero, as in tragedy or romance, but from the perspective of the audience (Frye, 182). Society on- and offstage judges the performance of the hero; he and they comment on whether he has been able to impress sufficiently to attain an unsullied heroism.

As we approach the remainder of the corpus, the observations about reading Cornelian theater mentioned in the preface should be kept in mind. These plays have inspired numerous critical appraisals and approaches. The open-endedness of Corneille's theater seems to call out for a variety of interpretations. Although those that stay close to the texts are the most convincing, there are no definitive readings of these plays. Analyses grounded in the seventeenth-century context are often very informative, but the reason we continue to read Corneille is that each successive generation of scholars has been able to illuminate the texts in new ways that permit readers to engage the texts over and over again, finding renewal in these fresh perspectives.

Chapter Four

Le Grand Corneille:
Pompée to *Pertharite*

The Entry into Tragedy

An artificial dividing line traditionally marks off the tetralogy from the rest of Corneille's oeuvre. Polyeucte represents the apotheosis of the archetypal Cornelian hero; the saint who attains eternal life and is able to bestow it upon his followers achieves the ultimate service to society. The human drive for distinction cannot outdo the accomplishments of divinity, however. After *Polyeucte,* Corneille, now considered the master of the French stage, continues to experiment with exceptional protagonists who often offer stunning performances, but their effect on the community is not as positive as in the tetralogy. In order to be considered a hero, the Cornelian protagonist must assume responsibility for the destiny of others. In the plays discussed in this chapter, from the middle period of his production—from *La Mort de Pompée* in 1643 until *Pertharite* in 1651—we find mainly protagonists who are unable or unwilling to achieve heroic status. In the tetralogy, as we have seen, personal sacrifice was necessary for Rodrigue, Horace, Auguste, and Polyeucte, but their reward was recognition as a savior. A world in crisis, on the edge of chaos, needs salvation more than ever in these later plays, but the hero seldom performs this function. On the rare occasions that he does, in only 3 of the 10 plays written during these years is there a miraculous aura attached to his accomplishments. Sacrifice becomes unnecessary, and the magical atmosphere of wish fulfillment reigns as in the happy ending of a comedy. The comic life force suddenly dissipates disorder, and disaster turns to triumph in a typically comic structure of reversal (Mauron 1954, 30–32).

Indeed, all of these plays end with the crisis resolved and the potential for a positive finale. But in 7 of the 10, the ones without an idealized hero/savior, the solutions found are problematic. All seven have in common protagonists who bear some resemblance to the heroes of the tetralogy but who, for a variety of reasons, fail to win the applause of the collectivity, on- and offstage. The possibility of social rebirth appears shaky with such inadequate leadership. These protagonists may win recognition from a love object, but when pleasing another individual becomes more important than serving society, Corneille's theater truly enters into tragedy. Earning the love of a partner cannot alone lead to salvation, since only in comedy is the formation of a young couple adequate in itself to establish social renaissance The final tableau of these plays projects not renewal but a false hope whose hollowness is even more disheartening than sheer despair would be.

The Cornelian spectator continues to function as the protagonist's judge and thus the comic structure defined by Mauron and Frye remains in place (Mauron 1954, 26–33; Frye, 163–85), even as the tragic intrudes. The sort of tragedy whereby the individual reader or spectator can identify with a suffering hero is rare in Corneille's corpus. The comic schema is further complicated by a new sort of depiction of the spectator onstage, no longer always a member of a cohesive group. Since the creation of the hero depends on the judgment of the group, any fragmentation in the onstage audience signals another difficulty for the character seeking to attain heroic status, and another source of tragic potential during this middle period.

Georges Forestier shows convincingly that Corneille was interested in plot construction first and foremost, before working on character development or any other aspect of his dramaturgy. Forestier sees Corneille's search for the sublime effects of surprise and suspense as paramount in his dramatic system. I share the view that Corneille put theatrical concerns uppermost, that is, how to make a successful play that would attract and hold his public. As Corneille himself says in an August 1660 letter to the Abbé de Pure, cited by Forestier (22), this preoccupation is more important to the dramatist than the task of portraying any political or moral concerns on stage. Corneille tells the Abbé that in his *Trois Discours* he has discussed "the principal questions of dramatic art," and no other important topics remain to be considered because whatever might be added about rhetoric, morals, or politics is "only embroidery" on the essential items he has already treated (*OC,* 3:6–7).

As we have already seen, Corneille was an innovator, insisting on flexibility in applying the rules of classical composition. He added to the structures of the basic genres by inventing new ones, such as the *comédie héroïque* in *Don Sanche d'Aragon, Tite et Bérénice,* and *Pulchérie.* In tragedy, Corneille experimented widely, as demonstrated by the originality of the tetralogy, the variations on the *tragédie chrétienne* (Christian tragedy) in *Polyeucte* and *Théodore;* he also created the machine plays *Andromède* and *La Conquête de la Toison d'or.* André Stegmann labels both *Othon* and *Agésilas* "a very audacious type of tragedy" in his edition of the complete works (664). As Corneille suggested in *L'Illusion comique,* the playwright must be a showman, ready to dazzle his audience with new exploits. In the preretirement group of plays, he returns to comedy, Christian tragedy, and mythological and political tragedy, while he introduces the tragedy of disintegration for both the hero and the group who judges him.

The Last Comedies

Le Menteur

With *Le Menteur* (*The Liar*), which premiered in 1643, the same season as the tragedy *Pompée,* Corneille returned to comedy for the first time since *L'Illusion comique* eight years before. He manipulates the standard plot of classical comedy as he had in the series of comedies from *Mélite* to *La Place Royale* by having one of the young lovers play the role of the blocking character. *Le Menteur* is based on a Spanish play, Alarcón's *La Verdad sospechosa* (1634), whose main character is, not surprisingly, an inveterate liar. Corneille follows the plot of the Spanish original, with the introduction of Parisian manners and local color.

Dorante is a provincial law student who, on arriving in Paris, presents himself as a sophisticated, noble warrior. From this more exalted position, he sets out to attract women with the help of his valet, Cliton, a farcical character whose running commentary on Dorante's exploits provides many comical moments.[1] Dorante quickly falls in love with Clarice, and his verbal virtuosity in making up stories to impress her would be admirable if his words could be backed up by action. His only goal is to conquer Clarice using whatever lies are necessary, since he imagines that she would not be interested in a lowly student.

Dorante's problems begin when he misinterprets her identity. A coachman tells Cliton that the most beautiful of the two women he sees is called Lucrèce, so Dorante pursues Clarice, believing her name to be Lucrèce. The theme of illusion is thus reinforced as Dorante's theatrical enterprise has more than one sort of faulty underpinning. His determination to forge his own existence in the manner of the hero of Cornelian tragedy leads him to resist his father's plan to marry him to Clarice. Believing it is Lucrèce he wants, Dorante invents a secret wife in the provinces so that he will not be forced to marry Clarice. He thus unwittingly loses Clarice even as he is challenged to a duel by Alcippe, Clarice's suitor. But as Jonathan Mallinson points out, Dorante remains undaunted because with his thoroughly theatrical approach to life, these problems are simply new inspirations for his talent as an actor (1984, 202–3). The real Lucrèce, impressed by his determined courtship of her, begins to fall in love, and Dorante's father, Géronte, agrees to help him obtain her hand. When Dorante finally realizes that he has mistaken Clarice for Lucrèce, he says that he finds himself equally attracted to both women. Thus, he is not disappointed to switch allegiances and marry Lucrèce—exhibiting the flexibility of a good actor able to change roles and highlighting his lack of emotional attachment to either woman. Play-acting is the thing for Dorante. The exploration of the passions we saw in the early comedies is absent from *Le Menteur.*

Dorante is not the only actor in the play. Clarice pretends to be Lucrèce in order to test Dorante's credibility, then Lucrèce and her servant role-play as well, in the belief that acting will serve to reveal Dorante's secrets. This practical approach is not very effective in pinning down Dorante's true character, however, because there isn't one. Dorante can only be counted on to be entertaining, not to form a stable marriage. The confusion Dorante sows in his community detracts from the joyous, ideal atmosphere of the final tableau of lovers united. Just as had been the case in several of the early comedies, Corneille makes the comic ending problematic as he also explores the role of the hero as society's benefactor.[2]

As Mallinson points out, when Corneille exploits the popularity in 1640s France of Spanish comedies full of plot twists, he creates a play much more comical than Alarcón's (1984, 188–90). In the Spanish drama, lying is a moral flaw, whereas in *Le Menteur,* the characters who are gullible enough to believe the liar appear ridiculous. Our hero, Dorante, is presented not as a sinner but as a creative artist, a dreamer who delights in invention. In the *Examen* in 1660, Corneille expresses great enthusiasm for the subject, which is understandable given that the creativity of Dorante's lies places him well within the comic structure we see throughout Corneille's corpus. Mallinson notes that "like an actor, {Dorante} looks for approbation in his audience . . . for the impressive performance he has just given" (1984, 201). Like Alidor in *La Place Royale,* Dorante is a successful performer, yet the audience's judgment of him can only be harsh when his lies turn out to be destructive of social rebirth rather than an aid to it. He affirms his greatness with an assured tone that recalls the heroes of the tetralogy, but the status of hero is only awarded to actors whose performance furthers society's aims.[3] Dorante sees himself as a hero but the other characters and the spectators do not, in spite of his inventive and entertaining exploits. Théodore Litman notes that the Cornelian hero always wants to overwhelm with his spectacular feats, but comic figures like Dorante or Matamore in *L'Illusion comique* provoke laughter because their words and acts bear little relation to reality, inside or outside the play (206). *Le Menteur* has always been in the repertory of the Comédie Française; Dorante's misdirected inventiveness keeps the audience fascinated even as we see the flaws in his performance and follow the plot to its less than ideal denouement.

Dorante is rewarded rather than punished in the end; as usual, Corneille avoids any overt didactic message in the comedies. Corneille explains in the dedication to his next play, *La Suite du Menteur,* that his notion of moral instruction in the theater is born out of the spectator's pleasure and does not require wrongdoers to be punished (2:95–98). Dorante provides a most diverting performance, and his obvious moral shortcomings do not lead to ostracism. Nonetheless, the instability of his attachments threatens social renewal and taints Dorante's claims to heroic status. His moral flaws can be easily evaluated by the audience even as they are amused by him. Corneille exploited the character's undeniable attractiveness in *La Suite du Menteur,* but this time his faults seem even more evident as the play begins.

La Suite du Menteur

In the continuing saga of the liar, produced during the very next season (1644–1645), the action moves from Paris to Lyon, and Corneille imitates a Lope de Vega play. We learn in the exposition that Dorante fled Paris before his marriage, taking Lucrèce's dowry with him. To restore honor, his father married Lucrèce in his place but died soon after, whereupon Lucrèce and her family quickly exhausted Géronte's fortune. This chilling scenario is made even bleaker when Dorante is arrested for murder after trying to separate two dueling aristocrats.

The play opens with Dorante in prison, receiving money and love letters from a young noblewoman, Mélisse, through her servant and intermediary, Lyse. Burlesque comedy is introduced in the scenes between Lyse and Dorante's ever present valet, Cliton, since the language of love seems absurd in Cliton's ridiculous delivery. Dorante and Mélisse echo the servants' love duet and bring the comedy back to the more serious tone of romantic tragicomedy. The adventure plot of tragicomedy is suggested by the appearance in the jail of the escaped duelist. Dorante would be freed if he identified the young man, Cléandre, but instead Dorante sacrifices his liberty to protect a fellow nobleman who had, after all, fought valiantly, ignoring the anti-dueling laws for the sake of honor. When Cléandre proves to be Mélisse's brother, Dorante is all the happier to have shown such magnanimity.

In this play, Dorante's untruths thus have a much different effect than in *Le Menteur.* He continues to lie, but with admirable motivations: to obtain a portrait of Mélisse, to protect her honor, to get rid of a rival for her affections. Unfortunately for Dorante's strategy, his rival turns out to be a friend who is able to free him from prison, Philiste. So Dorante lies in order to prepare his departure, a sacrifice for Philiste's sake. Mélisse's tears and public revelation of her love for Dorante make the sacrifice Philiste's instead of Dorante's, and the happy ending takes place ironically buttressed by the liar's performance.

The "moral of the story" is that the relatively selfless hero is no fun compared with the narcissistic Dorante of *Le Menteur.* In the 1645 dedication of the play, Corneille makes his first well-developed statement about the fundamental goal of the theater, which is solely to entertain, in Corneille's view. Moral instruction is often a by-product of the well-designed play, but in no way is the playwright obliged to present an explicit moral lesson (*OC,* 2:95 – 96). He points out that the Dorante of the second comedy offers an exemplary virtue, whereas in *Le Menteur,* he only displays moral imperfections. And yet, *Le Menteur* is a much better play, says Corneille, because in *La Suite,* Dorante loses along with his bad habits his capacity to entertain us (*OC,* 2:95). Dorante's performance is heroic in *La Suite.* He serves the interests of Cléandre and Philiste while establishing a sincere love relationship with Mélisse. He deserves the spectator's approbation. But the creativity we saw from the hero not only in *Le Menteur* but also in the early plays *and* in the tetralogy, is absent from *La Suite du Menteur.* The Cornelian heroes who continue to attract audiences today are those whose performance dazzles and overwhelms us as we witness the process of the creation of a persona. Mallinson notes that in all of the comedies, the protagonists are actors, and their language creates a role (1984, 219). The actor is the archetypal comic hero for Corneille, who "adapts comic techniques for an investigation of tragic dilemmas" (219). Acting in tragedies, the hero as performer attempts to come to terms with political or moral codes, or with his own self-regard, suggests Mallinson, and complexities of

motive, mixtures of strength and weariness, conviction and doubt characterize Cornelian tragic heroes (220). They use theatrical strategies in
the sometimes vain effort to define a role that will result in their designation by the audience as a hero.

The Tragedy of Recognition

The Multiple Meanings of *Recognition*

As was suggested in chapters 2 and 3, the notion of recognition can be
applied to Corneille's theater in several different but related ways. I have
used it most frequently to describe the spectator's or reader's role in the
creation of the Cornelian hero. The aspiring hero must obtain the recognition of his society in order to achieve the title, and Corneille links the
onstage and offstage spectators, who both must evaluate the protagonist's performance in terms of its value to the group. The hero's admirers onstage mirror the audience placed outside the frame of the play, a
process that is illustrated quite explicitly when we see Pridament play
the role of spectator in *L'Illusion comique*. Terence Cave points out that
the Greek term *anagnorisis* (recognition) is related to *anagnôstês,* which
means reader (260). Readers (and spectators) are, inescapably, recogniz-
ers. Corneille pushes his audience toward one of the several definitions of
the word, "the acknowledgment or admission of a kindness, service,
obligation, or merit."[4]

In the dramatic theory of the seventeenth century, including Corneille's
own, there was, of course, another sense in which the idea of recognition
was important, and it is this concept of anagnorisis in theater that is
Cave's starting point in *Recognitions: A Study in Poetics*. Corneille and
Cave return to Aristotle's use of the term in his *Poetics* as one of the three
components that can form the plot of a dramatic work, along with
peripeteia (different kinds of reversal) and pathos (varieties of
suffering).[5] Aristotle's discussion of anagnorisis has many implications,
according to Cave. At the most general level, it means the movement
out of ignorance and into knowledge, but it is also about how knowledge surfaces and how we are convinced of its authenticity (Cave, 27,
39). The sort of plot that results from anagnorisis usually involves the
recognition of persons or identity in the denouement, as, in the classic
example, Oedipus is revealed to be the son of Laïus, whom he killed, and
of Jocasta, whom he married.

The recognition plot persists in Corneille's theater, although
Corneille rejects Aristotle's order of preference when he finds the

"unknown identity" plot far inferior to the plot where characters act "à visage découvert," in full knowledge of the identities of the other characters (second *Discours; OC,* 3:152–55). Cave sees a combination of "ambivalent suspicion" and fascination with the standard recognition plot on the part of Corneille and his contemporaries during the middle years of the century. This popular plot device became less common and was used in forms that tend to disguise it and return it to the more vague meanings already to be found in Aristotle (Cave, 103, 221–23). Since the term *recognition* applies differently to various Cornelian contexts, an examination of Corneille's manipulation of it can help us trace the evolution of his comic structure, from the audience applauding the meritorious hero, to the playwright's very original use of the standard "unknown identity" plot, to the exploration of questions about knowledge and authority.

La Mort de Pompée

In *La Mort de Pompée* (*The Death of Pompey*), first performed during the same season as *Le Menteur* in 1643, the Egyptian King Ptolomée (Ptolemy) finds himself trapped between Pompée (Pompey) and Jules César (Julius Caesar) as republican Rome enters into the imperial period. Pompée has asked for asylum in Alexandria after losing the battle of Pharsalus, but Ptolomée knows that aid to the venerable Roman general will provoke César's wrath. Ptolomée allows himself to be convinced by his corrupt advisors not only to avoid helping Pompée but to have him killed in the hope of pleasing César. That Pompée holds the will declaring that Ptolomée must share power with his sister, Cléopâtre, is another motivation for Pompée's murder. Ptolomée's questionable character is further illustrated when he considers having both César and Cléopâtre assassinated. Dissimulation is his best weapon, as he pretends to accept the dominance of César and Cléopâtre, ready to play the role of accommodating brother until César's departure—or murder.

Cléopâtre seemingly demonstrates the heroic *générosité* we have come to associate with the Cornelian hero. She wants to assist Pompée no matter what the potential cost, since without him her claim to the throne would not have received the initial recognition it needed. Although Ptolomée questions her sincerity, she reveals that César is in love with her and will establish her on the throne in any case, rendering her motives pure in contrast with Ptolomée's egotism. Cléopâtre in turn is in love with César, and she sees a mutual respect for heroic virtue in their shared love. She recognizes herself as a worthy ruler whose *gloire* requires her to channel amorous passion into her heroic identity. The play ends with Cléopâtre on the throne, acclaimed by the people after Ptolomée is killed by the same mob who praises his sister. She displays all the regal virtue her brother lacked, lamenting his death despite its advantages for her. She refuses to marry César, preserving him from political trouble in Rome since the state would not accept a foreign queen. The throne seems ample consolation for her loss of a husband, especially since she knows that she has imprinted herself on his soul. Sacrifice is rewarded less spectacularly than in *Polyeucte,* but it remains a theme inextricably associated with heroism, along with the concept of recognition.

Cléopâtre seems to achieve heroic status easily, but the recognition theme in *La Mort de Pompée* is treated with great subtlety. Doubt is cast on the heroic identity of three out of four protagonists, with only Pompée's widow, Cornélie, exempt from any suspicion of pretense. Theatricality is particularly evident in *La Mort de Pompée,* according to Judd Hubert, because all of the characters function as actors, and as spectators evaluating the performances of others.[6] Ptolomée is not the only flawed protagonist; the text also looks critically at claims of heroic magnanimity or *générosité* on the part of Cléopâtre and César. Even Ptolomée puts on the mask of *générosité* in act 4, scene 2, and he is sure that Cléopâtre is also in disguise. The shadow of uncertainty hovers around Cléopâtre, forcing the audience to question her claims to purity. Perhaps the desire for power inspires only a superficial virtue.

Cornélie's accusations of hypocrisy against César are even more credible. Pompée's death, far from pleasing César, outrages him. Pompée was a Roman nobleman, and the Egyptians had no right to murder him so ignominiously. César further demonstrates his *générosité* when Cornélie arrives to declare her hatred of César and his destruction of the Roman republic. César treats her as an honored guest, not as an enemy, and expresses his regret at not being able to make peace with Pompée, but Cornélie finds César's performance unconvincing. She notes that honoring the memory of Pompée costs him nothing and is in his best interest politically—just as Cléopâtre can mourn Ptolomée's death in a gesture that may be empty.

When Ptolomée's plan to assassinate César is uncovered by Cornélie, she immediately moves to save César. She wishes her revenge on César to be an honorable one on the battlefield, not a shameful clandestine ambush. As Hubert says, Cornélie cannot bear Ptolomée's mediocre play and requires an appropriately theatrical, heroic death for her enemy in order to invest the spectacle of César's punishment with the meaning it deserves (1984, 127)—and the meaning of history is created through the representation of its dramatic moments.[7] The insoluble problem for the characters in this tragedy is their inability to create truly dramatic scenarios because of the strength of Pompée's presence in death. Hubert demonstrates that the characters cannot come close to the greatness evoked by the narrative of Pompée's life included in the text of the play. They continue to perform in order to rise above rather sordid events, even if Pompée's ideal can never be reached. César and Cléopâtre posture, but their performance is always called into question by the narratives of Pompée's life. In theatrical terms, Pompée was a dramatist and actor far superior to those we see on stage (Hubert 1984, 119). In *La Mort de Pompée,* Hubert sees a descending movement away from the ideal proposed in these narratives, and the representation on stage of what remains of Pompée reinforces this impression (122). The head of Pompée and the urn containing his ashes are often evoked; his presence is literally fragmented. Cornélie persists in her desire for vengeance, preferring to leave Alexandria with Pompée's head as her talisman rather than join in a funeral organized by César. But before she departs, vowing to raise another army, she recognizes his virtuous qualities. Can the spectator thus assume that César deserves our recognition as a hero?

Hubert shows that César performs in order to bridge the gap between virtue and ambition (1984, 122). In the tetralogy, suggestions of such a gap (for example, in Horace, or Auguste before act 5 of *Cinna*) mean the character is in danger of losing heroic status. This is even more true in *Pompée,* where political expediency provides a poor spectacle. César and Cléopâtre are contrasted with the ideal heroic couple, Pompée and Cornélie (Hubert 1984, 125). When the play ends, Cléopâtre is secure on her throne, and César is at the height of his power, while Cornélie is a wandering exile accompanied only by the remains of her dead husband. Superficially, Cléopâtre and César look like the triumphant winners in a contest of military and political might. But fragmentation looms: Hubert calls it a "failure in continuity. Instead of covering up and minimizing the various gaps between performers and spectators, between history and spectacle, *La Mort de Pompée* flaunts them throughout and thus points repeatedly to its own theatricality while affirming the more dubious theatricality or cover-up of history" (129). The audience's role is much less clear here than in any previous Corneille play. Cornélie is the least ambiguous of the three living "heroes," and she lives up to the comic structure's requirements that the hero be a selfless social servant. How should we react when the morally exemplary protagonist is expelled from the very society she claims to serve? Society is left at the mercy of creative but potentially untrustworthy rulers. Like the inventions of Dorante in *Le Menteur,* their performance, energetic as it may be, is not totally convincing to the spectators onstage, or off.[8] By introducing more difficulty in the recognition and interpretation of heroic behavior, Corneille was entering into a new phase of experimentation in his concept of tragedy and the tragic.

Héraclius, empéreur d'Orient

In *Héraclius, empéreur d'Orient* (*Héraclius, Emperor of Orient*) (1646–1647), Corneille experiments with the standard recognition plot by fashioning what might be the most complicated plotline of the century; even *Clitandre* is easier to follow. But convoluted action of *Héraclius* did not deter audiences from making this story of mistaken identity a great success. The problem of dubious authority is central, since the reigning emperor, Phocas, had acquired the throne in a coup d'etat 20 years earlier. At that time, Léontine, who was caring for three infant boys, sacrificed her own son in order to save the legitimate prince, Héraclius. Héraclius has been raised as Martian, Phocas's son, while the real Martian has been raised as Léontine's son, Léonce, who is actually dead. Having the usurper Phocas raise the former emperor's child leads to plot complications, to say nothing of the complex emotional reactions when the truth is revealed.

The possibility of sister-brother incest is suggested when Pulchérie, Héraclius's sister, is slated to marry him on two different occasions. The natural inclination of the siblings draws them to other partners, but the danger of incest hovers, along with painful confusion. When Martian is convinced that he is the true Héraclius, his innocent love for Pulchérie appears criminal, and the couple tries in vain to explain away their past feelings for each other. The threat of incest has to be traced back to its source, the regicide committed by Phocas when he took power; he is the rotten center at the heart of society. The possibility of parricide joins regicide when Léontine pushes Martian to kill Phocas. Despite Martian's penchant for honor and virtue, which distances him from Phocas, Léontine believes that his blood is tainted as the son of a usurper, and he should have no right to create a new, heroic identity for himself.

Unfortunately for the tortured characters, especially Martian and Phocas, *la voix du sang* (the voice of lineage), clearly heard by earlier Cornelian characters, is not at all reliable in this play. Héraclius is in the advantageous position of knowing who he is before the play opens, but Martian's situation is more complicated because a false revelation points to him as the missing Héraclius, an identity much preferable to him than being the son of the tyrant. But even in the role of Héraclius, Martian remains paralyzed, never able to act in order to save his kingdom. When he admits to filial feelings for Phocas (now dead) in the last scene of the play, so much resistance has come before that it looks like a very artificial sort of resolution, an imposition of acceptance necessary for the restored order of the "happy ending" to be complete. As for Phocas, he puts himself in the position of having to decide which of the two young men to execute as Héraclius and admits to total confusion, but with an inclination for the wrong victim (act 5, scene 3). Infanticide joins parricide, regicide, and incest as threatened transgressions. Even Héraclius is finally overcome with doubt in act 5, scene 2. He cannot bring himself to assassinate Phocas, who has loved him as a son.

In a magical, miraculous denouement, the virtuous are saved as Phocas's political maneuvering leads to his assassination without either Héraclius or Martian being forced to commit the crime. The hero has not played the primary role in society's salvation, so the audience's role as the body who must designate the hero becomes complicated. Where can authority be found? The assassination of Phocas leaves the throne momentarily vacant, until a letter from Héraclius's mother is produced, proving the identities of Héraclius and Martian. Authority and legitimacy depend on a written document fortuitously produced, after other attempts at the revelation of the "truth" had been found defective.[9] The precariousness of Héraclius's position is underscored at the end of the play when the recognition theme is further manipulated.

It falls to Héraclius as the new emperor to try to extend the recognition theme into its more usual Cornelian dimensions. Héraclius uses the vocabulary of recognition twice in the last four lines, speaking to the leaders of the conspiracy against Phocas:

> Et vous, dont la vertu me rend ce trouble heureux,
> Attendant les effets de ma *reconnaissance,*
> *Reconnaissons,* amis, la céleste puissance,
> Allons lui rendre hommage, et d'un esprit content
> Montrer Héraclius au Peuple qui l'attend.
>
> (5.7.1913–16; my emphasis)

[And you, whose virtue saved the day,

As you wait for the reward my gratitude will bestow,

Recognize, friends, the power of heaven,

Let us pay homage, and with happy hearts,

Show Héraclius to the People who await him.]

(my translation)

The translation of *reconnaissance* as gratitude reminds us that the public is always grateful for the hero's services, but in these lines, the gratitude is directed toward the conspirators and toward a helpful Providence, *not* toward the emperor/hero. Héraclius speaks of himself in the third person in the last line, suggesting an alienation between his identity as emperor and as an individual. In the tetralogy, the hero always ends up in complete identification with his role. The "I" used by Auguste in *Cinna* turns into "He" here, and the spectator's admiration is directed to a kingly entity that might be an empty signifier, a role that could just as well be filled by the virtuous Martian.

Lyons notes the distance between the spectator and the characters in the play: we know Héraclius's identity from the beginning and watch their confusion from a position of great dramatic irony.[10] This distance is a fundamental characteristic of Corneille's theater. Lyons shows that in *Héraclius,* this judging function reinforces a message about identity, especially political identity (1978, 124). The arbitrariness of the ending points to the tragedy's theatricality: we can see clearly that the characters are actors playing their designated roles, with no apparent internal necessity, "as the gap between the spectator's knowledge and the characters' beliefs about identity widens. At the last verse of the play . . ., the public not only recognizes the by now familiar distinction between Héraclius as a person and as power symbol but may identify with the waiting *peuple.* The populace within the play, like the public of the Hôtel de Bourgogne [the theatrical company that first performed *Héraclius*], depends on the same theatrical convention which concludes the work. Politics is theatre" (Lyons 1978, 124).

In the last lines of the play, the Emperor Héraclius's saving grace is the power to bestow recognition on others. In this spectacular role, he is able to enjoy his power in the reflected gaze of his people. But if *Héraclius* helps us recognize that politics is theater, and based on illusion, our identity with the larger society referred to in the play and our participation in the fantasy ending can only be troubled. The wish fulfillment we experience at the sight of a unified society at the end of *Cinna* and *Polyeucte* is damaged here. Cave suggests that Corneille's multiple evocations of such transgressions as incest and parricide generate enormous tension and anxiety within the play as well as for the spectator, tension and anxiety exacerbated by the text's attempts to repress them (298). The audience wants to "pass off this sleight of hand as the real thing," posits Cave, because "the threat of imposture and usurpation has not been exorcised" (305). Our role as the authorizers of the happy ending becomes much more problematic during the period between the tetralogy and Corneille's first retirement from the theater in 1652.

Pertharite

Pertharite, roi des Lombards (Pertharites, King of the Lombards), Corneille's last play before a seven-year retirement, was not well received when it premiered during the 1651–1652 season. Couton surmises that the political climate led to the play's failure. The Fronde erupted into civil war in the fall of 1651, and after the execution of Charles I in England in 1648, the story of the usurpation of royal power would have touched too many nerves for the public of 1651 to appreciate the play's appeal to loyalty to the monarch (*OC,* 2:1505–7)—especially one as flawed as Pertharite.

Both King Pertharite and the usurper of his throne, Count Grimoald, lack the drive for distinction as public servants. The inadequacies of César in *Pompée* and Héraclius and Martian in *Héraclius* become complete degradation in Pertharite and Grimoald. By placing their love for Queen Rodelinde above the duties of a ruler, they fail to convince Rodelinde, along with the audience, that they merit recognition as heroes, as Corneille points out in his 1663 *Examen* of the play (*OC,* 2:722). The mixture of a proclaimed desire for *gloire* with the apparent lack of ability to maintain a consistent heroic performance makes for unsatisfactory characters. At least César and the protagonists in *Héraclius* perform their role with conviction, if not with total success.

Set in Italy in the high Middle Ages, *Pertharite* reminded Voltaire of Racine's *Andromaque* because the deposed queen is threatened with the death of her son when she refuses to accept her captor's amorous advances (*OC,* 2:1499–1500). A major difference in Rodelinde's conduct is the way she calls Grimoald's bluff. She dares him to murder her son, for only then will she agree to marriage, believing her husband to be dead. Her bold proposal contrasts sharply with the male characters' love-sickness. The other female protagonist, Édüige, Pertharite's sister and Grimoald's former fiancée, is also a strong figure. She continues to love Grimoald even though he abandons her in favor of Rodelinde, but she fights back fiercely against the indignities she has to suffer as a rejected lover. The female characters exhibit a much stronger sense of duty than the men, although both Grimoald and Pertharite are active players in the power game.

Grimoald led a coup to acquire political power, and Pertharite fought bravely before being forced to flee. Grimoald has been a just and popular ruler, but a harmonious society cannot be founded on illegitimacy.[11] Pertharite returns, but his abdication means that he can never regain full potency, despite a renewed ability to act, demonstrated by his stabbing of the traitor Garibalde. Both men are ready to abdicate power and responsibility. When love overwhelms the duty to reign, they completely abandon any pretension to heroism. Even their generous treatment of one another in the denouement represents a corruption of heroic *générosité*. Grimoald returns Pertharite's crown and in turn is rewarded with his own kingdom. The recognition theme is subverted because instead of exceptional characters recognizing mutual merit, we have a waffling duo whose partners doubt their capacity for constancy. Grimoald and Pertharite cannot even manage to perform convincingly before an audience of one woman, whereas their chosen spectator, Rodelinde, consistently espouses heroic values, "the values of royal patriarchy," as Susan Read Baker puts it, which are rejected by the men (86). Rodelinde is the defender of "Father's authority," claims Baker (90), in an intriguing Freudian analysis of male and female positions in the text. As for Pertharite, Baker notes: "Because his role has been contrived to reflect feminine values of conjugal intimacy and fidelity, his ongoing promotion of these values onstage continues to emasculate him. Although the king's murder of Garibalde closes the gap between rank and deeds, the fracture in his role between rank, sex, and discourse persists" (89).

Anagnorisis is also full of confusion in the play because on his return to the kingdom, Grimoald and Garibalde refuse to recognize Pertharite, either as an individual or as king. Instead of identity immediately restored, recognition is deferred. Pertharite is accused of being an actor, impersonating a king, or a ghost, the mere shadow of the sovereign he claims to be (act 3, scene 4). His very existence is called into question, appropriately for a monarch who calls himself weak and impotent.[12]

Society is on a more solid footing at the end of the play than at the beginning as political harmony descends on the region, but the foundation for this happy ending is unsound. How can such unstable rulers form a solid base on which social rebirth can take place? The audience must recognize flaws both in the male antiheroes and in a denouement achieved by a sudden, implausible change of heart on the part of Grimoald.

Pompée, Héraclius, and *Pertharite* provide examples of the different sorts of recognition in Corneille's works of the "middle period," but all of the plays examined in this chapter have important connections to the theme. *Rodogune* and *Don Sanche d'Aragon* use variations on the "unknown identity" plot, while *Théodore, Andromède,* and *Nicomède* use recognition in other ways. I have abandoned strict chronological order in the treatment of these plays in order to highlight some of the other threads that tie them together, in the case of *Rodogune, Théodore,* and *Nicomède,* and to isolate some of Corneille's experiments with genre in *Andromède* and *Don Sanche d'Aragon.*

The Monstrous Mothers

Rodogune, princesse des Parthes

As he tells us in the *Examen* in 1660, *Rodogune, princesse des Parthes* (1644–1645) was Corneille's favorite of all his plays (*OC,* 2:199–200). His views on the use of history in tragedy, already articulated in the preface to *Héraclius* in 1647, are well illustrated in *Rodogune.* The subject of tragedy should *not* be *vraisemblable,* or plausible; the spectator derives pleasure from extraordinary, unbelievable, scandalous subjects (*OC,* 2:357). We should not forget that Corneille is involved in a doctrinal struggle with seventeenth-century theoreticians for whom *bienséance* (propriety) and *vraisemblance* (plausibility) are inextricably linked.[13] Intricate plots like those of *Le Cid* or *Héraclius* and extravagant, improper behavior, especially on the part of female characters, made Cornelian theater a subject of controversy among the critics despite the playwright's popularity in the 1640s. He had not forgotten *La Querelle du Cid* 10 years earlier, when Chimène's conduct came in for particular criticism. In the preface to *Rodogune,* also published in 1647, he cites his historical source at length, insisting on the authenticity of his story as justification for the inclusion of strong, even menacing female characters, and of incidents that might shock his audience; for Corneille, historical truth overrides the rule of plausibility (*OC,* 2:195–98). Corneille alters his sources substantially, a procedure easier with little-known historical events such as those in *Rodogune* and *Héraclius.* But he retains potentially explosive topics: incest, parricide, infanticide, and regicide haunt *Héraclius,* but in *Rodogune,* the instigators of such crimes are women. The main character is a monstrous mother, a type not seen in Corneille's theater since his first tragedy, *Médée.* In fact, mothers had been completely absent from his plays between *Médée* and *Rodogune.* The threatening feminine analyzed by Verhoeff and Greenberg in the tetralogy is indeed in evidence here.

Cléopâtre, queen of Syria (not the Egyptian princess we saw in *Pompée*), is the mother of twins. The eldest will inherit the throne, but she withholds this vital piece of information and will only reveal the identity of the future king in her own good time. This knowledge represents her primary remaining power, power essential to her but which will disappear once her son takes over. The idea that the future monarch will marry Cléopâtre's rival, Rodogune, makes the queen furious. Rodogune was also the fiancée of Cléopâtre's former husband, Nicanor, whose murder Cléopâtre had ordered. Cléopâtre is able to justify her act in the name of protecting her children's inheritance, since Nicanor was planning to reclaim his throne at their expense. But Cléopâtre's rationalization of her crime is complicated by the fact that she had married Nicanor's brother, believing Nicanor to be dead. Not just a victim of misunderstanding and circumstance, Cléopâtre is an aggressor.

The potential moral problems posed by Cléopâtre's behavior are compounded by the contrast between Cléopâtre and the other characters. Her sons, Antiochus and Séleucus, feel no rivalry and are indeed firm friends. Each is in love with Rodogune and would prefer her hand to the political power their mother cherishes. When Cléopâtre promises the throne to whichever son will kill Rodogune, she appears morally reprehensible, but her sons gloss over the horror of her request. Instead, they place themselves in Rodogune's hands, asking her to choose between them. When she says she will marry the prince who kills his mother, the virtuous but rather weak twins are caught between two strong female figures. Suspense is heightened, with no examination of the moral positions of the women. Instead, the tension builds until, in the striking climax, Cléopâtre, having already killed Séleucus, drinks poison onstage after failing to destroy Antiochus and Rodogune as well. Cléopâtre's performance is daring: she offers a ceremonial cup to the couple, but before they can partake, a warning arrives, referring to either Cléopâtre or Rodogune. Each appeals to Antiochus, who decides to continue with the ceremony, unable to believe that either his mother or his fiancée would poison him. Rodogune stops him, fearing the worst from Cléopâtre, who, in a last desperate gesture, takes the first drink. The poison takes effect before her intended victims can share her death.

The moral dilemma of Rodogune's earlier suggestion that Cléopâtre be murdered is swept aside with the positive tone of the last lines. Cléopâtre's evildoing far outweighs Rodogune's counterchallenge, which was really a matter of self-defense. The spectacular performer, the most interesting character by far is Cléopâtre. Marc Fumaroli demonstrates Cléopâtre's isolation within her society; she alone recognizes her grandeur.[14] Her treatment of her confidant, Laonice, illustrates her craving for an appreciative audience as she strives for *gloire,* but a glory based on the sublime, extraordinary nature of her acts rather than on any pretension to virtue (Fumaroli 1981, 28–38).

More recent readings of *Rodogune* stress the negativity of the final scene rather than the spectator's pleasure at the spectacle of Cléopâtre's dying exit. In a 1992 book, Mitchell Greenberg declares that the ending of *Rodogune* is the most pessimistic in all Cornelian theater, because of the ambivalence surrounding the projected wedding of Antiochus and Rodogune.[15] Indeed, Cléopâtre curses their union (5.4.1819–24), and Antiochus ends the play with an order that the temple be prepared for mourning instead of marriage. The spectator who admired Cléopâtre's grandeur must also acknowledge her destructiveness. Cléopâtre is far from heroic in the Cornelian sense of the hero as social servant, but neither is her son a hero. Social organization is threatened not just by Cléopâtre, as Harriet Stone observes, but by Antiochus's attachment to his mother (1987, 38).[16] Cléopâtre could be seen as the scapegoat whose elimination guarantees the restoration of order, but since she herself initiates the sacrifice, the cleansing power of her death is lost (Stone 1987, 44). Moreover, the disappearance of the threat to order is not a cause for celebration, as it would be in the Cornelian and classical comic structure. In Stone's words, "Antiochus's sustained identification with Cléopâtre confirms . . . that her death offers society no final release from the violence that she has engendered" (45).

A void at the center of power is felt even more keenly here than in *Pompée, Héraclius,* and *Pertharite.* Scholars such as Couton and Bénichou who are interested in interpreting Cornelian theater as a reflection of the political situation in France note the instability of the period after the death of Richelieu (1642) and Louis XIII (1643) as the cause for the pessimism of these plays. Whether or not such a connection exists, what remains true for the twentieth-century reader is the fascination of

intriguing characters and suspenseful plots in a dramatic structure full
of psychological resonance that can touch us across the centuries.

Théodore, vierge et martyre

The figure of the menacing mother must have intrigued Corneille,
because he developed it again in his next play, *Théodore, vierge et martyre*
(Theodora, Virgin and Martyr), prepared for the 1645–1646 season.
Here the evil mother is also the archetypal stepmother. Marcelle wants
her stepson, Placide, to marry her daughter, Flavie. Placide, however,
loves Théodore, the disinherited princess of Antioch to whom he plans
to return the throne held by Marcelle and Placide's weak, unworthy
father, Valens. Théodore's faith is so important to her that she has little
interest in Placide, but his love for her makes Théodore the target of
Marcelle's wrath. Like Polyeucte, Théodore suppresses human love (for
Didyme, a fellow Christian) and is ready for martyrdom. Marcelle's
threats build her road to glory.

Valens, Marcelle's cowardly husband, tries to save Théodore by tricking Marcelle. He suggests they place her in a bordello rather than execute her. He hopes that this bold act will convince Théodore to
renounce Christianity and prevent his son from venting his fury on Marcelle and on Valens himself. Théodore, however, prefers death to either
prostitution or marriage to Placide. Unable to rescue her by marriage,
Placide begs Marcelle to save her. In Marcelle's view, his submission only
proves the strength of his love for Théodore, and she is more determined
than ever to be rid of her daughter's rival.

Théodore escapes from prostitution by exchanging clothes with her
other admirer, Didyme. Placide now feels obliged to protect Didyme,
and in a contest of heroic *générosité,* both men declare that the other
should flee with Théodore. Théodore has other ideas, however; she
refuses to be cheated out of her martyrdom. Corneille respects classical
decorum as, in an offstage crime, Marcelle personally stabs both
Théodore and Didyme when she sees Placide coming to their rescue.
Placide faints at this gory sight, only to be greeted by Marcelle's suicide
when he regains consciousness. The rule of *bienséance* does allow Placide
to appear in the last scene, dying from a self-inflicted wound and full of
accusations against his father's cowardice when faced with the monstrous acts of Marcelle.

Corneille's taste for the scandalous is evident in *Théodore.* At a time
when the conservative religious lobby against the theater was growing,

the combination of Christianity and prostitution provoked cries of indignation from his critics, although the loudest protests arrived only after Varet's antitheater treatise of 1666.[17] The play was a failure, Corneille tells us in 1660, because the scenes in the brothel, full of dramatic potential, could not be depicted onstage. Once again at loggerheads with the doctrine of *bienséance,* Corneille blames an exaggerated prudery on the part of the doctrinaire theorists for robbing his heroine of her opportunity to express her torment fully. Corneille himself points out that as a determined Christian martyr, Théodore has few other possibilities for inner conflict, and thus for dramatic impact. He rightly stresses that Placide and Marcelle are the most interesting characters (*OC,* 2:270–73).

As in *Rodogune,* the monstrous mother dominates the action to the end. Baker contrasts the triumphant ending of *Polyeucte* with a world plunged into corruption and despair in *Théodore:* "The indiscriminate mingling of the blood of Théodore, Didyme, Marcelle, and Placide on the dagger which kills them all contrasts singularly with the purifying shower of Polyeucte's blood which baptizes Pauline and provokes her miraculous conversion. . . . At the dénouement, it is not salvation but again sanguinary violence which passes between Christian and pagan planes. The dagger furnished by the phallic Marcelle has its way with all its victims, giving accrued dramatic force to the threat of irremediable violation which constitutes the core of tragic vision in this play" (67).

The potential heroes are not just inadequate to the task, as in *Pompée, Rodogune, Héraclius,* and *Pertharite.* They die a futile death, one bringing no salvation or hope to those remaining onstage. In A. D. Sellstrom's words, the "liar" and "monster" plays of this period "represent modulations whose negativity the playwright seeks to contain."[18] Violence and destruction are indeed contained at the end of these plays, but with little to replace them. Social rebirth seems a lost ideal, but it returns to the oeuvre in new guises. Corneille's gift for experimentation had not abandoned him. His first machine play, *Andromède,* and the invention of a new dramatic genre with *Don Sanche d'Aragon,* both analyzed below, are followed by a very untragic tragedy, *Nicomède,* where the monstrous mother undergoes a radical transformation, and a healthy society can be reborn.

Nicomède

Nicomède (1650–1651) provides some of the clearest evidence of Corneille's allegiance to the comic structure I find in his theater. He begins his preface by proclaiming that he has once again introduced an original new formula to the French stage, a formula he proudly calls "extraordinary." Corneille portrays himself as the hero of a battle to keep innovation alive (*OC,* 2:639)—much as he would in the *Discours* nine years later. The originality of the tragedy lies in a total suppression of "tenderness and the passions" in favor of "the grandeur of courage," persecuted but unwavering in its devotion to the public good. In the *Examen* of 1660, Corneille elaborates further on the notion of the hero as a public servant whose performance is so impressive that the spectator experiences a new sort of "tragic emotion," unlike the cathartic fear and pity said by Aristotle to be necessary for the audience of tragedy. Corneille calls this new emotion "admiration," a complex word with the Latin *admirare* behind it—in other words, something visual, spectacular. He claims that awe for the hero will purge the spectator's passions with a more effective form of catharsis, since our admiration of the hero's extraordinary virtue will make us detest the vice-ridden conduct of his enemies (*OC,* 2:643). Not only does Corneille make the moral dimension of his theater explicit here, he also gives another example of his didactic subtlety. The familiar schema remains in effect: we can learn about virtue from his heroes because they perform spectacularly and because we are asked to participate actively in judging their performance. Corneille's heroes serve society, and only society (the audience on- and offstage) can determine who deserves heroic status.

Upon his return from the army, Nicomède, the eldest son of the king of Bithynia, faces political chaos at the royal court. His father, Prusias, is a weakling subservient to Rome and to his second wife, Arsinoé. The third of Corneille's monstrous mothers poses a greater threat to Nicomède than does the hostile Roman Senate, for her intent is murderous. She wants her son Attale to inherit the throne in Nicomède's place, and thus she pretends to support the Roman ambassador's plan to marry Attale and Laodice, queen of Armenia and a captive at the court of Bithynia. Laodice, a heroic figure in her own right, prefers Nicomède, who has returned to protect her. The threat of assassination hangs over both of them because they represent an anti-Roman political faction, waiting for leadership in order to revolt. Arsinoé is all too eager to take advantage of Rome's discomfort with Nicomède.

From the outset, Nicomède and Laodice distinguish themselves from the duplicitous Arsinoé and the cowardly Prusias and Attale. As Corneille states in the preface, the heroes act "à visage découvert," without masks (*OC,* 2:634). The use of this expression is noteworthy since in the second *Discours, à visage découvert* refers to the type of plot wherein the identities of all the characters are clearly recognized from the beginning (*OC,* 3:152–55). Although Nicomède and Laodice are recognized as heroic immediately, Attale's true character, even his political identity, remains hidden for much of the play. Corneille has surprises to spring on the spectator, surprises that arise out of the tension between characters acting *à visage découvert* and *à visage couvert,* surreptitiously.

Arsinoé cleverly hides her plots. Her surprise at Nicomède's return is feigned, and even the projected marriage of Attale and Laodice is a mirage she promotes in order to provoke Nicomède into losing his temper with his father. She uses all of her wiles to rid the court of Laodice and Nicomède, but Nicomède has always served his father loyally. Only the inability to recognize the purity of his son's virtue makes Prusias fear Nicomède. Political ingratitude and the lack of appropriate recognition are countered by Nicomède's recognition of his father's lack of courage. In act 2, scene 3, Nicomède calmly insults Prusias to his face and in front of the Roman ambassador and the rest of the court. He will continue to speak his mind throughout the play.

The refusal to disguise one's position is dangerous, but Laodice and Nicomède always maintain control of their emotions as they express their scorn for the sly tactics of the others. Dignity characterizes their every speech, so that we can but admire their frankness, especially in contrast with the evil ruses of Arsinoé. The virtue of Nicomède and Laodice is so impressive that it converts Attale to their cause, and he frees Nicomède from prison before the planned assassination can take place. Attale's capacity to recognize and appreciate his stepbrother's superiority sets the stage for a positive ending in which Prusias, the Roman ambassador Flaminius, and even Arsinoé are overwhelmed by the spectacle of Nicomède's virtue. He pardons his enemies as Auguste does in *Cinna,* and the effect is similar, only now Corneille furnishes an explicit theory to accompany the comic structure of his play. Heroic *générosité* is contagious, and it leads to mutual recognition. Nicomède uses the term in the last scene as he recognizes his blood ties to Attale as a sign of shared character traits (5.5.1824). Flaminius proposes a whole new, more respectful relationship between the kingdom and Rome when he recognizes that Nicomède will not descend to secret political maneuvers. Finally, Prusias ends the play in a manner reminiscent of classical comedy when he emphasizes the newly established social communion created by Nicomède's virtue.

In Mitchell Greenberg's view, Nicomède is a representative of traditional values who saves patriarchy from its undoing by Arsinoé and the

subversive threat she poses (1986, 150). Doubrovsky reads the play differently, seeing it as one in a series of Corneille's works depicting conflict
between Rome and a local king, and also between the king and a hero
who has heretofore served him. The king is tempted to manipulate his
subjects with Machiavelian intrigue, and his kingdom is rife with internal corruption; the hero is tempted to revolt and represents subversion
against the power in place (1963, 323). The divergent perspectives of
Greenberg and Doubrovsky can be brought together by reading the
play as an archetypal comedy. In comedy, the young tend to subvert the
corrupt, established society, and yet tradition remains, for the happy
ending restores a lost golden age, before the advent of disorder and corruption (Frye, 164, 171). The "golden age"may be patriarchal, but any
other social structure would have been difficult to imagine in the seventeenth century.

Nevertheless, Corneille's strong female characters are not all on the
losing side. Michel Prigent observes that Nicomède could not have
enforced social communion on his own. While he takes the lead and
inspires awe as well as emulation, the efforts of Attale *and* Laodice are
essential in bringing about the cohesive ending in the face of politics at
its most corrupt (Prigent, 293). Rather than see this as a sign of the
hero's increasing weakness as Prigent does, from the point of view of the
comic structure we can say that the greater the threat, and the more
participants in its defeat, the greater the satisfaction of the wish fulfillment experienced by the spectator.

In this last of the three "monstrous mother" plays, the menacing
maternal figure is reintegrated into society rather than expelled from it
in the manner of the comic scapegoat. The life force of comedy is felt all
the more strongly in this tragedy of admiration thanks to Arsinoé's conversion to group values. The threat of the powerful mother has been dissipated, and the only remaining mother in Corneille's corpus is the
mild-mannered Jocaste in *Oedipe*. Are Verhoeff and Greenberg correct to
see the feminine as threatening even in those plays where the female
characters are far from dominant? Corneille's women have justifiably
inspired a vast amount of critical commentary and generated at least as
much controversy as any other aspect of his theater.

Women and Power in Corneille's Theater

Analyses that focus on the female characters all address the topic of
power, but while some scholars consider Corneille's heroines to be as

powerful as the male heroes, with a great deal of influence over the developing action in plays throughout the corpus, others find them consistently less than heroic, even impotent. Proponents of the view that Corneille depicts women as powerless, usually passive objects, include Mary M. Rowan, whose 1979 article looks at the heroines from *Médée* through *Nicomède,* and Larry Gregorio.[19] At the other extreme, among the first studies of Corneille's female heroes, Charles Ayer's in 1898 and Maria Tastevin's in 1924 highlight their power, and even at times their superiority, over the male heroes, in both political and moral terms.[20] More recently, Marie-Odile Sweetser has discussed female access to power in Corneille's oeuvre: his woman can be just as ambitious and successful as men, and they often share male values.[21] Without making claims for the entirety of the corpus, Alice Rathé studies Corneille's queens and finds that he accords them power equal to that of the kings, although unlike the male monarchs, they must respect traditions, follow special strategies, and prove themselves worthy in order to hold onto political control.[22] Timothy Reiss examines equality of reason between men and women in Cornelian theater, a controversial topic during the seventeenth century.[23] Female Reason, he argues, is often depicted having the same qualities as male Reason, but without the male dependence on violence. Reiss sees an evolution toward more political violence in the corpus, as Reason exercised by women becomes "more marginal with respect to political authority" in Corneille's plays (1987, 21).

Moving away from a view emphasizing similarity and equality toward an insistence on the heroine's difference from the hero, Josephine Schmidt uncovers "heroic codes and ethics that pertain to females alone," ethics based on love (4). In this look at the tetralogy, she finds Corneille's heroines exercising political and moral power, but only to the extent that they conform to the demands of patriarchal society, rather than to female values (137). In a study of the differences among Corneille's female characters, as opposed to their differences from the male heroes, Mary Jo Muratore sees an evolution in the Cornelian heroine when considering the entire corpus.[24] She maintains that a certain power is available to all of Corneille's protagonists, who "are called upon to make a decision that will profoundly affect both themselves and those around them" (Muratore 1982, 4). She groups the heroines into four categories, according to their motivation to act: the idealists, the public servants, the individualists, and the reactive heroines. Muratore sees a progression from idealism to a more humane realism over the course of Corneille's career. She thus follows in the footsteps of Claude Abraham,

who finds in Corneille's post-retirement plays that "those heroines seeking their fulfillment in the 'glorious' manner find their path more and
more difficult, not because of outside barriers, but because of a growing
awareness of their true nature and because of hearts that will not be
stilled" (152–53).

But what is the "true nature" of the Cornelian female protagonist?
Even considering just the plays from *Mélite* to *Nicomède,* we have seen an
enormous variety of reaction to all of the characters. Indeed, a survey of
the Corneille criticism on the "woman question" illustrates a problem in
literary criticism in general and in the study of Corneille's very inter-
pretable texts in particular. How can, for example, Serge Doubrovsky
and Claude Abraham make directly contradictory statements about the
heroines of the post-retirement plays? Doubrovsky claims that these
women take the political initiative away from the male characters, that
they alone maintain the heroic ethic of mastery and become the "real
men" in the plays from 1658 through 1674 (1963, 292), while Abraham insists that these same heroines focus entirely on love (152–53).
Such conflicts occur because reading is a risky business, inevitably
guided by our prejudices, conscious and unconscious. While there is no
definitive, perfect, unassailable interpretation available to us, those critics who are clear about their methodology make it easier for the reader
to understand why certain aspects of the text are being promoted as
important.

On the "woman question" in Corneille, the psychoanalytic approach
that became particularly popular in the 1970s has produced some illuminating analyses, firm in their theoretical grounding. Harriet Allentuch's articles initially insisted on the similarity of values between the
male and female heroes, both inspired by "aristocratic and neo-stoic
aspirations and convictions."[25] But in her 1979 article, Allentuch distinguishes between the heroine as the conscious mistress of her will on the
one hand, and her function on an unconscious level as the hero's antagonist on the other, a frightening combination (for the hero) of tenderness
and aggressive potential (1979, 64). This sort of analysis heads in the
same direction as the work of Verhoeff and Greenberg, as I have already
suggested (see chapter 3, note 12). From this perspective, also present in
the work of Baker and Harriet Stone, the threatening presence of the
heroine exists independently of the values she holds and of her success or
failure as a power seeker in a play's sociopolitical context. This aspect of
the impact of the female characters is particularly useful since it remains
constant throughout Corneille's oeuvre, despite the heroine's changing

political status and the variety among female characters, even within the same play.

In terms of my more global notion of comic structure, the recognition of a female character as society's (even partial) savior never happens in the corpus during the middle period—with one exception, the "heroic comedy" *Don Sanche d'Aragon.* Of course, during this period male heroes disappear as well in this sense, since social renewal is not promised at the end of most of these plays, with the exception of *Nicomède, Andromède,* and *Don Sanche d'Aragon.* Although the heroine participates in social rebirth in the comedies, in *Clitandre,* in the tetralogy, in *Nicomède* and in *Andromède,* her role as a public servant always remans secondary to male initiatives. In Muratore's "public servant" category, she includes Rodogune (a choice I find problematic) and Dona Isabelle of *Don Sanche d'Aragon.*[26] The remaining female public servants, in Muratore's view, are from the period after 1658. We will indeed find an evolution in the Cornelian heroine, including the public servants, in the final plays.

I return to the comic structure because I find it a helpful framing device for understanding Corneille's vast corpus. With a focus on the female characters, however, the critics using a psychoanalytic method have invaluable insights to offer, insights that can harmonize with other, wider visions of this oeuvre.

Myth and Machines: *Andromède*

Andromède is a machine play written for the 1647–1648 season, but it was not performed until 1650 because Louis XIV had been ill and the troubles of the Fronde were brewing. Machine plays contain special effects (thanks to machinery), as well as music and, often, dance. This was Corneille's first mythological subject since *Médée,* and the spectacular elements of the story lent themselves to the use of visually impressive machines, constructed by the Italian expert Torelli but designed by Corneille himself. The visual spectacle begins in the prologue, where the muse of tragedy, Melpomène, sings the praises of the young Louis XIV, who was 11 at the time. The play incorporates song as well as mobile stage sets, showing clearly its roots as a French imitation of the Italian opera being promoted by Mazarin. His sponsorship of an Italian *Orpheus* in 1647 was much criticized, so the production of a French machine play was seen as an attempt to divert the attention of Mazarin's critics (*OC,* 2:1393–94).

Corneille's first machine play introduces the conventions of opera to the French stage two decades before French opera was officially born, according to Perry Gethner.[27] Andromède has been promised to Phinée, but Persée has spent the last month discreetly courting her. When Andromède is selected for sacrifice to a vicious sea monster, Persée saves her with the help of his winged stallion, Pégase. Despite Andromède's initial love for Phinée, she rejects him in favor of Persée, accusing Phinée of cowardice in not being willing to die for her, thus justifying the switch in love objects. Phinée then further degrades himself by attacking Persée while the latter is giving thanks in the temple of Juno. In *Andromède*, the hero's performance goes beyond human capacities a second time, as Persée single-handedly defeats Phinée and his henchmen thanks to Medusa's head, a trophy Persée had stuck in his belt after slaying the dreaded she-monster. The happy couple ascends to the heavens, along with Andromède's parents, Cassiope and Céphée.

Gethner lists the elements of operatic discourse present in *Andromède* and notes that they are not typical of Corneille:

> [L]yricism, by which I mean the unashamed expression of intimate feelings without attempting in any serious way to combat or suppress them; the almost total domination of the action by deities or sorceresses, thus, in effect, substituting divine assistance and magical devices for human valor; the redefinition of the *généreux* as preordained, not self-created; the importance of poetic justice, assured by one supreme deity who can rectify any harm done by gods or men; the dismantling of the heroic fusion of private person and noble rank; the primacy of passion over reason and will; and finally, the dramatically superfluous prologue that serves only to lavish extravagant praise upon the king. (64)

Nevertheless, certain of these elements conform easily to the basic structure of Cornelian theater. Despite the absence of purely human valor and a hero dependent on supernatural aid rather than self-creation, a spectacular performance does take place. Persée is a savior, recognized as such explicitly in seventeenth-century France when he is associated with Louis XIV in the only complete history of Louis's reign, the history in medals struck beginning in the 1660s.[28] Gethner sees Persée's status as a demigod as a sign that, in this play, "[t]rue heroic status is determined at and by birth" (61)—as is the case with Louis, I would note. The argument can be made that this is not an anomaly and that the biological imperative, the call of familal duty, or the "voice of lineage" (*la voix du sang*) is heard by the hero from *Le Cid* on. The hero recognizes his own potential, usually with explicit reference to this heritage.

In an echo of Doubrovsky's *Corneille et la dialectique du héros,* Gethner finds divine assistance just as important for Andromède as for Persée: "While heroes in many of Corneille's other tragedies must undergo the painful process of sacrificing a part of themselves in order to attain the ideal of self-mastery, Andromède is free to express her all-too-human fears and hesitations because her heroic stature comes as a 'grace' from heaven" (62). But Andromède earns her grace just as most Cornelian heroes do, first in her acceptance of her fate and then in her refusal to blaspheme the gods as do Phinée and Cassiope. The overt effort to suppress the fear of death does distinguish her from the typical Cornelian protagonist, and she does epitomize "the lyrical, as opposed to the heroic view of death, focusing on suffering and destruction, rather than triumph and glory" (Gethner, 55). Cassiope says in the first scene that Persée's virtues are visible to all, and Andromède's superiority is acknowledged even by the gods. *Both* innate qualities and heroic performance illustrate the basic (comic) schema of Cornelian drama even as the playwright continues to experiment with it.

Heroic Comedy: *Don Sanche d'Aragon*

In the dedication to *Don Sanche d'Aragon* (1649–1650), Corneille congratulates himself on the originality of the play. Always proud to be an innovator, the dramatist claims to have invented a new theatrical genre, the *comédie héroïque,* or heroic comedy. Normally, comic characters are not aristocrats, let alone royalty. When he says that the quality of the characters' actions is more important than their social class in defining a play's genre, Corneille takes a clearer stand on the question of genre designations than at any time before the *Discours* in 1660. In *Don Sanche d'Aragon,* the noble personages do not face deadly peril as do the characters of Cornelian tragedy, so the play deserves to be called a comedy. Corneille elaborates: suffering in love is not enough for tragedy, and laughter is not necessary for comedy. In this work, most of the characters are royal, and the tone is serious, but political questions are subservient to the love story (*OC,* 2:549–53). Thus, a new genre is born, a comedy about heroes.

The play lacks the accumulation of adventures characteristic of tragicomedy, a genre that was becoming outmoded in any case. Nevertheless, *Don Sanche d'Aragon* ends on a note familiar to the audience of tragicomedy. Anagnorisis resolves the troubles of royal lovers whose story could have turned to tragedy without it.[29]

The hero, Carlos, is a valiant soldier, but not a nobleman, let alone of royal birth. Therefore, Queen Isabelle of Castile's love for him is totally misplaced, despite his obvious moral merit and many military victories. Scorned by his rivals at court, he always maintains a dignified stance, as does the queen. Both hide and repress their love because it is socially and politically impossible. When Carlos's true identity as Don Sanche, prince of royal blood, is revealed, the couple comes together for the sort of social rebirth typical of classical comedy. As in most Cornelian tragedy, Carlos/Sanche and Isabelle are both public servants by virtue of their inclinations and actions as well as their position. Service to society is a duty they gladly assume as heroes, and this is what distinguishes them from the purely comic characters who only contribute to social rebirth by forming a healthy young couple. Heroic comedy is indeed the most accurate description possible for *Don Sanche d'Aragon*.

As in Corneille's previous works, the hero and heroine serve society differently, although they share the same heroic values. While Don Sanche has been active on the battlefield, Isabelle's main contribution to social harmony has been her resistance to marriage until the revelation of her soul mate's true identity. The play once again demonstrates that a woman not willing to go to the extraordinary, criminal lengths of the "monstrous mothers" has a limited capacity for action on her own. The expansion of female power in the post-retirement works becomes all the more intriguing in this light.

As is typical for Corneille, different sorts of recognition come into play. From the theatergoer's or reader's point of view, we believe, as in *Héraclius,* that we know the hero's true identity from act 2, scene 3: he is the son of a poor fisherman. John Lyons reminds us that Corneille toys with the concept of dramatic irony in *Don Sanche d'Aragon,* since we too are taken by surprise with the revelation of the hero's identity in the denouement (1978, 125–28). But like the spectators onstage, we have also been looking for the appearance of the eponymous character—and who else could it be but the heroic Carlos? The idyllic atmosphere that permeates the play makes the characters' problems seem not at all grave and encourages us to expect the best possible outcome.

The anagnorisis that reveals Carlos to be Sanche combines with the genetic imperative of *la voix du sang.* Not only do Sanche and Isabelle recognize each other as exceptional beings, Sanche's sister and mother, the princess and queen of Aragon, also feel a strong attraction for him from the moment they see him. The incest theme evoked so menacingly in *Héraclius* is suggested, only to be immediately tamed. In *Héraclius,* incest becomes part of the deformation of patriarchal law, imposed by the false emperor. Here, Elvire's admiration and possibly desire for her brother, Sanche, expressed in the first scene of the play, is counterbalanced by her respect for her own rank and her attraction to her eventual husband, Don Alvar. Her feelings for Sanche signal his merit rather than the possibility of a criminal love.

Society also recognizes Sanche as a hero, an invaluable contributor to the public good. He much prefers the recognition of his merit to attempts by other characters to assign him Don Sanche's identity before the moment of anagnorisis. But as in *Pertharite,* merit alone cannot legitimize a monarch. In Sanche, the ideal combination of birth and ability to perform heroic acts furnishes society with the perfect sovereign, doubled by an equally virtuous queen.

The seventeenth-century audience could participate in yet another recognition, that of the contemporary political context. Queen Isabelle strongly asserts the Crown's rights when faced with the arrogance of an aristocracy whose feudal values contest her authority. In the *Examen,* Corneille tells us that the play was applauded by the court and all of Paris, until it was criticized by a "famous supporter" whose dislike caused it to lose its audience (*OC,* 2:556). Couton surmises that the Prince de Condé, a powerful leader of the French nobility during the rebellions of the Fronde, took exception to *Don Sanche d'Aragon* as a work supportive of Anne d'Autriche and Mazarin (*OC,* 2:1423–24).[30] But as Lyons insists, this interesting theory represents only a surface preoccupation: "[T]he deeper themes of identity belong not to a specific incident, date, or author, but betray a more generalized fascination with the social and sexual system . . . which underlies aristocratic and monarchic society. . . . [T]he significance of the plot structure seems greater as a measure of the temper of the time than a few verses of political doctrine" (1978, 134–35). I would add that not only the preoccupations of the seventeenth century but also our own preoccupations, fears, and pleasures can be explored by reading the theater of Pierre Corneille.

Corneille would return to the *comédie héroïque* twice more, in *Tite et Bérénice* in 1670 and *Pulchérie* in 1671, indicating not only his love of experimentation but also his attraction to the comic structure seen throughout his corpus. Social renaissance is always a Cornelian subject, examined from many different angles. Corneille's last plays continue to introduce variations on his basic themes.

Chapter Five

The Theater of Introspection

The Pleasures of Cornelian Tragedy

The pleasure derived from plays with a comic structure is the pleasure of an unconscious wish fulfillment, as described in chapter 2. To witness the expulsion of a scapegoat or blocking character who had threatened social cohesion, to participate in the spectacle by judging such a character, to see the threat exorcised and society renewed by the formation of a healthy young couple: all these elements are sources of psychic satisfaction available to the audience of archetypal comedy. Skillful dramatists play with variations on this basic theme. Pierre Corneille's special contribution to seventeenth-century dramaturgy resides partly in the transformation of this model derived from comedy. As we saw in chapters 2 and 4, a major innovation introduced in his comic plays was the assignment of the role of blocking character to one of the young people rather than to a heavy father, and as in Molière's theater, the blocking character is sometimes reintegrated into society, sometimes not. This strategy, influenced by the pastoral, helped Corneille to renew comedy as a dramatic genre. Borrowing from one genre to renew another is a hallmark of his theater, as demonstrated by his use of the comic schema in tragedy.

In the tetralogy, there is always a young couple who is separated by a double obstacle, as both a paternal figure *and* a member of the couple in some way block their union. Obstacles are removed thanks to the performance of the hero, an exceptional being who serves society so spectacularly that social renaissance can take place, and the young couple can be reunited.[1] Even in these four plays, considered Corneille's greatest, there are many variations on the comic structure. Most interesting in terms of spectator pleasure is the enormity of the threat to society posed by a double obstacle, the extreme nature of the hero's response, the audience's active participation in evaluating his performance, and the satisfaction of the wish fulfillment when the hero triumphs and society is saved from disintegration. This combination of elements takes the comic structure to a new plane in its impact on the spectator, who is *ébloui,* or overwhelmed, by the hero's extraordinary feat, mirroring the reaction of the characters onstage who marvel at what he has accomplished.

During Corneille's "middle period," from *Pompée* to *Pertharite,* the protagonists' performances in the tragedies degenerate to the point that it becomes difficult to designate any character as the hero in the manner of the tetralogy. There is no savior, and society seems headed not for renewal but for stagnation in plays like *Rodogune, Théodore, Héraclius,* and *Pertharite.* Nonetheless, the more positive comic schema remains in *Nicomède* and in the plays not designated as tragedies. What is true of all of these works is that Corneille continued to experiment with a fundamental structure, and the spectator remains in the same position throughout the corpus. As if we were watching classical comedy, Corneille forces us to judge performances rather than to identify with the characters' suffering. The pleasure of the Cornelian text is rooted in this role, which we can play whether the character blocking the union of a young couple is a tyrannical king, a monstrous mother, or an unfaithful lover, and whether the hero performs inadequately or spectacularly.

Corneille's use of the comic structure in tragedy is strikingly clear in *Oedipe,* first performed in January 1659, after he ended his seven-year retirement from the theater. It was a structure he never abandoned in the 16 years remaining in his theatrical career, although the variations continued to develop. The dominant trend among these 10 plays is a more intense exploration of the characters' desires and fears than the brief internal debates Cornelian heroes engaged in prior to 1659. Self-questioning becomes more prevalent, which could push the spectator toward the sort of identification with the protagonist's suffering that Mauron uses to define tragedy as opposed to comedy (1954, 26–33). But even with more introspective characters, Corneille creates situations in which we remain more judge than fellow sufferer. This positioning of the spectator is the major characteristic distinguishing Cornelian tragedy from that of Racine. Corneille's would-be heroes maintain their pretension to social service. The discourse of duty is never absent from their role for very long, and their desire always goes beyond the love object. They want to capture the wider recognition of society and bask in its power to declare the individual exceptional. H. T. Barnwell has noted that pathos in Cornelian theater always involves a struggle with duty, but duty is not really a moral imperative, "because duty, whatever form it takes, is a passionate desire for self-fulfillment."[2] The outer-directedness of the heroes forces us to evaluate them in social terms, but since social renewal must include the formation of a young couple, the hero's performance is complicated by the intersection of love and politics. This had been the case since the tetralogy, but the conflict is more pronounced in the last plays because self-fulfillment depends more than it ever had before in the corpus on recognition from both society and the love object. This double recognition is much more difficult to obtain and dilutes the strength of the hero's performance so that both the group and the lover may remain unsatisfied. This does not mean, however, that the theatergoer or reader is necessarily dissatisfied with the play. The pleasure of an active role remains, even when the hero fails in his drive for distinction.

Corneille Tackles Oedipus

The story of Oedipus is of course one of the founding tales of Western tragedy. Aristotle treats it as exemplary in the *Poetics,* and Freud assured its place in the twentieth-century imagination. Sophocles and Seneca had presented Oedipus as both a victim of fate and a guilty man, having unwittingly killed his father and married his mother. Corneille reverses both guilt and victimization, turning them into innocence and the exercise of free will. The enormous changes he makes in the plot structure not only form the basis for these reversals, they also add another completely original frame to the story, a frame that contains all the elements of the Cornelian comic structure.

Corneille, having prepared the *Trois Discours* and the edition of his theater that would be published in 1660, was looking for a project with which to end his retirement. He had received the largesse of the minister of finance, Nicolas Fouquet, whose eventually failed quest to be the young Louis XIV's next chief minister led him to become a patron of the arts, in the manner of Richelieu and Mazarin. Corneille offered to write a tragedy on any subject proposed by Fouquet, and Oedipus was one of the three choices given the author in the summer of 1658 (*OC,* 3:1366). Such a challenge represented the perfect platform from which the master could reclaim his place of prominence among French playwrights. *Oedipe* was indeed a triumph at the time, although today it is usually considered to be seriously flawed, and it has not been performed since the eighteenth century.

In Corneille's version, love flowers between a character invented by Corneille, Dircé (the daughter of the dead king, Laïus, and Queen Jocaste), and Thésée, the legendary Athenian prince, not normally a player in the Oedipus drama. Dircé and Thésée are the idealized royal couple, but their union is disrupted by Oedipe, a cruel stepfather and, in terms of the comic structure, a blocking character. Oedipe also plays the role of tyrannical usurper to Dircé's noble, disinherited princess. Corneille combines the love plot and politics, since Dircé vigorously disputes Oedipe's place on the throne that is hers by birthright, while Oedipe blocks her marriage to Thésée because of the political clout it would give her. The kingdom of Thebes is further disrupted by the plague, and as in Sophocles, an oracle is consulted in order to learn what must be done to end the disaster.

When Laïus's ghost says in act 2 that his blood must be shed, Dircé steps to the fore demanding to be sacrificed. In act 3, Thésée is thought to be Laïus's son, and he too is ready to die. Oedipe's behavior contrasts markedly with the young couple's courage: even after Oedipe is identified as the murderer of Laïus in act 4, he puts off self-sacrifice in the hope that Thésée will be the victim of the gods. But when in act 5, scene 3, he learns that he is Laïus's son as well as his murderer, and that his wife Jocaste is his mother, a tragic denouement seems certain. Jocaste commits suicide, but Oedipe's final words and gestures attenuate the tragic at the end of the play. When Oedipe at last assumes his burden in act 5, scene 5, he transforms it into heroism. The gods have given him the opportunity to save his people, he says, but his virtues are his own creation, and owe nothing to any deity (5.5.1833 – 40). The admiration expressed by Thésée and especially Dircé underscores the effect of Oedipe's conversion to virtue.

The archetypal tragic story becomes in Corneille's hands the archetypal Cornelian tragedy. Oedipe plays the hero's role and gains the approbation of a society unified in praise of him. His onstage admirers are echoed by the people, although the masses are evoked, as is often the case in Cornelian theater, with some scorn in act 5, scene 1, before the healing moments of the denouement. But as is always true in the tragedies that end positively, the views of the elite and larger public opinion harmonize in the last scene in their validation of the hero.[3]

Oedipe the tyrant becomes Oedipe the savior only when he is recognized and he recognizes himself as the killer of his father and the husband of his mother. Terence Cave highlights the great irony of Corneille's approach to the subject: Oedipe can disclaim responsibility for his involuntary guilt in this matter (319)—while the crimes of his behavior as king and toward Dircé are washed away by his conversion to the role of social servant. Oedipe does gouge out his eyes (offstage, of course), and the blood that flows from his wounds not only removes the plague from

Thebes, it also immediately cures three of the disease's victims in a miracle reminiscent of the magical powers of Polyeucte's blood (5.9.1995–2000).[4] In sacrificing himself, Christian Biet notes, Oedipe gains salvation as he saves humanity.[5] He must be replaced as sovereign, but Thésée stands ready to renew the monarchy doubly, by joining with Dircé in the formation of a young, vital couple who is also royal, possessing all of the biological and moral qualities necessary to relegitimize the institution and thus reestablish society in general on new moral ground.

Biet interprets this ending in the seventeenth-century context with reference to Corneille's Jesuit worldview and the imminent coming to power of Louis XIV in 1661 (507). Certainly, Thésée's declaration in act 3 that free will can triumph over an arbitrary predestination promotes the Jesuit perspective (3.5.1149–78). The role of free will in Oedipe's conversion from criminal to hero is evident because guilt is suggested only when he seeks to avoid his destiny rather than assume it. There is a marked contrast with Thésée and Dircé, who fight to take on the burden of the horrible accusations of the oracle during a series of false recognitions.

Along with most scholars, Harriet Allentuch surmises that *Oedipe*'s lack of popularity since the eighteenth century is caused by a confusion of genres, an aesthetic dissonance between two plots that don't mesh, as Corneille supplements the oedipal plot with a romance (1994, 571–72). Corneille notes the absence of a love plot in the original story, and since his public expected one, he furnishes it. But along with additions, there are omissions: *la bienséance* would not allow him to show Oedipe tearing out his eyes, for example (*OC*, 3:20). Delicacy reigns in the language of the lovers as well, the language of *préciosité,* that delicate and euphemistic expression of elevated sentiments.

Patriarchy and politics are the glue that holds the disparate elements of Corneille's version of the Oedipus legend together in a more unified whole than critics see when they focus on the way the Greek tragedy is deformed by the addition of Dircé and Thésée. The traditional denouement of the tragedy, the recognition of Oedipe's true identity, brings into harmony the love plot, the political dilemma of an illegitimate ruler, and the horror of Oedipe's transgressions. The resolution remains true to the Cornelian comic schema in its most life-affirming form. Social rebirth is not the spectator's final impression in the versions from antiquity nor in the other seventeenth-century treatments of Oedipus (see Biet).

Oedipe also exhibits one of the new characteristics of the post-retire-ment Cornelian hero in a scene of puzzled self-questioning in act 3, which has been read by some critics (for example, Cave, 316, and Allen-tuch 1994, 574) as an awkward attempt to justify his sudden conversion in the denouement. Oedipe abruptly ends his persecution of Dircé and Thésée, and he says that he feels extreme confusion at his own desire to alter the situation (3.4.1045–64). He expresses his former fear that their union could damage him politically, now replaced with a more general-ized dread that the audience well understands. If this scene is also read in the context of the plays to come, it is the harbinger of a Cornelian hero whose doubts, fears, and desires are given more play than in the years prior to *Pertharite,* where Grimoald and Pertharite have already lost the easy path to a heroic solution. Oedipe's certainty at the end of the play will be obtained with much greater difficulty in the works to come.

La Conquête de la Toison d'or

With *La Conquête de la Toison d'or* (The Conquest of the Golden Fleece), Corneille returns to the myth of Jason and Medea. Unlike his first tragedy, *Médée,* this is a machine play, his second and last one. As in *Andromède,* the use of machines, music, and the mythological source cre-ate a fairy-tale atmosphere in which the tragic potential is greatly atten-uated. The play was performed in 1661 for the joyous occasion of the marriage of Louis XIV to Maria Theresa of Spain in 1660, although the original impetus came from a Norman noble seeking to fill his home-built theater with a stunning spectacle (*OC,* 3:1412–19). The prologue celebrates the royal marriage and the Peace of the Pyrenees, so the tone is set for a tragedy we expect to end well. Indeed, it ends spectacularly.

John Lapp demonstrates that "in *La Toison d'or,* feats of magic and metamorphosis provide the central interest."[6] The magic begins in a magnificent garden setting created by the sorceress Médée, who has transformed one area of her native, barren Colchos into a place of beauty. Lapp notes that one "type of metamorphosis that runs through the play illustrates the change from the wretched and repulsive to the harmonious and beautiful" (180). Spectators could fully appreciate these metamorphoses since this was "a production whose machines and set-tings, by all contemporary accounts, far surpassed any that had so far graced the French stage" (177).

As in *Médée,* the heroine's love for Jason causes her suffering, while he again plays the role of "a scheming gigolo," as Lapp so aptly puts it

(191). The beautiful settings become repulsive at Médée's order, and only when Médée is expressing her anger at Jason's possible betrayals. In act 3, scene 4, she transforms a pleasure palace into a monster-filled cave after a debate with his former mistress, Hypsipyle, queen of Lemnos. The somber forest that hides the golden fleece, created by Médée to protect this treasure, suggests the depth of her mistrust before she gives in to Jason's request that she take it for him. In so doing, her father's kingdom will be destroyed, but Jason cannot return home without the golden fleece. In the end, Jason is satisfied, and Médée makes her spectacular exit on the back of the dragon who had guarded the fleece. The "happy couple" will leave for Greece together on Jason's waiting ship. Peace and beauty reign in the last scene, as the palaces of the Sun, Juno, and Jupiter appear magically in the sky. Corneille's lengthy description makes the elaborate grandeur of the sets clear even to the reader. Although the dispossessed King Aète at first seeks vengeance against his daughter and Jason, when Jupiter assures him that destiny will eventually reestablish his throne, he ends the play with words of contentment and prepares to leave Colchos with his son and Hypsipyle, an entirely happy couple whose kingdom he will share.

Hypsipyle's new love, Médée's brother, Absyrte, has conquered the queen with help from Médée to make him look heroic. Médée's power asserts itself throughout the play. She is the dominant figure and the main hero in the Cornelian sense of social service, as emphasized at the end of the prologue when she is specifically given credit for the creation of the garden of Colchos (lines 239–40). Médée lauds Jason in the first scene of the play as the savior of the state (1.1.310), but it is Médée alone who brings about the denouement. Jason may fight the ferocious bulls and soldiers who guard the fleece, but the ultimate guardian, the dragon, is tamed by Médée. These events are guided by Providence, says Jupiter (5.7.2194), but destiny is realized through Médée's acts. She will be punished eventually for choosing Jason over family loyalty, but the end of this segment of the story affirms the life force, "since in the end all the characters depart from the dismal, desert Colchos for sunnier shores" (Lapp, 188). Médée's transgression against her family is also downplayed by the very presence of her brother, whom she kills as an infant in some versions of the myth. Her status as a Cornelian hero is problematic, since the notion of service to society that she mentions in act 1, scene 1 disappears in favor of an exclusive focus on Jason. But the transformations in the legend effected by Corneille go a long way toward placing Médée in the Cornelian heroic mold.

Médée closely resembles the other heroes of the last period of his production in her repeated self-interrogation. The primary recognition she seeks is Jason's love, but acquiring it seems doubtful to her to the end. She questions his love as an illusion, a magic charm that has enchanted her and that she wishes she could resist, to no avail (2.2.758–71), and her hesitations continue (see 4.1.1446–51, the soliloquy in 4.2, with more questions in the next scene [4.3.1520–25], for example). The fact that her desire centers on love rather than *gloire* distinguishes her from the majority of Corneille's protagonists throughout the corpus, who usually do not separate the two, as indeed Jason cannot (3.3.1206 and 4.4.1705 are quite explicit in this regard). But Médée signals the increasing difficulty of harmonizing desires in an oeuvre in which the seamless melding of love and *gloire* is challenged by the hero him- or herself.

Sertorius

Corneille insists in the preface that *Sertorius* (1662–1663) contains "neither the tenderness of love nor uncontrolled passions" (*OC,* 3:311), yet he invents two female characters whose presence inspires tender sentiments indeed. The Roman general Sertorius, the conqueror of Aragon, has problems on several fronts, all concerning identity and the passions that are born of conflicting allegiances. He loves republican Rome, which he claims to represent, but he is ready to rebel against the current Roman government, led by the tyrannical Emperor Sylla. On the Iberian peninsula, Sertorius is under attack from traitors in his own camp. His lieutenant, Perpenna, opens the play by revealing his failed attempt to assassinate Sertorius out of jealousy of his military supremacy as well as Sertorius's conquest of the heart of the Iberian queen, Viriate. Only the villain Perpenna allows his passions to explode, but strong currents of emotion affect all of the characters.

Viriate seeks independence for her kingdom of Lusitania (now Portugal and part of Spain). Sertorius's army represents the road to freedom from Roman dominance, and Sertorius himself symbolizes Roman strength and heroic virtue for Viriate, whose wish to marry the general is based on a combination of political aspiration and esteem. Viriate experiences no conflict between her *gloire* and her love interests. In the manner of so many Cornelian heroes of both sexes, desire is inspired by the love object's virtue and political standing, inextricably linked.

From this perspective, Sertorius should be able to return her love, and the heroic couple could reign triumphant. But the old general is not

ready to abandon Rome in favor of sharing Viriate's throne. To further
muddy the waters, when his rival, the much younger general Pompée,
arrives at the head of another Roman army, he tells Sertorius that Sylla
has reformed, that he is ready to abandon dictatorship as soon as his
enemies abroad (i.e., Sertorius) put down their arms. Sylla thus deserves
the loyalty of all true Romans (3.1.958–64). In the face of Pompée's
youthful energy and pragmatism, can Sertorius continue to claim that
he alone represents the authentic "Rome," especially when Pompée
highlights the resemblances between Sertorius and Sylla as iron-handed
rulers (3.1.893–900)?

Sertorius's relations with Perpenna add another layer of complexity,
since Sertorius fears his lieutenant's threatened mutiny and encourages
Viriate to marry Perpenna in act 2, scene 2. Sertorius continues to voice
his fears in act 4, scene 2, even as he agrees to marry Viriate. Viriate is
indignant at this derogation from the image of the heroic ideal couple
that she wants to form with Sertorius. Sertorius's motivations are further
complicated by his love for Viriate. The stern old general experiences
tender passions, even if Viriate herself does not (see in particular scenes 1
and 2 of act 4). Early on, he expresses great regret at the idea of a political marriage without love (1.3.370–72). The hero divided between personal and public concerns, further troubled by conflicting sociopolitical
alliances, is in a poor position to deal with his antagonists—and even
with those who claim to be his allies.

The second female protagonist, Aristie, also vies for Sertorius's hand
in marriage. The former wife of Pompée (who divorced her at Sylla's
insistence), Aristie seeks a political alliance with Sertorius much as Viriate does. But as is most often the case in Corneille's theater, the heroines
have aspirations that cannot be realized without the assistance of male
military might. So the best interests of society are in Sertorius's hands,
and he is in a state of confusion that paralyzes him.

For the first time in Cornelian theater, the fragmentation of the
onstage audience spreads to divide the collectivity it represents into
opposing camps whose rulers have equally valid claims to legitimacy.
This fracture is deepened by Sertorius's feelings for Viriate. When Perpenna does manage to assassinate Sertorius, the spectator is almost
relieved to see the impasse end. There is truly no way out for a would-be
hero who is not sure whom he should serve. As John Lyons notes, Sertorius has outlived the society that made sense to him (1996, 138). This
variation on the Cornelian comic structure comes close to being one of
the most tragic in his corpus because the lack of a solution to Sertorius's

dilemma points to one of the fundamental definitions of tragedy: unrelieved open-endedness, an infinite continuation of suffering.[7] With his death, however, Sertorius does end up serving society's best interests. When he and Pompée meet, it is Pompée who expresses an ethic of social service (3.1.781–88). Nevertheless, Pompée is only present in two scenes until the close of the play. This is Sertorius's tragedy. But Pompée is there at the end to confirm Sylla's abdication, to punish Perpenna, to assure Viriate's power, to remarry Aristie and provide a new basis for social rebirth, and generally, to restore order. His final words are a recognition of Sertorius's greatness, a heroic status that can now only exist in the legend of long-ago exploits. The comic structure has been penetrated by the tragic, but in the end, a positive note is sounded in this subtle and affecting play, long considered one of Corneille's masterpieces. As a hero who wishes to live up to the social servant model, Sertorius faces an insoluble dilemma. Where and what is the society he wishes to serve?[8] Is it with Viriate, among the Iberians, or is it in Rome? Sertorius wants to believe that the Roman values he holds dear are no longer located in the city of Rome, but rather remain exclusively with him: "Rome n'est plus dans Rome, elle est toute où je suis" (3.1.936). But Lyons notes that recognizing his difference from Rome really means betraying Rome (1996, 147).

Gordon Pocock illustrates how Corneille smooths out the inconsistencies of register in a play full of political content, yet with naturalistic love scenes (127–32). As he had since *Le Cid,* Corneille joins love and politics together, but with varying strategies throughout the oeuvre. Pocock notes that Pompée's political role in act 3, scene 1 is countered by his role as a lover in the meeting with Aristie in the very next scene: "[T]he two opposites, his love for Aristie and his self-interest, are presented clearly, without any mixture. The two values are held . . . in suspense. We may infer that it is precisely this ability to hold the conflict sharply in focus without striking attitudes or rushing to heroic extremes which is presented by Corneille as admirable" (132).[9] Flexibility is Pompée's finest quality, one that was highly valued in Louis XIV's France, where the *honnête homme,* the skillful social actor, replaces the warrior hero as the only attainable ideal.[10] Pompée's supple performance is a pragmatic blend of self-interest, in both love and politics, with the social servant role of the hero.[11]

Corneille was evolving with the times toward a recognition of the importance of *amour-propre,* the love of self, as part of the hero's makeup. A destructive force in Racine's tragedies, in Corneille it would always be attenuated by other, finer inclinations. Nonetheless, the bold certainty attained at the end of each play in the tetralogy gradually eroded in favor of a more complex series of dramatic experiments.

Sophonisbe

Corneille acknowledges in the preface to *Sophonisbe* (first performed during the same season as *Sertorius* in 1662–1663) that he is following in the footsteps of Jean Mairet, whose own *Sophonisbe* had appeared almost 30 years earlier, in 1636. Corneille's play became the subject of a literary quarrel, initiated by the Abbé d'Aubignac, the well-known theoretician and a recent enemy.[12] D'Aubignac's main point of attack was Corneille's lack of respect for *bienséance:* the playwright had offended the sensibility of his public by the scandalous existence of two husbands for Sophonisbe, which Corneille justified by historical fact, always a resource when he wanted to go beyond the bounds of seventeenth-century decorum (*OC,* 3:1463). Corneille needed to treat Mairet's subject with new effects, and allowing the two husbands to coexist was one way to demonstrate his originality. Another was the invention of Queen Éryxe of Getulia, Sophonisbe's rival for the love of her former fiancé, Massinisse. Sophonisbe had married the elderly Syphax instead in order to make him an ally of Carthage, the principal rival of Rome in Africa. She sacrificed her love willingly, out of patriotism. Sophonisbe makes it quite clear to Syphax that *gloire* is more important than love, but his devotion to her influences his political decisions, much to Sophonisbe's disgust. Her love still rests with Massinisse, and the determination to serve Carthage by marriage to Syphax seems all the more unfortunate when Syphax is in danger of being subjugated by Rome, whose enemy he has become because of Sophonisbe. Sophonisbe could be a loser in love and in *gloire.*

H. T. Barnwell highlights "the unity and consistency and of heroine," whose concern for *gloire* brings together love, jealousy, and politics.[13] But heroic *gloire* contains only a small remnant of the idea of service to the state, since in Sophonisbe's case, "the driving force behind her ideal of *gloire,* patriotic, regal or jealous, is an overwhelming desire for independence" (1984, 580). The two key contaminators of heroism in Corneille's depiction of Sophonisbe are jealousy and the desire for independence. The heroes of the tetralogy had been independent actors, but their exceptional gestures benefited society and secured its approval. After *Polyeucte,* we often see the failure of heroism when the drive for distinction leads away from social service, or when love and *gloire* do not reinforce one another. The discordance here occurs precisely because Sophonisbe insists until act 5 that her conflicting impulses do harmonize. She sees herself as the embodiment of Carthage, but this image is shown to be less than unified as early as act 1. Unlike Viriate in *Sertorius,* love and *gloire* do not find a focus in one man for Sophonisbe. Sophonisbe is the dominant player by far in the tragedy, so her consistency or lack thereof should be an important component of any analysis.

Peace with Rome depends on a marriage between Éryxe and Massinisse, who appear to be a unified couple. Sophonisbe is the only royal personage involved to refuse this solution, on grounds of patriotism and resistance to Roman domination. But in act 1, scene 2, she clearly exposes her true motivations to her confidant. She pushed Syphax to make war on Éryxe simply out of jealousy, and Éryxe is now her prisoner. Sophonisbe had wanted Massinisse to marry Syphax's sister, since a marriage arranged by Sophonisbe would demonstrate her domination of her former lover: "A slave who escapes is always cause for embarrassment," she says (1.1.130). This strategy, reminiscent of Alidor's "gift" of his fiancée Angélique to a friend in *La Place Royale,* shows Sophonisbe's passion for power, in love and politics. When she invokes patriotism, and the royal pride of an independent sovereign, the notion of saving her people is nowhere evident. Her sheer egotism is emphasized by the repeated return to the theme of her jealousy. The link with Alidor is significant: prevention of the Massinisse-Éryxe wedding is her primary impetus for action, so that she functions more like the blocking characters of Corneille's early comedies than any of his protagonists since the 1630s. What takes *Sophonisbe* into the register of tragedy besides its royal characters and serious tone is the searching exploration of her self-love. Sophonisbe is a daring performer in the mode of the monstrous mothers, especially Cléopâtre in *Rodogune,* but unlike them, her position in relation to her adversaries evolves during the course of the play. Barnwell astutely remarks that "as Corneille became older he became more interested in uncovering the secret motives of his characters than in their 'poetic' expression" (1984, 591).

Sophonisbe seems to believe only in absolutes. She scorns Éryxe, Massinisse, and Syphax for their willingness to compromise with Rome, although they all point out to her that such a compromise is inevitable when faced with a much stronger enemy. Sophonisbe would prefer to fight on, whatever the cost to Syphax's kingdom of Numidia. No social servant she, despite her protests of love for Carthage. Two different states face Roman domination, and Carthage's struggle might be considered noble in comparison to the desire for peace in defeat expressed by the other protagonists. But when Sophonisbe says that Carthage must not be crushed, she really is defending first and foremost her own *gloire*. Her actions reveal more and more clearly the selfishness behind her demands. Provoking rivalries is Sophonisbe's favorite sport. In act 1, scene 4, she reminds Syphax of her preference for Massinisse, along with his debt to Carthage, as she goads him into risking his crown and his life for her once again by continuing to fight the Romans. In her manipulation of Syphax, she goes so far as to cry, acting as cleverly as she says Rome will in tricking Syphax.

After the battle, Sophonisbe is bitterly disappointed that Syphax allowed himself to be captured rather than be killed, or better yet, killing himself. She turns to Massinisse, using strategies similar to the ones that had kept Syphax on the battlefield, a combination of tears and threats. The Romans require that Sophonisbe be turned over to them, to be led as a captive through the streets of Rome. After act 1, this fate hangs over Sophonisbe, but she ends act 2 on a note of triumph: Massinisse will marry her. Love, vengeance, and *gloire* come together to seal her apparent victory at the expense of Éryxe and Syphax. Loyalty, at least to individuals, is not one of her characteristics. When Syphax, in chains, is brought to see her, after berating him for his cowardice, she says that she will again abandon Massinisse for him if he can arrange her escape to Carthage. "My only desire is my freedom," she declares (3.6.1107), but her freedom has meant slavery for others. She calls Massinisse her slave in act 1, scene 2, she imprisons Éryxe, and Syphax recognizes himself as her slave in act 4, scene 2, after the Roman general Lélius frees him from the literal chains he had worn because of his service to Sophonisbe. The Roman chains that Sophonisbe would avoid at any price are actually sought by Massinisse in act 4, scene 3, as preferable to losing Sophonisbe, although as Syphax learned, becoming enchained for Sophonisbe's sake is more likely to inspire her scorn than her praise. Such ironies abound. At the end of act 4, for example, Sophonisbe refuses to join Massinisse in a tearful plea for mercy from the Romans, even though she used tears to manipulate both of her husbands. She can dominate Syphax and Massinisse with tears and with the chains of love, but her weapons against Rome are her husbands themselves. Feminine power is always at one remove from the physical might that is necessary for lasting victory in Cornelian tragedy.

When Sophonisbe recognizes her imminent defeat in act 5, scene 1, she also recognizes the inconsistencies in her conception of the *gloire* she holds so dear. She feels panic at the pull of her love for Massinisse as it breaks into her allegiance to Carthage, and she admits that marrying Massinisse was a political mistake, made in the throes of her jealousy of Éryxe. Another recurring motif, the metaphor of poison, combines with the vocabulary of slavery that still appears throughout act 5. Syphax had said that he would joyfully return "the poison he is stealing from me" to Massinisse, in an unflattering description of Sophonisbe (4.2.1226). In act 5, scene 2, Massinisse sends Sophonisbe poison so that she may commit suicide rather than be Rome's slave, but she sends it back. In control of herself once more, she already has her own poison ready, and besides, Massinisse should take it himself since, if he becomes an ally of Rome, he is as much a slave as she is. Poison means freedom, and when Sophonisbe liberates herself in death, the Romans admire her proud gesture. But admiration in Cornelian theater does not necessarily imply moral grandeur. It means aesthetic triumph, a stunning performance that can be appreciated even if the character is ethically problematic. Sophonisbe's admission in act 5, scene 1 of mixed motivations sullies the purity of her *gloire* and affects the interpretation of her suicide. Barnwell believes that her grandeur remains unimpaired, but he also notes that the idea of *gloire* in *Sophonisbe* is a *gloire* whose objectives diminish in comparison with the Cornelian tradition (1984, 592).

A diminished *gloire* hangs over the play, affecting both Massinisse and Syphax, who abdicate their responsibility as rulers in order to serve the interests of Sophonisbe. Sophonisbe claims to serve Carthage, but as we have seen, her effect on the political situation is a negative one because personal animosities so often drive her actions. The only character who consistently displays a commonsense concern for practical solutions is Éryxe.[14] Her love for Massinisse does not provoke from her the destructive behavior Sophonisbe exhibits. Hers is the voice of the future, of the reasonable compromise with Rome that the men abandon when under Sophonisbe's spell. Éryxe is a less dramatically satisfying creation than Sophonisbe, but as Susan Read Baker points out, she is the only character to recognize and fully accept the political reality of Rome's power (111). The comic structure has again been called upon, and altered, in order to explore new dimensions in Cornelian tragedy as we judge the correctness of Éryxe's evaluation of the situation. Barnwell's observation about the diminished objectives of *gloire* applies to Éryxe as well as to Sophonisbe. Éryxe is the only candidate for hero, but the quiet calm of her performance lets us know that the objectives of heroism have been severely limited here.

Othon

"And I can say that there has never been a play where so many marriages are proposed without one taking place" (preface to *Othon; OC,* 3:462). Indeed, no fewer than five different matches are discussed in the tragedy. This reference to the disintegration of the marriage plot signals another twist in comic structure that subtends Corneille's theater. The playwright has changed history in order to "place all the blame on an evil man"(*OC,* 3:461). This blocking character, Vinius, is also a "heavy father" figure and the scapegoat the audience can hold ultimately responsible for an incomplete social renaissance, although conditions in a corrupt royal court lend themselves to the sort of intrigue Vinius finds irresistible. A virtuous young couple struggles to defeat the political schemes put into motion by Vinius and others, but as was the case in Cornelian comedy, trouble also comes from within the ranks of the young people themselves. When Corneille tells us that he will show Othon's virtues in all their brilliance, but without hiding his vices (*OC,* 3:461), the imperfect but high-performing characters of the comedies may come to mind. Othon lacks their energy and drive, however, and only a partial wish fulfillment combats Vinius's negative illusion in the end.[15] Moreover, Othon's role playing has its own destructive potential, and the final scene is colored by sadness rather than triumph.

Othon takes place in the court of the Roman emperor Galba. The political context fits Corneille's definition of tragedy in the first *Discours:* there is life-threatening peril, along with ambition and the desire for vengeance (*OC,* 3:123–24). But never before in the corpus had he produced a tragedy with such a tense, claustrophobic atmosphere. *Othon* was first performed in November 1664; Racine's first play, *La Thébaïde,* had premiered in June, so the rivalry between them had not yet had a chance to develop. It is noteworthy that the "Racinian" ambiance of *Othon* was created without the younger playwright's influence, so often seen to haunt the works of Corneille's last decade in the theater.

In the eyes of critics primarily interested in Corneille as the chronicler of French political life, another possible influence on the plays of this period is, of course, the beginning of Louis XIV's personal reign in 1661. Couton reads *Othon* as a piece in praise of the young king, who would not let himself be influenced by ministers (*OC,* 3:1493–95).

Jean-Claude Joye provides a more subversive political interpretation, finding in the play a critique of the divine right of kings (87–98). The text can support both views; a look at the dramatic structure as always produces a wider perspective.

Political intrigue traps all of the characters like a giant spider web whose interlocking threads make escape impossible. Othon is engaged to Plautine, whose father, the Consul Vinius, is systematically pillaging the state for his own gain. Vinius has enormous power, and he has guaranteed Othon the succession to Galba's throne, provided he marries Plautine. Othon justifies his willingness to make this political partnership, since alliances are a necessity in a court where corrupt advisors exercise power over the weak emperor. Othon stands out in his relative virtue. He has come to love Plautine, which reinforces the spectator's impression that they represent hope for new leadership with a foundation in sincerity rather than hypocrisy.

Othon's friend Albin advises him to vie instead for the hand of Camille, Galba's niece (a Cornelian invention). But love, fidelity, *and* politics reinforce Othon's ties to Plautine. Encouragement to abandon Plautine arrives from a surprising quarter when Vinius announces in a panic that Othon *must* court Camille for all their sakes: if his enemies choose Camille's husband, every ally of Vinius will be in danger. Camille is obviously attracted to Othon, and Othon should profit from her inclination, according to Vinius. Othon and Plautine wish to remain faithful to each other, but the political reality of imminent death for those out of power makes their idealism difficult to practice. Plautine is ready to sacrifice her marriage to save the lives of her fiancé and father, and she proposes an enduring, Platonic love to Othon instead. But in a lover's quarrel more typical of comedy (act 1, scene 4), Othon refuses to give up on their original dream. It is as if only the happy ending of the marriage plot will satisfy him. But the necessity of political, emotional, and moral compromise moves the play into the realm of tragedy, the tragedy of tainted, unsatisfactory solutions.

When Othon is convinced that he must disguise his true feelings and pursue Camille, he is forced to recognize the difference between his mask and his "real" identity, a situation rare in Corneille's tragedies. It is in the comedies that acting and trickery go hand in hand for the protagonists, whereas the heroes who adopt a new role in the tetralogy and beyond do so as part of a permanent change in identity, as when Rodrigue becomes le Cid, or Octave becomes Auguste in *Cinna*. Even some of the more questionable changes of role in the plays of the middle period, such as César's magnanimous conduct in *Pompée* and Grimoald's last-minute conversion in *Pertharite,* claim to be permanent metamorphoses. Only the "monstrous mothers" are actors who seek to dupe others, and Othon, with his pretension to virtuous heroism, would prefer not to consider himself a mere actor, despite the fact that he was a courtier under the extremely corrupt Emperor Nero.[16] Nevertheless, instead of just another player on the political scene, Othon wants to be the savior of his society. He imagines that when he accedes to the throne, virtue will reign for the benefit of all. But if his power is founded on duplicity, can he hope to replace corruption with rectitude?

Like many of the heroes from this last period of the oeuvre, Othon suffers from divided desire (Plautine versus the throne) and from fear: fear of losing what he desires, and fear of losing his life, while seeing Plautine killed as well. His fears and desires are tortuously linked, because if he loses the throne, he and Plautine will probably be assassinated in any case. Either match will damage him, and Plautine faces the same dilemma when the freed slave Martian offers to help Othon win the empire, with Plautine's hand in marriage as the price.

While Plautine and Othon see clearly that there is no satisfactory way out of their dilemma, Camille is able to blind herself into believing that Othon loves her. She pursues him with all the more enthusiasm and justification when Galba chooses Pison instead of Othon as his successor. Only Camille can save Othon from death now. She manages to convince her uncle to let her marry Othon—but his permission comes with the understanding that the throne is not part of the bargain. Othon feels as though he has been tricked into declaring love for Camille, but she tries to convince him that when Galba is dead, her link to the crown will enable him to topple Pison. Their debate in act 3, scene 5 over which scenario is more likely to lead to Othon's death illustrates just how hopeless his situation is. He expresses despair and sees only threats of ruin and death all around him. He has dishonored himself by declaring a love that is false, with no political gain to show for it.

Plautine is determined at this point (act 4, scene 1) to save Othon and make him emperor when she marries Martian. Othon is horrified at the thought, since his reign would be founded on an even more corrupt base than he had imagined by marrying Camille. Another layer of corruption is introduced by Vinius, the most skilled actor and manipulator among all the characters. While on the one hand, the army is offering to follow Othon, on the other, Vinius has approved the marriage of Plautine and Pison, for if Camille marries Pison, Vinius will have no tie to the throne. Plautine's refusal of such a shameful bargain is strengthened by horror that her father would go so far as to build his power on Othon's corpse.[17] "You would see a thousand lovers die with joy," Vinius tells her, if only you could know the exhilaration of holding power (4.3.1318–22). The illusion of victory floats before all those who seek it, but the definitive identity of Galba's successor is elusive, as the emperor receives conflicting advice from every quarter.

Othon's death is announced, but this is just another illusion. A series of murders leaves Othon in power, but Vinius is dead, and Plautine wants to be left in peace to mourn her father, despite his treachery. Enormous ambiguity surrounds the final tableau. As at the end of *Le Cid,* we can imagine an eventual marriage, based on love but tainted by past events. Othon's last words are a declaration of friendship to the absent Camille, who only wants his love. Irony attends this triumph of the lonely hero in a world, as Helen Bates McDermott says, where "heroism is utterly out of place."[18] The corrupt elements, Vinius, Galba, Pison, and Lacus are dead, killed by their obsessive drive to obtain power. Martian lives on, though in disgrace, a symbol of the impossibility of eradicating vice from the court entirely. McDermott finds in the weary Othon "a rich and burdensome *savoir* [knowledge] rare in a seventeenth-century hero (1978, 651). I would agree that in the plays of Corneille's last period, this deepening of knowledge is the norm, and it provides much of the interest of these complex and fascinating works.

Agésilas

Agésilas, Corneille's only play written in free verse, was not a success when first performed in 1666. Thirty-five years later, one of Corneille's more acid-tongued detractors, Racine's friend Boileau, published an epigram that suggested it was time for Corneille to retire: "Après l'*Agésilas,* / Hélas! / Après l'*Attila,* / Holà." Couton observes that Corneille's reputation was still so great in 1666 that Boileau didn't dare reveal his witticism, but critics since the 1660s have usually taken Boileau's judgment as authorization to pass over both *Agésilas* and the tragedy that follows it, *Attila* (*OC,* 3:1518–19). While *Attila* is the more compelling of the two works, *Agésilas* holds interest as another example of Corneille's continuing effort at innovation. As is so often the case in his theoretical writings, Corneille's preface conveys his willingness to experiment as a heroic gesture: just as the Romans renewed Greek tragedy, the modern

French playwright must dare to strike out in a new direction, despite the
risks involved when one leaves the well-trodden path (*OC,* 3:563–64).

The risks taken here are impressive. The standard 12-syllable alexan-
drine is varied with 8-syllable verses, and a variable rhyme scheme at
times replaces the standard rhyming couplets. A rhythm new to tragedy
was created, perhaps under the influence of opera, a budding form of
theater in France of the 1660s. Corneille had experimented with rhyme
and meter ever since the 1630s by introducing *stances* in his characters'
monologues. The length of lines and the sort of rhyme used vary in
stances, which we find only at moments of extreme emotional intensity
for his characters. In the most famous example from Corneille's theater,
Rodrigue works out his decision to duel with Chimène's father in *stances*
at the end of act 1 of *Le Cid.* Corneille's decision to write in free verse in
Agésilas was not well received in 1666, but it highlights the importance
of strong emotion in the play and suggests a focus on individual desire.
Agésilas is one of a group of "matrimonial" plays of Corneille's last
period, since the pairing of six young, aristocratic characters forms the
subject. Politics and tender passion mix as they always have in Cornelian
tragedy, but individual desire takes center stage. The theme of sacrifice,
still very important in *Othon* in the heroine Plautine, becomes increasingly less idealistic. As Couton puts it, in *Agésilas* we have six characters
in search of a happiness that satisfies not only their hearts but also their
ambition, their vanities, and their love of self (*OC,* 3:1521).

In political terms, Agésilas, king of Sparta, is faced with a minister so
powerful that the monarch's sovereignty is threatened. Of course, this
theme continued to be topical in France after the Fronde, after the disgrace of Fouquet, the finance minister, and only five years into Louis
XIV's personal reign. This is a political theme Corneille would return to
in his last play, *Suréna,* and the more general examination of royal prudence in the face of a potentially threatened monarchy was one that
interested Corneille throughout his career.[19] But the weight of the story
presented in *Agésilas* is given to the love plot, as marriages are proposed,
rejected, and rearranged to great emotional effect. There is no risk of
death, and the absence of mortal peril along with lengthy debates
exploring personal sentiments seem to orient the play more toward
heroic comedy in the manner of *Don Sanche d'Aragon.* In calling *Agésilas*
a tragedy, Corneille altered his own definition of the genre in favor of yet
another experiment. The playwright's use of language reinforces this
impression: the *précieux* language of love is accompanied by a great deal
of irony, and even the sort of sarcasm that can cause a reader to chuckle.

André Stegmann goes so far as to call it a *tragédie enjouée,* or "joyful tragedy" (1968, 2:630).

When viewed from the perspective of Corneille's comic structure, the situation that inspires such irony and such passion begins with a father figure. Lysander is a powerful Spartan captain under Agésilas. Lysander has two daughters to marry, and two suitors arrive to pursue these young women in order to cement a political alliance with Sparta, and in particular with Lysander. One of the suitors is the king of Paphlagonia, Cotys, and the other is a grand Persian noble, Spitridate. Lysander is an indulgent Cornelian father rather than the "heavy father" of classical comedy: he wants his daughters to marry for love, but this proves difficult to achieve. The eldest daughter, Elpinice, has been promised to King Cotys, but Elpinice and Spitridate are in love. Aglatide, the younger daughter, loves Cotys, but he prefers Mandane, Spitridate's sister, who is also the love object of Agésilas. As in Corneille's early, pastoral-influenced comedies, the potential for forming happy couples is troubled by the young people themselves.[20] Cotys refuses to trade Aglatide for Elpinice unless Spitridate makes sure that Cotys can have Mandane, but Spitridate is reluctant to break their agreement with Lysander by leaving one of the daughters unwed . Mandane loves Cotys, so at least two happy couples out of three seem possible, were it not for the problem of political alliances. Yet political decisions are constantly reviewed and changed in order to justify romantic preferences, and Agésilas is not exempt from these machinations. Agésilas adds another layer of complication when he declares that Lysander's daughters cannot make such politically powerful marriages. The king's dispute with Lysander means that Spitridate can marry Elpinice only if Agésilas marries Mandane, since the alliance thus formed with Spitridate through his sister would solve the political problem—and satisfy Agésilas's desire. But this solution comes at the expense of the feelings of Mandane and Cotys, and with a dubious political effect, since Agésilas would be marrying a foreigner, against the expectations of his society, and King Cotys would have an excuse for aggression. Neither is Lysander free from emotional swings even as he engages in political intrigue against Agésilas. His motivations include a combination of the desire to conserve power, the perceived need for self-protection against an ungrateful king, hurt feelings, and the desire for vengeance. The overwhelming impression for the spectator is of the generalized instability of the male characters and the dissatisfaction of the women.

The plot thickens even further when Aglatide refuses to break her engagement to Spitridate because she is afraid of being left out of the

multiple marriage scenario. She will give in only if Cotys or Agésilas
agrees to marry her, even though she is aware that neither man is in love
with her. With bitter irony, she pushes Mandane to choose one of the
kings, so that she may have the other. The risk to her sister's happiness
should Mandane follow her heart and marry Cotys is of little concern to
Aglatide in her jealousy. Mandane in turn is bitter that Cotys seems all
too ready to renounce their love in an apparently futile effort at political
harmony. Spitridate meanwhile makes it clear that he has no intention
of giving up Elpinice: heroic sacrifice in service of a harmonious society
has no appeal for him, but then, Cotys and Agésilas are the only kings.
At moments, they seem likely to live up to their responsibility as monarchs, but they waver in their resolve. As Jacqueline van Baelen has
noted, "No one is ready to sacrifice personal happiness for that of others
or for the general good."[21] Agésilas takes Mandane for himself and
allows the Elpinice-Spitridate union. When Mandane makes it clear that
she loves Cotys, however, Agésilas gives in to her desire to marry the
other king. His sacrifice appears less than heroic in the context of her
feelings and his previous actions, inspired as they were by his hatred of
Lysander and his desire for Mandane at least as much as by any sense of
duty to his role as monarch. Van Baelen makes an astute remark about
Agésilas as compared with *Pompée:* "The rhetoric of heroism is displaced
into a non-heroic world and Corneille achieves in both these plays, a
density, a level of irony and pessimism lacking in the earlier tragedies"
(77–78). In *Agésilas,* this irony and pessimism are more evident than in
Pompée, especially given the tone of the final scene.

Agésilas takes Aglatide as his wife, and since he had courted her in
the past, for a moment there is a suggestion that this third couple could
represent a thoroughly positive pairing. Aglatide's sarcastic comments
about Agésilas's unfaithful character show rather the opposite, however.
She reminds him of his past attentions to her and remarks: "Not that
I'm thinking of them any longer. I've learned from you my lord, / That
time can change one's desires, heart, and soul" (5.8.2085–86). The primary royal couple is formed on a note of cynicism.[22] Aglatide has the
throne she sought, and at the end of the play, all the characters declare
their allegiance to Agésilas in the generosity of his sacrifice of Mandane.
Yet Agésilas's reluctant gesture seems a parody of the sacrificial *générosité*
of earlier heroes. Nevertheless, Corneille was correct to call *Agésilas* a
tragedy rather than a heroic comedy. Although the positive ending is
damaged and degraded, and the egotistical causes and effects of passionate love are too clearly exposed to speak of an ending commensurate

with his comic structure, Corneille once again used this structure to interesting effect.

Attila, roi des Huns

In *Attila, roi des Huns* (Attila, King of the Huns, 1667), we see a monster even more menacing than the monstrous mothers of *Théodore, Rodogune,* and *Nicomède.* Once again the monstrous character is royal and holds political power. Attila is in fact an absolute ruler, unlike Marcelle, Cléopâtre, and Arsinoé, who as women were dependent on weaker male characters to hold the formal reins of power. Attila is thus all the more threatening, and his disappearance from the scene represents an even stronger wish fulfillment than the deaths of Marcelle and Cléopâtre, or the pardon of Arsinoé. The plot is relatively simple: the tyrannical Attila holds supreme political power in what is now central Europe, and he holds the balance between a fading center of influence in Rome and the developing state of the Franks. Attila must decide whether or not the Franks will take supremacy over the Romans, and his choice will be signaled by his marriage plans. He holds two princesses hostage: Ildione, sister of the Frankish king, and Honorie, sister of the Roman emperor. His political decision is complicated by his love for Ildione, a love that represents his only point of vulnerability. The feminine remains threatening in Cornelian theater, but Attila combats it by repression and manipulation. He proposes first to Honorie, then switches to Ildione later on, provoking tension between the princesses as part of his larger political strategy. He also holds two kings hostage, Valamir of the Ostrogoths, who wants to marry Honorie, and Ardaric of the Gepidae, who is passionately in love with Ildione. The cruelty of the kings' situation is evident when Attila asks them to make the decision about which woman he should marry. He takes a sadistic glee in their anguish and addresses them with great sarcasm. Attila's move to divide the two allies from each other underscores his role as a destroyer of existing social and political structures. But in the end, Attila himself is destroyed by an unstanchable nosebleed. Although his death occurs offstage, the recounted image is spectacular. Attila's fury literally bursts his veins, which spout blood like fountains and streams (5.6.1755–60).

Attila is the scapegoat upon whose death social rebirth can be founded. In Northrup Frye's model of society's foundations in comedy as I have used it throughout this study, the *pharmakos,* or scapegoat, is a powerful monomaniac determined to impose his deformed vision of the world (Frye, 164–65). Attila represents a truly foreign, cancerous growth on the social body. Scapegoats in Corneille's tragedies, those characters who threaten to destroy social structures and who are not reintegrated into the group, have always been members of the ruling elite. Their behavior has been damaging and abhorrent to others, but even extreme acts of violence such as Pymante's attempted rape and murder of Dorise in the tragicomedy *Clitandre*, Ptolomée's murder of Pompée and attempted regicide of César in *Pompée*, and Cléopâtre's infanticide of Séleucus and attempted regicide of Antiochus in *Rodogune* are contained by reaction from other characters. Attila has already committed regicide, the most inexcusable crime by seventeenth-century standards, doubling it with fratricide since the first king he killed was his older brother, Vléda, from whom he stole the throne. Six other regicides have followed before the opening scene of *Attila,* with two more threatened during the play. Not only is Attila's violence not in the least restrained by others, it is monstrous in its extent and diversity, and the risk that it will become universal is clearly felt by the spectator. John Lyons points to his death as the moment when France acquires its identity, the moment of the nation's birth or origin, founded on a marked difference from what came before (1996, 161–62).[23] Attila functions as a sign of difference in several ways.

In terms of the comic structure, Attila is clearly a blocking character, preventing the formation of two well-suited couples. Lyons notes the structural resemblance with the early comedies in the imbalance in the number of available mates: three men vie for two women (1996, 155). In the comedies, the odd man out plays a socially destructive role, as does Attila here.

Socially, Attila compares his position and values to the kings' aristocratic code of honor. He has acted without scruples and acquired power by force, while their sense of royal, ethical conduct leaves them completely vulnerable to his aggression. When he goes so far as to force them to duel, they appear all the more impotent as they are forced into a parody of their standards. Politically, the situation is ironic: Attila notes how a veritable league of nations has been formed to fight against him, so that his aggression has built new political links among his enemies, which he will combat with ignoble deviousness. Another irony in the strategy Attila uses against the pitiable kings is pointed out by Lyons: Attila gains power "by apparently avoiding the exercise of power. By giving Valamir and Ardaric the right to decide whether he should ally with Rome or with the Franks, Attila will not only eliminate an annoying minor king but will do so without any responsibility in this fate. Attila will simply be following the advice of one of his allies and placating the anger of the others by drawing their anger onto a scapegoat" (1996, 163). Attila almost succeeds in provoking a deadly rivalry and in making one of his victims the scapegoat. Nevertheless, the comic schema will prevail, and Attila himself will be the only *pharmakos*.

Attila's behavior presents an interesting twist on the notion of the Cornelian hero as a social servant. The abdication of responsibility is impossible for the character deserving of the title of hero in Corneille's theater, but not only does Attila *refuse* to serve society, he is proud to be the object of the public's hatred (5.3.1564–65). Renaissance must be built upon the elimination of decay in favor of the pure freshness of the new. The scapegoat serves society with the necessary role of agent of change, but whereas the hero's participation in a social renewal suggests the continuation of his role into the future, the scapegoat must either mend his ways and make reparation to society (as Arsinoé does in *Nicomède,* for example), or meet his deserved end.

Attila's death is the most dramatic in Cornelian theater, but it is not brought about by any of the other protagonists. Valamir and Ardaric do not really measure up to the standards of the Cornelian hero since they are largely passive. Although the women are more active characters than the men, Attila's absolute control paralyzes his captives, even Ildione, who plans to murder Attila after they marry.[24] In fact, most of her energy during the play is taken up by her competition with Honorie. They are caught in the paradoxical situation of vying for the hand of the tyrant neither wishes to wed. But the one not chosen will be dishonored: once again, Attila divides and conquers.

Attila's death brings a positive resolution to their dilemma in the manner of a *deus ex machina,* the god who arrives fortuitously in Greco-Roman comedy to restore order to the chaotic situation caused by the scapegoat.[25] In another of the play's ironies, Attila presents himself as the envoy of God (5.3.1572–82), while he will also be punished by God.[26] But as in the case of Attila's doubly ironic role as builder and destroyer of alliances, his death contains a further irony. Attila is at least partially responsible for his own demise. He who used apparent indecision and silence as a weapon against Valamir and Ardaric is only apparently a victim, because it is his rage that provokes the fatal hemmorhage. He must bear responsibility for his own death, in a reinforcement of the notion that abdication of responsibility is not only nonheroic; in a ruler, it is inadmissible.

Lyons makes the connection between this play and the monsters that inhabit Racine's theater. Attila recalls horrible figures like the sea creature who kills Hippolyte in *Phèdre,* for the Hun has some of the "nonhuman physical qualities" associated with monstrosity (1996, 156). His name resonates with twentieth-century North Americans as a sign of barbarity, even bestiality. Attila is deformed in every possible way: the outside reflects an inner rottenness. Once again Corneille is shown using "Racinian" devices at a time when Racine had only produced two plays, and the possibility that the younger dramatist influenced the older seems remote. One of the reasons critics have given for the modern preference for Racine over Corneille is that the relatively more naturalistic, historically based approach of Corneille does not have the same universal appeal as Racine's mythical stories.[27] But Corneille's theater does resonate with archetypal structures skillfully manipulated by the dramatist. Corneille also offers a door to understanding the local historical concerns of seventeenth-century France, but his corpus provides stories of much wider import.

In *Attila,* as in all of the post-retirement plays, the protagonists tend to exhibit socially destructive behavior whose roots are located in *amour-propre.* Attila is able to manipulate others partly because, as their jailer, he can develop any scenario he wishes, but his task is made easier by their blindness to the advantages of working together to defeat him. Translated variously as vainglory, egotism, or self-love, *amour-propre* was carefully explored by Racine, the Jansenist writer Blaise Pascal, and the worldly author of maxims, La Rochefoucauld, to name only the best-known authors to make *amour-propre* a central theme in their work.[28] Corneille in the 1660s joined in the discussion of the very human tendency to place the self at the center of the universe, while remaining blind to the potentially destructive force of *amour-propre,* dangerous to society as well as to the self. In his earlier work, the Jesuit concept of free will had seemed to influence Cornelian characters, and this is true as late as *Oedipe,* as I suggest in the earlier discussion of that play. Corneille does not replace Jesuit free will with Jansenist predestination in his oeuvre after *Oedipe,* but he gradually includes more characters whose motivations are clearly less than selfless, and whose desires and fears are visible to the spectator, often thanks to sarcastic humor or irony on the part of other characters.[29] In a marked contrast with the tetralogy, heroes who perform with confidence are difficult to find, and yet increased self-questioning does not necessarily lead to insight or to mastery of a difficult situation. Not only did Corneille continue to experiment with the dramatic structure of his works, he was also interested in exploring the pre-occupations of his day.

More Heroic Comedy

Tite et Bérénice

With *Tite et Bérénice,* Corneille returned to heroic comedy in order to take on Racine in direct competition. Racine's *Bérénice* premiered one week prior to Corneille's play, in November 1670. Corneille's play was a box-office failure, while Racine had a stunning success. Corneille blamed his failure on the bad acting of Molière's company (*OC,* 3:1606), but the relative neglect of *Tite et Bérénice* since the seventeenth century suggests serious aesthetic flaws.

Tite (Titus), the Roman emperor, has long loved Bérénice, a queen of Judea, but a Roman emperor can never wed a foreign queen, so their marriage is seemingly impossible. Racine's tragedy begins with some hope of marriage, followed by the gradual realization that, out of respect for his office and the Senate's decree, Titus must renounce Bérénice. She leaves Rome in an atmosphere of dignified sadness (*tristesse majestuese,* says Racine in his preface). Corneille assumes that the separation has already taken place, but Bérénice returns from exile just as Tite is preparing to marry a Roman noblewoman, Domitie. Domitie has been in love with Tite's brother, Domitian, but her passion for the title of empress is stronger than her passion for Domitian. Bérénice and Domitian try to prevent the union of Tite and Domitie.

Two dreamed-of love matches are blocked by an obstacle arising from within the couples. With the invention of Domitie, Corneille sets up the sort of conflict among young lovers that we see so often in his theater. The political dilemma of the royal characters whose story is tragic in Racine's *Bérénice* becomes material for a heroic comedy in Corneille's treatment because Corneille gives his characters much more apparent control over their fate. Where Racine depicts victims of destiny, Corneille portrays victims of their own egotistical desires.

Tite superficially resembles the Cornelian hero who strives to serve his society, but his lack of resolution from start to finish makes it impossible for the spectator to admire him. The pity inspired by the suffering of Racine's Titus is greatly attenuated here because of Tite's bad faith at the end of the play. In a noble sacrifice to his duty as emperor, he is prepared to send Bérénice away for the second time, even though the Senate has approved their marriage—but this is only after Bérénice has already decided to leave him. Tite was in fact ready to abdicate for her sake in act 3, scene 5 and again in act 5, scene 4; even in the last scene of the play, he resists the heroic gesture toward which Bérénice pushes him. Tite's decision at the very end of the final scene is to accept Bérénice's departure, to renounce marriage to Domitie, and to share power with Domitian. This signals a conversion to heroic duty, brought about by Bérénice's virtue. Corneille came as close as the well-known facts of history would allow him to a happy ending. The marriage of Domitian and Domitie, and the satisfaction of Domitian's love along with Domitie's ambition adds a positive note completely at odds with Racine's somber tragedy.[30] Indeed, *heureux* (happy) is the last word of *Tite et Bérénice*. Nevertheless, heroism is greatly attenuated in this *comédie héroïque*. While some critics interpret Tite's last words more favorably, I agree with Jonathan Mallinson, who sees the emperor's renunciation of Bérénice as an act of lassitude and despair.[31]

Domitie's ambition reminds us of the Cornelian hero's drive for distinction, but her desire for the throne serves only to satisfy her ego. Anger and jealousy are her dominant emotions, and they signal her egotism to the spectator. The cruelty of asking Domitian to defend her marriage to Tite before the Senate is striking, especially when she says "Love me as I want you to [i.e., make sure I marry your brother], or love me no longer." (4.3.1230). The insult to her *gloire* at possibly losing the throne is compounded by her jealousy of Bérénice, which in Mallinson's view makes Domitie want to seduce Tite as well as to wed him (1989, 89). In her last appearance onstage in act 5, scene 2, she threatens Tite with a fight to the death if he refuses to marry her. Domitie's obsession with rank does not suggest a solid foundation for the empire if she attains her goal.

Neither are Domitian and Bérénice idealized lovers, nor are they social servants. Domitian may describe for his brother in act 1, scene 2 the purity of the love he shares with Domitie, but when the couple is alone, he repeatedly castigates her for her ambition and rather sadistically imagines her being punished for abandoning him (act 1, scene 3). In a logical and successful strategy, he courts Bérénice in the hope of making Domitie and Tite as jealous as he feels.

Bérénice, for her part, tries to goad Tite into braving the Senate by making a grand ideal of the emperor's independence (3.5.989–96). But jealousy movtivates her just as much as it does the others. Moreover, Bérénice's jealousy has a double source: besides becoming Tite's beautiful and distinguished wife, Domitie as empress would be her political superior. When Tite does agree to give up the empire for Bérénice, she berates him for his weakness and lack of character (5.4.1643–46). A transformation occurs in the last scene of the play, however. Bérénice shows much more *générosité* than any of the other protagonists. She makes the decision to quit Rome in order to protect Tite from the enemies he would inevitably make if her married her. She appreciates the Senate's gesture in accepting her as empress and declares that she and Tite should in turn recognize the favor by renouncing their marriage, which would trouble the peace of the empire as well as threaten Tite's life. She wants to preserve their *gloire* for posterity. Her triumph is based on excepitonal sacrifice: "I would be yours, if I loved in the ordinary way," she tells Tite (5.5.1732).

With the return to the theme of conversion to socially beneficial conduct thanks to the recognition of exceptional merit in a leader, Corneille was true to his comic schema, offering yet another variation on it in the story of Tite and Bérénice. In *Cinna* in 1642, we see a similar situation for a Roman emperor: all the protagonists are less than heroic until Auguste's sudden decision to be magnanimous leads to a mass conversion to virtue and to a recognition of his worthiness. Why does Bérénice's gesture, which has the same effect for the onstage spectators as Auguste's, not operate to overwhelm theatergoers and readers? Is it the displacement of the gesture onto a female character other than the emperor? A more likely answer lies in the insistent development of the theme of *amour-propre* in *Tite et Bérénice*. In act 1, scene 3, Domitian's confidant Albin exposes a theory of *amour-propre* that colors our view of the characters' actions for the rest of the play:

> Self love is the source in us of all other loves,
> It is the sentiment underlying all other sentiments,
> It alone lights up, crushes, or alters our desire.
> The objects of our wishes are object of our pleasures:
> You who love with such faithful ardor,
> Do you love Domitie, or your pleasures?
> And when you aspire to such sweet relations,
> Is it for love of her or for love of yourself?
> The cherished idea of possessing her
> Has enchanted and obsessed you,
> But if you imagined a better fate,
> You would soon point your affections in another direction.

Conquering her is the pinnacle of delight,
You imagine nothing but suffering without her,
And that is why she charms you,
Yet you love only yourself, when you think you love her.

(1.3.279–94)

Domitian is too caught up in his passion to protest this interpretation of his love, which is shown to pertain to all of the protagonists, including Bérénice: Mallinson sees an egotistical *gloire* even in her final renunciation of Tite (1989, 93). Whether we are impressed by the force of the conversion she effects or not, it has been so tainted that it cannot come close to the magic of Auguste's metamorphosis.

Corneille never wrote an uninteresting play, but in *Tite et Bérénice* he did write a relatively unsatisfying one. The clash between *amour-propre* and the claim to heroism produces aesthetically pleasing works by Racine and by Corneille himself. *Tite et Bérénice,* however, suffers ultimately from a problem of recognition. The best-developed text on *amour-propre* of the seventeenth century, La Rochefoucauld's *Maxime supprimée no. 1,* shows that blindness to its workings is the most salient characteristic of *amour-propre* (La Rochefoucauld, 133–36). Domitian's dismissal of Albin's warning explanation, and the other characters' reluctance to examine their motivations, gives a hollow ring to the happy, heroic ending of *Tite et Bérénice.* In this play, Corneille denies his characters the flashes of lucidity experienced by Racine's potagonists in the midst of their tortured blindness. The audience sees the contrast between blindness and insight; Bérénice, Tite, Domitie, and Domitian do not. Introspection increases in Corneille's last plays, but *Tite et Bérénice* remains a comedy whose players are more interested in ostentation than in painful self-reflection.

Psyché

Psyché, a "tragedy-ballet," was the result of collaboration between Molière, who laid out the plot, the playwright and opera librettist Quinault, who wrote the words for the parts to be sung, and Corneille, who wrote the most of the free verse for the spoken parts. Louis XIV had ordered an entertainment for January 1671, to be performed several times before Lent, and the foreward to the published version of *Psyché* claims that Corneille had only two weeks to finish all the versification (*OC,* 3:1079).

Psyché is worth mentioning because, as Couton points out, the play contains some of Corneille's best, and most tender, love poetry. His nephew, Fontenelle, wrote in his biography of Corneille that the old author wanted to demonstrate his ability to follow the fashion for a sort of tender sentimentality not usually associated with the poet of noble heroism (*OC*, 3:1629). An examination of Corneille's post-retirement plays shows that well before *Psyché*, his protagonists were exposing their conflicting emotions more thoroughly than in the tetralogy that had made him so famous.

In the generic scheme of Corneille's work, *Psyché* would have been more properly labeled a heroic comedy like the plays that precede and follow it in his production. The mythological characters can end the play happily, thanks to their supernatural powers. Even deserving mortals like the long-suffering heroine, Psyché, can live forever in a fantasy afterlife.

Pulchérie

In the preface to his last heroic comedy, performed during the 1672–1673 season, Corneille claims to have written *Pulchérie* against the grain of the obsessions of the time (*OC*, 3:1172). In other words, he castigates Racine's emphasis on the inability to control violent passions. Nonetheless, *Pulchérie* contains several characters whose desires are not easily denied.

When the play opens, Princess Pulchérie has reigned as empress of the Orient for 15 years. Although her brother had held the title of emperor, she had exercised power independently and well. With her brother's death, she will lose the throne unless another male figurehead is elected emperor. This situation reflects French political tradition: under Salic law, a woman could not inherit the throne, although both Marie de Médicis and Anne d'Autriche had been able to act as regents for their young sons, Louis XIII and Louis XIV, respectively. Pulchérie has a candidate in mind, the man she loves, Léon. But she makes it clear to him that her role as empress takes precedence over their relationship: she will marry whomever the Senate chooses as emperor. Duty supersedes love for Pulchérie, in a dichotomy that recalls the declarations of Chimène in *Le Cid*. Pulchérie's fiancé, Léon, does not share her values, for he would readily abandon duty in favor of their love. But Pulchérie feels an immense responsibility to her country, to her family, and to her conception of herself. An ethic of service makes her a true Cornelian hero, and her certainty and lack of self-questioning at this point are reminiscent of Rodrigue and the other male heroes of the tetralogy. Corneille's remarks about an unfashionable viewpoint in this play do seem to apply to Pulchérie. Nevertheless, there is tension from the first scene between Pulchérie's idea of Léon and his own words and deeds. She insists in the opening lines that her love is based solely on reason and on esteem for his virtue. No "blind desires" affect her, she says (1.1.1–12). But in Léon's reply, it is precisely the sort of blind devotion to love refused by Pulchérie that he promotes (1.1.45–76). A flaw is thus revealed in this, the principal match, from the start.[32]

Two of the other characters even more obviously share the preoccupation with self-questioning that we see so often in the post-retirement plays. Once again we have a group of young lovers with the potential to achieve sentimental harmony, but several obstacles block their way.[33] As in *Tite et Bérénice,* the political duty of the ruler is a key factor, along with the ambition of one who seeks to share the power of the empress through marriage. Aspar and Léon's sister, Irène, are in love, but Aspar is another leading candidate for emperor, and like Domitie, the desire for the title appeals to him more than his desire for Irène. And like Domitian, Irène vows to avenge herself on her unfaithful lover.

The conflicts among the four are further complicated by another potential emperor, Martian, the elderly senator. When we learn that Martian is in love with Pulchérie, the dynamic of comedy is suggested more strongly. Because of his age, Martian recalls the "heavy father" of comedy who threatens to prevent the union of the young couple. The heavy father who wants to become a young lover has another resonance with comedy for fans of Molière: Arnolphe in *L'École des femmes* (*The School for Wives*) appeared in 1662, although this comical blocking character is authoritarian rather than sweetly noble like Martian. The *vieillard amoureux,* or elderly lover, also appears in several of Corneille's early comedies, as well as in *Médée.* Normally, Martian would remain the odd man out, but there is hope for equilibrium in this play of only six characters. Martian's daughter, Justine, is also in love—with Léon. Can desires be readjusted so as to form three happy couples and a stable poltical solution?

When Pulchérie is elected empress between acts 1 and 2, she is given the power to control her own destiny along with everyone else's. Martian suffers mightily from the supposition that she will marry Léon, but at great sacrifice to himself, he has supported her independence. He has loved her devotedly, in silence, for 10 years, but he plans to commit suicide when all hope of having her is lost. He will continue to serve her while she needs his support, which is necessary with Aspar conspiring to try to take power. Martian comments that Aspar is not only a manipulative politician, he is also unfaithful in his love for Irène. Like Léon, Martain has the values of the perfect courtly lover, making Aspar look like the most flawed of the characters, lacking respect for both duty and love.

Only Martian is able to experience a complete correspondence between his political dealings, all on Pulchérie's behalf, and his devotion to her as a lover. In light of this relative perfection, his recuperation into the set of happy couples at the end of the play is not surprising. Indeed, he is the most appropriate match for Pulchérie, because Léon continues to declare that being emperor does not interest him. Martian agrees to help Léon convince Pulchérie to satisfy her love by naming him emperor, despite Léon's unsuitability for the role. Martian believes that he best serves Pulchérie by continued sacrifice. Only Pulchérie puts service to the empire before love; only Martian comes close to being worthy of her.

Justine shows herself to be as virtuous as her father, vowing to help Léon obtain Pulchérie, who retains hope in act 3, scene 3, that the Senate will elect Léon emperor, for she will never name him herself. Even this solution would be damaging to the empire, and Pulchérie is able at the beginning of act 5 to renounce completely the idea of marrying Léon. She gains insight along with her title, and realizes that Léon would be a poor emperor. She admits that her dream in act 1 of harmonizing love and duty was only an illusion. In a continuing echo from *Le Cid,* she chooses to value duty as completely as Rodrigue does, but like Chimène, she has a higher price to pay than the warrior-hero who may someday possess his beloved without compromising his role as a social servant. She will give the Senate an emperor in Martian, whose love she will not return, but with whom she can form a chaste partnership that leaves her power intact.[34]

The force of Pulchérie's moral and political will forges at least one other union, as Justine is given to Léon, who becomes the heir to the throne. Aspar is encouraged to accept Irène rather than to dream of a power he does not merit. A double and possibly triple marriage ends this heroic comedy, but on a note of desire only partially satisfied. Even Pulchérie's autonomy is questioned by Domna Stanton as self-deception, since she cannot sit on the throne alone (243–44). While the text of the play does not really support this contention, neither can I agree with

Marie-Odile Sweetser that Corneille shows in *Pulchérie* his Jesuit confidence in human perfectability, founded on the exercise of free will and extreme effort (Sweetser 1994, 121). Two so diametrically opposed readings of the same text are possible because the play contains interesting ambiguities. Despite the empress's undeniable sacrifice and service, she is not exempt from desire. The desire for autonomy replaces and sublimates her desire for Léon, and even this desire is not solely a function of values like the desire to serve or the noble desire for glory. Pulchérie is also motivated by fear: "I tremble to think that I will be his wife / And one does not marry the most cherished lover / Without immediately giving oneself a master as well as a husband" (5.1.1442–44). Even an admirable heroine cannot achieve unquestioning moral certainty in the plays of Corneille's last period.

It is significant that Racine's *Mithridate* appeared in 1673, with an elderly lover as its main character. Mithridate's cruel jealousy and sensuality could not have been further from Martian's respectful courtliness. Corneille renewed favorite themes by examining them in more depth and by continuing to interrogate the heroic ideal, yet the destructiveness of unbridled passion would never triumph in his theater. The Jesuit world view so strongly communicated in the tetralogy becomes more nuanced, but it never gives way to the Jansenist pessimism, whose influence is nonetheless felt in the corpus after 1660.

Suréna, the Tragedy of Fear

With his final play, the tragedy *Suréna, général des Parthes* (1674–1675), Corneille returns to the theme of the monarch threatened by a powerful subject, last treated in *Agésilas* and also seen in *Le Cid*. Often called the most "Racinian" of Corneille's tragedies, *Suréna* focuses on those passions of the flesh so central to Racine, in a plot much simpler than those of most Corneille plays of any period. As Georges Forestier demonstrates, however, *Suréna* is not an attempt to imitate Racine but is rather an affirmation of Corneille's usual preoccupations with dramatic structure (Forestier, 34, 40). In this, his last experiment in a career full of innovations, he continues to bring new perspectives to bear on his favorite structures and themes.[35]

Eurydice, an Armenian princess, loves Suréna, a powerful Parthian general, but she is engaged to the heir to the Parthian throne, Pacorus. Pacorus has willingly abandoned Suréna's sister, Palmis, in favor of the important political alliance with Armenia—and because he has fallen in love with Eurydice. Suréna has been ordered to marry the (never shown) Parthian princess, Mandane, which is the only way he can reassure King Orode of his complete loyalty. Suréna and Eurydice both put off the marriages that would destroy any hope of happiness, but they do so at Suréna's peril. The combination of Pacorus's jealousy and Orode's fear eventually do prove deadly, and Suréna is assassinated—though by whom is never explicit.[36]

Suréna had been a faithful servant of his king and his society, but his forbidden love for Eurydice puts him in a state of paralysis that affects her as well. She cannot bring herself to make the sacrifice necessary to save Suréna's life. All of the protagonists are self-centered to a destructive degree. Pacorus is obsessed with knowing the name of Eurydice's lover so that he can punish the transgressor. Palmis wants to see Pacorus tortured by unrequited love for Eurydice. Orode puts his kingdom in danger by killing his most successful military leader because he owes Suréna too much. Suréna assures him of his loyalty and suggests that the marriage between Pacorus and Palmis could seal their trust, but the thought of Suréna married to a foreign queen terrifies Orode. The king must be prudent, even if Suréna reassures Orode as to his loyalty.

Noteworthy in its absence is any concern with ambition or the acquisition of political power. That particular dimension of the Cornelian protagonist is subsumed by other passions, with fear dominant among them. Orode is conservative, not grasping: he seeks to preserve what he has by the defensive measure of the two proposed marriages, possibly followed by murder, but at one or more removes. His son, Pacorus, seems to want to possess Eurydice out of desire, but fear of Suréna haunts him as well. Eurydice and Palmis both fear for Suréna's life and fear the loss of love. Even Suréna, though fatalistically ready to die, leaves the stage after repeating the verb *craindre,* to fear, twice in his last line of the play (5.3.1680). He fears not death but the women's tears: "Tenderness has no part a Hero's love," he says (5.3.1675). Fear of the weakening effect of an attack from feminine sentiment has been a constant in the Cornelian oeuvre. Here, it is part of a constellation of fear so pervasive that it must touch the spectator.

When Corneille discusses the notion of catharsis in the second *Discours,* he is skeptical about Aristotle's "purgation of the passions" in tragedy and that the spectator feels fear and pity: "I doubt that it ever happens" he concludes (*OC,* 3:145). Corneille's own idea of the viewer's response to tragedy is built on the concept of admiration he describes in the *Examen* of *Nicomède* (*OC,* 2:643). Admiration requires the distance

for judgment that we see at work throughout his theater, as the spectator is in a "comic" rather than "tragic" mode of reception, from the perspective of Mauron and Frye. Corneille places his audience in a position
to evaluate his characters, not to identify with them. *Suréna* does not
fundamentally change that position because responsibility and judgment are explicit topics throughout the play, but particularly in the last
three scenes. Suréna is killed "by an unknown hand," at a distance, with
three arrows (5.5.1713–17). This announcement in the final scene
seems to leave no one responsible for Suréna's death. But Suréna
declares in his last appearance that if Orode wants him dead, he hopes
that everyone will recognize his death as a crime rather than an accident
and that the guilty party becomes "abominable to the human race" even
if he tries to hide his identity (5.3.1605–14). Orode seems to bear the
brunt of this accusation, but Palmis blames Eurydice as well: "He runs
to his death and you are the cause," she charges (5.5.1681), an accusation she reiterates after Suréna has been killed. Suréna's own passivity
and refusal to leave Orode's kingdom are desperately criticized by
Palmis in act 5, scene 3. Is he not partly responsible for his own death?
    The refusal to act, to perform publicly, distinguishes Suréna and
Eurydice from heroic Cornelian characters. Escape and revolt seem futile
to them, and joining in the political and matrimonial manipulations
proposed by Orode is distasteful. They do have a sense of honor, of
gloire, but it is not directed toward activity on the public stage. Suréna
gives the spectators of his dilemma no act to admire. The people are
heard to cry in the last scene that Suréna had been taught a lesson, not
to disdain the orders of a king (5.5.1720). Pacorus and Orode hide
behind their royalty, masking any role in Suréna's death. Only Palmis,
the only character invented by Corneille and the only character to
appear in all five acts, attemps to change what the others see as
inevitable.[37] Unlike Eurydice, she enourages the politically expedient
marriages, even though she would forever lose Pacorus. Eurydice ends
the play in a faint, but Palmis vows revenge on Orode. Of course, Palmis
as a woman is in no position to combat the violence of the monarch, but
she represents the voice of resistance to fear, to the fear Orode feels and
spreads throughout his domain. She judges Orode, Pacorus, Eurydice,
and even Suréna severely, and the spectator participates in her judgment, even as we may pity their end.
    Emotion is expressed with great intensity in *Suréna,* and the self-
questioning that Corneille had introduced in his characters of the late
plays reaches its most concentrated form here. But self-examination

leads to dissolution rather than solution of the impass in which they find themselves. The eloquent words of Eurydice communicate their despair: "I want, without the release of death, / Always to love, always to suffer, always to die" ("Je veux, sans que la mort ose me secourir, / toujours aimer, toujours souffrir, toujours mourir"; 1.3.267–68). Solutions in Corneille's theater come from positive action, especially self-sacrifice. In the absence of outer-directed sacrifice, a self-centered self-immolation is the result for Suréna and Eurydice, and for Orode and Pacorus as well, according to Suréna's diagnosis of the illness with which their fear has infected society: murder has founded their reign, and their violence will play itself out within their family once Suréna, their supporter now seen as the external enemy, is exterminated (5.3.1637–62).

No recognition of the hero's service and fidelity, no magical conversion to virtue, prevents social disintegration or attenuates the tragic ending of *Suréna*. But even as Corneille terminated his career on a note of pessimism, he found a new way to use the comic structure underlying his entire corpus. The play's profound sadness does not signal a change in Corneille's conception of tragedy, affirms Forestier: the hero is never a victim of fate because he could choose at any moment to act to avoid death (Forestier, 59). Suréna has the Cornelian hero's drive for distinction, but the stage on which he chooses to exhibit it is limited to Eurydice's quarters. The causes of this shrinkage of ambition, this turning away from service, may be located in French political ideology; Greenberg posits a crisis in the absolutism of Louis XIV.[38] Another possible influence is the Jansenist ethic and aesthetic more closely associated with Racine, but which shows up in Cornelian theater as part of the exploration of characters who face head-on the insidious malady of *amour-propre*. Never hapless victims, Corneille's characters continue to evaluate their own actions, usually with a more positive social outcome than Racine's tortured creations ever achieve. With the fundamental human desire for recognition as his starting point in the 1630s, Corneille found a formula that allowed him to experiment with various forms of performance in a social context entertaining to audiences then and now. Both universal and particular to its time, his examination of love, heroism, and social organization led him from a celebration of the desire for recognition to the painful consideration of the obstacles, both internal and external, that prevent human beings from obtaining the recognition they crave.

Chapter Six

Conclusion

In his more than 30 plays, Pierre Corneille experimented with several dramatic genres and constantly sought new effects with which to stun and please his audience. His success owes much to his taste for innovation, his talent as a poet, and his ability to construct plots that always contain the sublime: the spectator is overwhelmed by the spectacular performances of his heroes, in "a climate of excitement, expectancy, and possibility" (Nelson 1963, 278). Corneille was a man of the theater, a constructor of stories with their sources in history, mythology, or romance. His primary goal, as he said explicitly and often, was to entertain theatergoers and readers, despite the insistence of the doctrinaire theorists of his era that drama must impart a moral lesson. Corneille's plays are instructive, but in his first *Discours* he sharply criticized the necessity for the onstage punishment of vice and reward of virtue that is promoted by most seventeenth-century French treatises (*OC*, 3:129–34). Pleasure comes first because, in Corneille's view, without the complete engagement of the spectator in the drama, the playwright has not fully communicated with his audience, and any attempt at didacticism would be ineffective.

One goal of this study has been to show how Corneille's texts solicit our active participation in the drama due to what I call a comic structure, a structure that functions across theatrical genres, including tragedy. This comic structure is born of the spectator-centered definitions of comedy and tragedy developed in the 1950s by Charles Mauron and Northrup Frye. The relationship between text and audience throughout Cornelian theater is a "comic" one, in that the spectator is always a judge of the protagonists rather than a fellow sufferer, as would be the case in archetypal tragedy. Corneille's plays force the consumer to participate not in any identification with characters but rather as a sort of drama critic. Corneille's characters are actors, trying to convince the onstage audience of fellow Cornelian creatures that their performance merits applause. The spectator, on- and offstage, judges the performer according to criteria implicit in the structure of the play. Themes such as sacrifice, recognition, and conversion return repeatedly; heroes who serve the community by their personal sacrifices receive in return public recognition of superior moral, social, political, and aesthetic status, and the most successful are able to convert others to their view of the world. The text guides the theatergoer or reader into sharing the perspective of the onstage spectator, as "positive" illusions that benefit the group convert observers into fans, while "negative," socially destructive illusions are subject to harsh judgment, and their creators are expelled from society. Protagonists who represent the creation of evil can give spectacular performances, but such characters always know defeat by the end of the play. We are far from the simple punishment of vice and reward of virtue, however, for all Cornelian protagonists have in common the aspiration to attain superiority over others, to be exceptional. Evildoers can be heroic in this sense, sometimes until the last scene of the play. Cornelian heroes are at times flawed and may fail to achieve the objectives they envisage, but they always seek to stand above the crowd by large appetites and dramatic gestures that require the spectator to evaluate their effectiveness as the action proceeds.

Another fundamental element of the archetypal comic structure is the love plot. The formation, destruction, and resurrection of couples is the primary story line in Cornelian comedy as in archetypal comedy. Corneille borrows from the tradition of the pastoral romance as well, eliminating the father figure of classical comedy as the character blocking the union of a young couple and the social rebirth their marriage represents. In Cornelian comedy, one of the protagonists belonging to the ranks of young lovers functions as the blocking character, creating chaos from within the very group that is responsible for society's renaissance. When this schema is continued in Cornelian tragedy, more weighty concerns such as political machinations among royalty or the threat of death are added. The formula we see in Corneille's first play, *Mélite,* is constantly altered, but the basic outline of the Cornelian plot remains in place throughout his oeuvre. All of Corneille's plays contain one or more couples, an obstacle to their union, performances from protagonists designed to elicit recognition (be it as a hero or a villain), and a denouement in which social regeneration (or its glaring absence) is a key element.

The projection of a renewed society that is a staple of the final scene of archetypal comedy can be found in all genres in Corneille's corpus. Influenced by a Jesuit education rich in the optimism of the Renaissance and the Counter-Reformation as well as by the relative stability brought by the end of the wars of religion at the close of the sixteenth century,

Corneille's works are also affected by the traumas of a monarchy and a religion still in turmoil during the seventeenth century. Nonetheless, the plays retain the emphasis on the human aspiration for recognition. Thomas Pavel observes that both Christian humanism and classicism in the seventeenth century are in profound discord with the social milieu where they prospered as intellectual movements. He finds the effort to promote humanism heroic, given the impossibility of making the empirical world coincide with the imaginary.[1] Even writers like Corneille, formed in Jesuit schools to believe in the capacity to improve human existence, must turn away from the "real" world in order to preserve the humanist ideal, in Pavel's view (153–58). Preserve it he does, thanks to a perspective that has so many features in common with archetypal comedy. Comedy, like classicism, is founded upon a vision of social stability; the Cornelian comic structure shares humanism's impulsion to value exceptional individual effort.

Optimism never disappears from Corneille's oeuvre, although some influential critics have seen the evolution of his theater as the story of a heroism that reaches its apogee in *Polyeucte* in 1642, only to depict a gradual decline in the hero's abilities and fortunes over the course of the next 32 years (see, for example, Doubrovsky 1963, and Stegmann 1968). But the failure of the hero should in no way be equated with the failure of the play. Because the Cornelian hero continues to declare his or her exceptional status in the face of seeming defeat, the notion of failure stands out in the majority of his works that are not part of the consecrated literary canon. A major pursuit of the present study has been to suggest the richness of the plays outside the tetralogy.

The fascination of the Cornelian corpus for twentieth-century readers can be located in several areas. Cornelian tragedy, tragicomedy, and heroic comedy have been explained by well-known scholars such as Georges Couton and Paul Bénichou in terms of events in seventeenth-century politics and society, reflected in Corneille's interpretation of incidents from (mostly Roman) history or, more rarely, from Greco-Roman mythology. They see Corneille as a recorder and interpreter of contemporary problems in the body politic such as relations among the aristocracy, the monarchy, and the rising bourgeoisie, while Mitchell Greenberg uses psychoanalytic criticism to uncover Corneille's exploration of a society in painful evolution toward the absolute monarchy of Louis XIV. Greenberg also highlights the role of female characters in the corpus, a preoccupation of many critics such as Muratore (1982), Rathé, Schmidt, Allentuch, and Rowan. Octave Nadal's important study of love in the

Cornelian canon also places the plays in their seventeenth-century context. Corneille has been considered the defender of Jesuit free will in the face of Jansenist predestination in the work of Marc Fumaroli, or the purveyor of a message about the providential nature of history (see, for example, the works of André Stegmann and Marie-Odile Sweetser). Cornelian theater examines the nature of tragedy in its relationship to history, in the view of John Lyons. These various ways of linking literature and society are the product of very diverse methods for reading Cornelian texts. They all yield interesting results, but other types of analysis prove equally stimulating: with a completely different orientation, another group of critics focuses on aesthetic questions. Georges Forestier studies how Corneille constructed his plots; Mary Jo Muratore (1990) and Judd Hubert, in all of his work on Corneille, for example, emphasize how Corneille reveals from within his plays the nature of theater itself.

Throughout this book, I have illustrated and drawn on many among the vast number of interpretations that Corneille's theater has inspired. The explanatory force of the comic schema resides in its ability to harmonize aesthetic, historical, psychological, and moral perspectives, while providing a touchstone for understanding the corpus. This is not to say that Corneille consciously adopted such a strategy; noting its presence underpinning the oeuvre is sufficient to enable the reader to profit from an approach general enough to encompass the entire corpus, while furnishing a framework for reading individual plays. The method chosen here is certainly not the only recommended one, but it allows the reader to trace an evolution over the course of Corneille's almost 50-year career. The major alteration to the comic structure is in the amount of introspection indulged in by the characters. As the exploration of desire deepens, especially in the plays written after 1660, fear is more often in the forefront than it was in the tragedies of the tetralogy. But the spectator stays in a position of superiority and judgment, and our pleasure remains that of the audience of comedy, as we applaud the expulsion of scapegoats who threaten social stability and recognize the efforts of protagonists who continue to try to distinguish themselves as they serve others.[2] While there may be tragic potential in the hero's sometimes futile attempts to bring salvation to his society, no Cornelian hero lacks the drive for distinction. Awe is always elicited from the spectator.

As Corneille places us at a psychic distance from his protagonists, forcing us into a position of judgment, he also implicates us in the value systems he portrays. Exploring the concept of recognition in chapter 2 of this study, I quote Timothy Hampton, who introduces the idea of a recognition that is different from the recognition spectators accord a hero. Hampton uncovers the way a text can make "people become subjects of political and social systems" when they recognize themselves in a text (6). Although we do not identify with Cornelian protagonists, the text encourages us to identify with their audience onstage and to ponder its values. Corneille's theater manipulates spectators and readers at the same time that we are given an illusion of freedom: he implies that we are judges, but active judgment is a charge we cannot escape.

What social and political systems does Corneille encourage us to consider? Patriarchy and monarchy are subjects of almost every Cornelian play, but his portrayals of these institutions are not clear cut.[3] Attila, Galba in *Othon,* or Orode in *Suréna* are hardly advertisements for the exemplary monarch, nor do Valens in *Théodore,* Prusias in *Nicomède,* or Vinius in *Othon* enhance our image of paternal authority figures. The playwright demonstrates that many questions can and should be asked when exploring social and political arrangements throughout the history of the Christian era. Corneille promotes an optimistic view that the most basic structures of Western civilization can continue to function well, yet he pushes us to interrogate them. His is the worldview of comedy, a genre that harks back, in Frye's view, to a golden age in the past, even as it moves from one kind of society to a new and better one (Frye, 163, 171). Both the golden age and the new age remain only vaguely defined. What they represent most clearly is a refusal of the system in place at the beginning of the play (Frye, 168). Change is sought and effected, usually in aid of a reborn society, but solutions to sociopolitical problems differ widely.

It is difficult to find wholly convincing the sort of reading proposed by Couton or Greenberg that insists on seeing these plays as a mirror for seventeenth-century French politics. Although enticing linkages often appear, there is too much variety in the oeuvre for such analyses to hold up completely. Nevertheless, I hope to have suggested the interest inherent in diverse approaches to Corneille, especially since his theater lends itself so well to a variety of reading strategies.

To read while conscious of the diverse possibilities for interpretation is an important message transmitted by Corneille's texts. In making the spectator/reader an active participant in the act of analysis, Corneille encourages us to keep an open mind, and he promotes a viewpoint that could be called, in terminology popular today, postmodern, in the sense that the denouements of his plays defy definitive interpretation, especially when we try to find firmly fixed sociopolitical positions in them. By using the drive for distinction as the sturdy, unifying thread that binds such a varied corpus together, we can locate a solid base for reading, one that leaves many questions open for discussion, while emphasizing the audience's active responsibility in trying to interpret Cornelian texts. In portraying characters for whom the drive for recognition, for difference, saves them from the dissatisfaction and disappointment of being ordinary, Corneille also suggests the saving grace offered by creativity to all human beings. Circumstances may prevent success in worldly terms, but as the suffering of Suréna shows, distinction can be achieved even amid an illusion of passivity. Passions move Corneille's characters just as violently as those of Racine, but Corneille's protagonists assume their predicament with a spirit of affirmative engagement absent from Racine's victimized characters. Cornelian characters exhibit the desire to experience passions, from the exultation of Rodrigue in *Le Cid* to the suffering of Eurydice in *Suréna*. Hunger for experience underlies Cornelian theater and makes reading it the pleasure Corneille intended it to be.

Notes and References

Chapter One

1. Although Fontenelle is not always the most reliable of witnesses, certain of his verifiable remarks are interesting, especially when he is discussing his uncle's character. The partial, 1702 version of Fontenelle's biography can be consulted in *Corneille: Oeuvres complètes,* ed. André Stegmann (Paris: Seuil, 1963); see *La Vie de Corneille,* 24–25; hereafter cited in text.

2. In his edition of the *Théâtre complet* of Corneille (Rouen: Publications de l'Université de Rouen, 1984–1986), Alain Niderst provides a list of the principal modern productions of each play. For an update, see also Cynthia B. Kerr, "Opération sauvetage: La Mise en scène moderne des dernières pièces de Corneille," in *Onze études sur la vieillesse de Corneille dédiées à la mémoire de Georges Couton,* ed. Madeleine Bertaud and Alain Niderst (Boulogne: ADIREL, and Rouen: Mouvement Corneille-Centre International Pierre Corneille, 1994), 171–85. Kerr mentions some of the earlier plays as well as Corneille's last works. See also *Corneille vivant, Bulletin annuel du Mouvement Corneille,* which furnishes information on recent productions.

3. René Guerdan's biography, *Corneille ou la vie méconnue du Shakespeare français* (Lausanne: Ed. Pierre-Marcel Favre, 1984), is an entertaining tale of Corneille's life and times. The book is well researched but avoids recent scholarly interpretations of Cornelian theater in favor of traditional views dating from the nineteenth century.

4. Georges Couton, *Corneille* (Paris: Hatier, 1969), 10–12; hereafter cited in text.

5. Georges Couton, introduction to *Oeuvres complètes,* by Pierre Corneille, ed. Georges Couton, vol. 1 (Paris: Gallimard, 1980), xlix–l; hereafter cited in text.

6. Marc Fumaroli, *Héros et orateurs: Rhétorique et dramaturgies cornéliennes* (Geneva: Droz, 1990), 20–24; hereafter cited in text.

7. Alain Viala, "Corneille et les institutions littéraires de son temps," in *Pierre Corneille: Actes du colloque de Rouen,* ed. Alain Niderst (Paris: Presses Universitaires de France, 1985), 200; hereafter cited in text.

8. Pierre Corneille, *Oeuvres complètes,* ed. Georges Couton, 3 vols. (Paris: Gallimard, 1980–1987), 1:780; hereafter cited in text as *OC.*

9. Milorad R. Margitic, "Sociological Aspects of 'La Querelle du *Cid*,'" in *Homage to Paul Bénichou,* ed. Sylvie Romanowski and Monique Bilezikian (Birmingham, Ala.: Summa Publications, 1994), 61.

10. Armand Gasté, ed., *La Querelle du "Cid"* (1898; reprint, Geneva: Slatkine, 1970), 40–42; hereafter cited in text. Gasté reproduces all the docu-

ments of the quarrel and includes in his introduction a poem about a crow (*une corneille*) trapped by a falcon—Jean-Louis Faucon de Ris, seigneur de Charleval, the aristocrat who cornered Corneille and threatened to beat him.

11. Corneille's contemporary Paul Pellisson, in his *Relation contenant l'histoire de l'Académie française* in 1653, suggests that Richelieu might have been jealous of the success of *Le Cid* since he himself wrote plays (*OC*, 1:803).

12. See Claire Carlin, "Corneille's *Trois Discours:* A Reader's Guide," *Orbis Litterarum* 45 (1990): 49–70, for a discussion of Corneille's use of the rules of classical composition; hereafter cited in text.

13. Couton notes that the failed playwright and theoretician the Abbé d'Aubignac had published his *Pratique du théâtre* in 1657. This treatise is respectful of Corneille's work, but it contains many criticisms. The appearance of *La Pratique* no doubt convinced Corneille of the necessity to spell out his own dramatic theory in more systematic terms than he had done before (Couton 1969, 151).

14. Georges Forestier, *Essai de génétique théâtrale: Corneille à l'oeuvre* (Paris: Klincksieck, 1996), 273; hereafter cited in text.

15. Couton notes emblematically that in 1675 Boileau published his famous *Art Poétique,* which includes a summary of the century's literary accomplishments. Corneille appears in only a few lines, wherein his best-known plays, those of the 1640s, are briefly evoked, with regret that Corneille was no longer capable of producing great poetry. Indeed, Boileau does not even touch on the variety of Corneille's work and his enormous influence over a period of almost 50 years.

16. Thomas Corneille began his theatrical career in 1647 with a comedy imitated from a Spanish model, as Pierre's *Le Menteur* had been in 1644 (Couton 1969, 126–27). Although Thomas wrote the most performed play of the seventeenth century, the tragicomedy *Timocrate* (1656), his plays never had the impact of his brother's.

17. The importance of the pastoral in theater can be attested by the great success of plays like *Les Bergeries* of Racan (first published in 1625) and Jean Mairet's *La Sylvie* (1628) and *La Sylvanire* (1631), all influenced by Honoré d'Urfé's five-volume novel, *L'Astrée.* See *Théâtre du XVIIe siècle,* vol. 1, ed. Jacques Scherer (Paris: Gallimard, 1975); hereafter cited in text. For a discussion of *précieux* poetry or *poésie galante* as it was known at the time, see Odette de Mourgues, ed., *An Anthology of Seventeenth-Century French Lyric Poetry* (Oxford: Oxford University Press, 1966), 18–20.

18. Attempting to define *la préciosité* has proven difficult for scholars since the 1650s, but the 1990s have seen enormous progress in the historical verification of the movement and in outlining its basic tenets. See Linda Timmermans, *L'Accès des femmes à la culture (1598–1715)* (Paris: Champion, 1993).

19. For a history of the Jesuit order, see Alain Guillermou, *Les Jésuites* (Paris: Presses Universitaires de France, 1963). The development and decline of

Jansenism is described by Louis Cognet, *Le Jansénisme* (Paris: Presses Universitaires de France, 1964).

20.   Paul Bénichou, *Morales du Grand Siècle* (Paris: Gallimard, 1948); hereafter cited in text.

21.   Couton 1980, xliii. Corneille's other religious works include translations such as *Louanges de la Sainte Vierge* (*In Praise of the Blessed Virgin,* 1665), the translation of a Latin poem by the Jesuit, Father de la Rue (1667), *L'Office de la Sainte Vierge* (*The Office of the Blessed Virgin,* 1670), and the ode to Father Delidel in 1668.

22.   John D. Lyons, *The Tragedy of Origins: Pierre Corneille and Historical Perspective* (Stanford, Calif.: Stanford University Press, 1996), 10; hereafter cited in text.

Chapter Two

1.   See the fine analysis of Gabriel Conesa, *Pierre Corneille et la naissance du genre comique (1629–1636)* (Paris: SEDES, 1989), 10–47; hereafter cited in text.

2.   In one of the best-known works of Corneille criticism, *Le Sentiment de l'amour dans l'oeuvre de Pierre Corneille* (Paris: Gallimard, 1948), Octave Nadal finds the roots of Cornelian comedy in the pastoral (22). In *Le Premier Corneille: De "Mélite" à "L'Illusion comique"* (Paris: SEDES, 1982), chapters 4 and 5, Robert Garapon also sees the pastoral as the strongest influence on the comedies, and he stresses the influence of *L'Astrée* on Corneille's comic production. Both hereafter cited in text.

3.   For a succinct overview of the characteristics of New Comedy, see Andrew Calder, *Molière: The Theory and Practice of Comedy* (London and Atlantic Highlands, N.J.: Athlone Press, 1993).

4.   Northrup Frye, *The Anatomy of Criticism: Four Essays* (Princeton, N.J.: Princeton University Press, 1957), 44–50, 163–85; hereafter cited in text. Harold Knutson has amply demonstrated that this archetypal schema functions throughout Molière's theater; see *Molière: An Archetypal Approach* (Toronto: University of Toronto Press, 1976).

5.   Serge Doubrovsky, *Corneille et la dialectique du héros* (Paris: Gallimard, 1963), furnishes a nicely nuanced discussion of the notion of realism in the theater in general, and in these comedies in particular. *Realism* is a relative term, and the representation of elements of everyday "reality" in the theater, or mimesis, does not imply an accurate reproduction of real social conditions. See pp. 34–36; hereafter cited in text.

6.   Nadal, 80; Doubrovsky 1963, 29–72, 81, and passim. Jacques Scherer, *La Dramaturgie classique en France* (Paris: Nizet, 1950), 321; André Stegmann, *L'Héroïsme cornélien: Genèse et signification,* 2 vols. (Paris: Colin, 1968), 1:56, 2:570–78. Both hereafter cited in text.

7.   Charles Mauron, *Psychocritique du genre comique* (Paris: Corti, 1954); hereafter cited in text.

8.   I first proposed that this theatrical structure is fundamental to Corneille's oeuvre in "The Woman as Heavy: Female Villains in the Theater of Pierre Corneille," *French Review* 59 (February 1986): 389–98.

9.   The *nourrice* was a stock character of drama, seen also in the old nurses prevalent in English theater of the sixteenth and seventeenth centuries. *Nanny* is a more modern rendering of the term for this character, always played by a man (*OC,* 1:1284).

10.   See Lawrence Harvey, "The Dénouement of *Mélite* and the Role of La Nourrice," *Modern Language Notes* 71 (March 1956): 200–203.

11.   For an interesting and subtle meditation on the significance of the title, see Jacqueline Lichtenstein, "What Is the Subject of *La Place Royale?*," trans. M. Dobie, *Yale French Studies* 80 (1991): 41–69.

12.   Constant Venesoen, *Corneille apprenti féministe de "Mélite" au "Cid"* (Paris: Lettres Modernes, 1986), 46, 78 n.50; hereafter cited in text.

13.   Han Verhoeff, *Les Comédies de Corneille: Une Psycholecture* (Paris: Klincksieck, 1979), and *Les Grandes Tragédies de Corneille: Une Psycholecture* (Paris: Lettres Modernes, 1982); hereafter cited in text. In both studies, Verhoeff relies less on Mauron's 1954 book on comedy than on his later work, *Des Métaphores obsédantes au mythe personnel* (Paris: Corti, 1964).

14.   Cynthia B. Kerr, *L'Amour, l'amitié et la fourberie: Une Étude des premières comédies de Corneille* (Saratoga, Calif.: Anma Libri, 1980), 124–32; hereafter cited in text.

15.   Garapon, 1982; Théodore Litman, *Les Comédies de Corneille* (Paris: Nizet, 1981); G. J. Mallinson, *The Comedies of Corneille: Experiments in the Comic* (Manchester: Manchester University Press, 1984). Both hereafter cited in text. Another source of diverse perspectives on Cornelian comedy can be found in the articles collected in *Corneille comique,* ed. Milorad R. Margitic, *Biblio 17,* vol. 4 (Paris, Seattle, Tuebingen: Papers on French Seventeenth-Century Literature, 1982).

16.   Jean Starobinski, *L'Oeil vivant* (Paris: Gallimard, 1961), 29–68; hereafter cited in text.

17.   Frye delineates six phases of comedy, ranging from irony to romance (177). While Corneille's early comic plays lean toward ironic comedy, we will see that his tragedies fit Frye's description of the sort of comedy that is closer to romance.

18.   Marie-Odile Sweetser, *La Dramaturgie de Corneille* (Geneva: Droz, 1977), 246; hereafter cited in text. See also Angela S.-M. Goulet, *L'Univers théâtral de Corneille: Paradoxe et subtilité héroïques* (Cambridge, Mass.: Harvard University Department of Romance Languages and Literatures, 1978). Goulet also founds her interpretation on paradox as the organizing principle of Corneille's theater.

19.   Milorad R. Margitic, "Mythologie personnelle chez le premier Corneille: Le Jeu de l'amour et de l'amour-propre de *Mélite* au *Cid*," in *Pierre Corneille: Actes du colloque de Rouen,* ed. Alain Niderst (Paris: Presses Universitaires de France, 1985), 548–50.

20.   Alain Couprie, "Corneille et le mythe pastoral," *XVIIe Siècle* 151 (April–June 1986): 159–66.

21.   Jean Rousset, *La Littérature de l'âge baroque en France: Circé et le paon* (Paris: Corti, 1954); pp. 204–18 specifically address Corneille's theater; hereafter cited in text. Kerr also discusses the baroque qualities of the comedies, highlighting ostentatious behavior. See also Jean-Pierre Dens, "Alidor et le baroque cornélien," in *Actes de Fordham,* ed. Jean Macary, *Biblio 17,* vol. 9 (Paris, Seattle, Tuebingen: Papers on French Seventeenth-Century Literature, 1983), 47–55.

22.   Timothy Hampton, "Introduction: Baroques," in *Baroque Topographies: Literature/History/Philosophy, Yale French Studies* 80 (1991): 6; hereafter cited in text. The term *recognition* presents its own semantic richness. I have already used it in the sense of the character seeking recognition from others, and in Frye's notion of the recognition that occurs at the end of comedy (Frye, 163). I will return to Hampton's context when discussing the tetralogy. In chapter 4, I will examine another related meaning, Aristotelian anagnorisis, which is thoroughly treated in Terence Cave, *Recognitions: A Study in Poetics* (Oxford: Clarendon Press, 1988); hereafter cited in text.

23.   For a discussion of tragicomedy see Roger Guichemerre, *La Tragicomédie* (Paris: Presses Universitaires de France, 1981).

24.   Louis Rivaille, *Les Débuts de Pierre Corneille* (Paris: Boivin, 1936), 99–100, considers the political elements to have been grafted onto the plot line of *Mélite* and the comedies that follow. Marie-Odile Sweetser notes that the royal intervention in the protagonists' marriages would be taken up again in *Le Cid, Horace, Cinna, Pompée,* and *Rodogune* (1977, 107).

25.   David Clarke, *Pierre Corneille: Poetics and Drama under Louis XIII* (Cambridge: Cambridge University Press, 1992), 119–20; hereafter cited in text.

26.   Susan Read Baker, *Dissonant Harmonies: Drama and Ideology in Five Neglected Plays of Pierre Corneille* (Tuebingen: Gunther Narr, 1990), 26; hereafter cited in text.

27.   Germain Poirier, *Corneille témoin de son temps I: "Clitandre" (1631), Biblio 17,* vol. 53 (Paris, Seattle, Tuebingen: Papers on French Seventeenth-Century Literature, 1990); hereafter cited in text.

28.   Jacques Truchet, "A propos de *Clitandre*," in *Héroïsme et création littéraire sous les règnes de Henri IV et de Louis XIII,* ed. Noémi Hepp and Georges Livet (Paris: Klincksieck, 1974), 258.

29.   See Joseph Marthan's study, *Le Vieillard amoureux dans le théâtre de Corneille* (Paris: Nizet, 1979), for a complete exposition of this topic.

30. Pierre Corneille, *Médée*, ed. André de Leyssac (Geneva: Droz, 1978), 38. De Leyssac analyzes Corneille's borrowings from Euripides and Seneca. Corneille combines his sources in order to arrive at the portrait of Médée in pursuit of justice as well as vengeance, victim as well as menacing sorcerer. Her desire to keep her children with her and the fact that Créuse and not Médée initiates the offer of the dress also make her a more sympathetic character (47–50).

31. Marie-Odile Sweetser, "Refus de la culpabilité: Médée et Corneille," *Travaux de Littérature* 8 (1995): 114; hereafter cited in text.

32. Mitchell Greenberg, *Corneille, Classicism, and the Ruses of Symmetry* (Cambridge: Cambridge University Press, 1986), 19; hereafter cited in text.

33. André Stegmann, "La *Médée* de Corneille," in *Les Tragédies de Sénèque et le théâtre de la Renaissance,* ed. Jean Jacquot and Marcel Oddon (1963; reprint, Paris: CNRS, 1973), 125.

34. An interlude in Corneille's production occurred in 1635 when, as one of the Five Authors, he wrote the third act of *La Comédie des Tuileries,* probably according to a plot outlined by Cardinal Richelieu himself. Richelieu could not decently present his own creations on stage but contented himself with this indirect form of theatrical glory. This play appears to be the only one of the Five Authors' creations in which Corneille participated, according to Couton (*OC,* 1:1408).

35. The reader is told that these clothes belong to actors; the surprise of act 5 remains intact for the first-time spectator of the play. Ralph Albanese provides an interesting discussion of the question of social class in the play in "Modes de théâtralité dans *L'Illusion comique,*" in *Corneille comique,* ed. Milorad R. Margitic, *Biblio 17,* vol. 4 (Paris, Seattle, Tuebingen: Papers on French Seventeenth-Century Literature, 1982), 141–45; hereafter cited in text. He suggests that Clindor functions as a mediator between the noble and bourgeois modes of existence. In my view, Clindor's final status as an actor makes social theorizing about him in particular somewhat problematic, given actors' ambiguous social position in the seventeenth century.

36. Robert Garapon, *La Fantaisie verbale et le comique dans le théâtre français du Moyen Âge à la fin du XVIIe siècle* (Paris: A. Colin, 1957), analyzes Matamore's language in the context of similar characters.

37. Couton cites, for example, *Célinde* by Baro (1628), two plays entitled *La Comédie des comédiens,* one by Gougenot (1631) and the other by Georges de Scudéry (1632) (*OC,* 1:1425). He doesn't mention the other most celebrated example of the period, perhaps because it is not a comic play: Rotrou's *Le Véritable Saint Genest* shows the conversion, while acting, of the patron saint of actors.

38. Corneille changed the title in 1660 to simply *L'Illusion.* Robert Garapon's edition of the play (Paris: Didier, 1957) explores Corneille's use of a variety of typical techniques of comedy and tragicomedy.

39.   Robert J. Nelson, *The Play within a Play: The Dramatist's Conception of His Art* (New Haven, Conn.: Yale University Press, 1958), 52; hereafter cited in text. Nelson notes that Georges May, in *Tragédie cornélienne, tragédie racinienne: Etude sur les sources de l'intérêt dramatique* (Urbana: University of Illinois Press, 1948), sees the arousal of surprise and curiosity as Corneille's favorite effects. Georges Forestier's exploration in *Essai de génétique théâtrale* of the sublime in Cornelian tragedy also emphasizes surprise, but from the angle of the plays' construction.

Chapter Three

1.   Many critics have seen honor and virtue as part of a didactic message Corneille is trying to send the spectator, but Robert J. Nelson, in *Corneille, His Heroes, and Their Worlds* (Philadelphia: University of Pennsylvania Press, 1963), correctly observes that Corneille uses honor and virtue as *themes* of his plays rather than preaching them as an ethic (293); hereafter cited in text.

2.   See Cordell W. Black, *Corneille's Denouements: Text and Conversion* (Madrid: Studia Humanitatis, 1984), for a discussion of the open-endedness of Corneille's plays. Black's analysis of "the uniquely significant role that the audience, both inner and outer, plays in Cornelian tragedy" (125) is insightful, although he emphasizes too strongly "a sense of painful and irreparable loss which challenges [the] sense of dazzling accomplishment" in the tetralogy (3).

3.   A critical decision for editors is whether to use the original text of 1637, the much-revised 1660 version, or the 1682 edition, the last one prepared by Corneille. Georges Forestier has edited the play twice in recent years, choosing the 1682 version for one edition (Paris: Magnard, 1988) and the 1637 version juxtaposed with that of 1660 for the other (Paris: STFM, 1992). I agree with the choice made by Georges Couton in editing the *Oeuvres complètes:* the original versions of all of the plays tend to be more lively, especially for the early ones that Corneille later tried to make conform to classical rules. The most thorough recent edition is the one by Milorad Margitic (Amsterdam and Philadelphia: John Benjamins, 1989). Others editions since 1970 include those by Renato T. De Rosa (Napoli: I.E.M., 1970); Peter H. Nurse (London: G. G. Harrap, 1978); H. Carrier (Paris: Hachette, 1991); Catherine Eugen (Paris: Presses-Pocket, 1992); and Jean Serroy (Paris: Folio Gallimard 1993). Two useful student guides to the play are W. D. Howarth's *Corneille: Le Cid,* in the Critical Guides to French Texts series (London: Grant & Cutler, 1988), and Alain Couprie's *Pierre Corneille: Le Cid,* in the Études Littéraires series (Paris: Presses Universitaires de France, 1989).

4.   This excellent verse translation is by Vincent J. Cheng, *Pierre Corneille, Le Cid: A Translation in Rhymed Couplets* (London and Toronto: Associated University Presses, 1987).

5.   In an insightful article based on speech act theory, Suzanne Toczyski observes that "Chimène's very silencing of her love for Rodrigue has been, in

effect, an attempt to claim a place in a world which would exclude her and which ultimately refuses any force to her (public) words." See "Chimène, or the Scandal of the Feminine Word," *Papers on French Seventeenth-Century Literature* 22 (1995): 518.

6. Lines 1832–33 of the 1637 version authorize hope that Chimène will eventually agree to the marriage: "Sire, is this sad wedding bearable? / Should *the same day* begin and end my mourning?" (my translation, my italics). "The same day" suggests that time is the main obstacle to the marriage; this reference to the same day disappears in 1660.

7. Georges Couton, *Corneille et la tragédie politique* (Paris: Presses Universitaires de France, 1984), 112.

8. Michel Prigent, *Le Héros et l'État dans la tragédie de Pierre Corneille* (Paris: Presses Universitaires de France, 1986), 25; hereafter cited in text.

9. Évelyne Méron, *Tendre et cruel Corneille: Le Sentiment de l'amour dans "Le Cid," "Horace," "Cinna," et "Polyeucte"* (Paris: Nizet, 1984), 13.

10. Milorad R. Margitic, *Essai sur la mythologie du "Cid"* (University, Miss.: Romance Monographs, 1976), 33–40; 166; hereafter cited in text.

11. The best development of these symmetrical oppositions is to be found in an article by A. Donald Sellstrom, "The Structure of Corneille's Masterpieces," *Romanic Review* 49 (1958): 269–77. The role of the Infanta in adding to structural balance is examined by E. J. Mickel, "The Role of Corneille's Infanta," *Romance Notes* 7 (1965): 42–45; and Eric Leadbetter, "Corneille's Infante: An Explanation of Her Role," *Romance Notes* 11 (1970): 581–85.

12. Greenberg 1986, 49. Greenberg uses many of the tools of feminist psychoanalytic literary criticism in his study, especially those developed by French critics such as Luce Irigaray, Sarah Kofman, Michèle Montrelay, and Eugénie Lemoine-Luccioni. Prior to Greenberg's work, in the 1970s Harriet Ray Allentuch was a pioneer in the application of the psychoanalytic literary theory of Mauron to the Cornelian corpus, often with a feminist slant missing from Verhoeff's work. See "Mauron, Corneille, and the Unconscious," *French Forum* 4 (1979): 55–68, for an excellent example of Allentuch's approach; hereafter cited in text. She arrives at the conclusion that although Corneille's heroines "are inspired by the same aristocratic and neo-Stoic aspirations and convictions that drive the men"(63), they represent for the heroes, on the unconscious level, "a tenderness the hero both fears and longs for and at the same time an aggressive potential that threatens him. . . . On the manifest level of the text she is a complex character, mistress of her will; on the unconscious level, a defeated antagonist representing an alienated part of the psyche" (64). Allentuch comes to many of the same conclusions as Verhoeff and Greenberg, but Greenberg reinscribes "the woman question" in a seventeenth-century political context, making his work both more ambitious and more controversial.

13. Barbara Woshinsky, *Signs of Certainty: The Linguistic Imperative in French Classical Literature* (Saratoga, Calif.: Anma Libri, 1991), 32; hereafter cited in text.

14. According to Josephine Schmidt's *If There Are No More Heroes, There Are Heroines: A Feminist Critique of Corneille's Heroines, 1637–1643* (Lanham, Md.: University Press of America, 1987), Corneille's female characters in the tetralogy reject the male split between public and private. They reject the male ethic based on brutality and injustice, as they try to develop an ethic of their own based on love. Her conclusion is that patriarchy triumphs in the tetralogy (33–42); hereafter cited in text. Despite some interesting points, Schmidt's book is a feminist analysis only in the themes emphasized. A more up-to-date feminist methodology can be found in Greenberg's books, for example, which use contemporary French feminist and Lacanian theory.

15. Serge Doubrovsky, "Corneille: masculin/féminin, réflexions sur la structure tragique," in *Autobiographiques: De Corneille à Sartre* (Paris: Presses Universitaires de France, 1988), 11–41; hereafter cited in text.

16. See Sharon Harwood-Gordon, *The Poetic Style of Corneille's Tragedies: An Aesthetic Interpretation* (Lewiston, N.Y.: E. Mellen Press, 1989), for a detailed discussion of Corneille's use of language.

17. See Germain Poirier, *Corneille et la vertu de prudence* (Geneva: Droz, 1984), 32–45. Poirier highlights Valère's allegorical role as the representative of prudence, as contrasted with Horace's violence. Horace and Valère complement each other, in Poirier's view: Horace fought the enemy outside Rome, while Valère combats the enemy inside—Horace himself. Poirier finds characters representing prudence throughout the corpus as he develops this allegorical reading, carefully grounded in the philosophy of the period.

18. Louis Herland, *Horace ou la naissance de l'homme* (Paris: Editions de Minuit, 1952), 195–202; hereafter cited in text.

19. Harriet Stone, *The Classical Model: Literature and Knowledge in Seventeenth-Century France* (Ithaca, N.Y.: Cornell University Press, 1996), 44–45; hereafter cited in text.

20. Hélène Merlin, *Public et littérature en France au XVIIe siècle* (Paris: Les Belles Lettres, 1994), 280; hereafter cited in text. The "public" in the seventeenth century was a shifting term that could refer in literary terms to an imaginary ideal, to the educated reader, or to the people of all classes who crowded into theaters in increasingly large numbers. Moreover, deciding what were uniquely private concerns became more difficult as the absolute monarchy gained power over what had previously been decisions taken within the family, as *Horace* demonstrates.

21. Jacques Ehrmann, "Structures of Exchange in *Cinna*," *Yale French Studies* 36–37 (1966): 169–99.

22. Gordon Pocock, *Corneille and Racine: Problems of Tragic Form* (Cambridge: Cambridge University Press, 1973), 62; hereafter cited in text. For more discussion of the characters, see Roger Zuber, "La Conversion d'Émilie," in *Héroïsme et création littéraire*, ed. Noémi Hepp and Georges Livet (Paris: Klincksieck, 1974), 261–76; and Odette de Mourgues, "Coherence and Incoherence in *Cinna*," in *Form and Meaning: Aesthetic Coherence in Seventeenth-Century*

French Drama: Studies Presented to Harry Barnwell, ed. W. D. Howarth et al. (Amersham, England: Avebury, 1982), 51–62.

23. Susan Tiefenbrun, "The Big Switch: A Study of *Cinna,*" in *Signs of the Hidden: Semiotic Studies* (Amsterdam: Rodopi, 1980), 181–208; hereafter cited in text.

24. The Prince de Conti, in his *Traité de la comédie et des Spectacles selon la traditions de l'Eglise* (Paris, 1666), targets *Polyeucte* in particular because he finds the love story more compelling than the religious aspect of the play. See George Couton's comments on Conti's treatise in his edition of Pierre Nicole, *Traité de la comédie* (Paris: Les Belles Lettres, 1961), 29–30. Nicole attacks Corneille's *Théodore* but does not specifically address the problem of *Polyeucte.*

25. Ronald W. Tobin, "Le Sacrifice et *Polyeucte,*" *Revue des Sciences Humaines* 38 (1973): 597; hereafter cited in text.

26. The Cornelian hero is often called a *généreux.* As used in the seventeenth century, the term derives from the Latin root *genus,* or literally, of good race (*Petit Robert* 1, 19th edition). The notions of the *généreux* and *générosité* combine noble birth and exemplary moral qualities.

27. Tobin notes that Félix is also implicitly contrasted with the Christian God, the other authority figure in the play. Félix's hesitations and contradictions are highlighted, as well as his attempts to suppress the free will whose exercise God promotes (592–93). This emphasis on the importance of free will reminds us of Corneille's Jesuit roots.

28. Verhoeff has explored the notion of the woman as gift in the comedies and in the tetralogy. See Verhoeff 1982, 85–92 for his remarks on *Polyeucte,* particularly p. 90.

29. One critic who finds Pauline's conversion completely implausible is John Cairncross in his article "*Polyeucte,* a Flawed Masterpiece," *Papers on French Seventeenth-Century Literature* 9 (1982): 571–90; see pp. 583–84 for his comments on Pauline.

30. Greenberg emphasizes "the survival and continuity in Christianity of Roman Partriarchy" (1986, 143). Michel Beaujour, "Polyeucte et la monarchie de droit divin," *French Review* 36 (1963): 443–49, also sees the affirmation of the Roman Empire in the play, the forerunner of the French monarchy.

31. In seeing a fundamental conflict between sainthood and heroism, Cairncross follows in the footsteps of Doubrovsky (1963, 223–61) and Bernard Dort, *Corneille dramaturge* (Paris: L'Arche, 1957), 64. Dort's Marxist approach arrives at the conclusion that the play is about heroism, not Christianity. Jeanne Bem's Freudian approach in "Corneille à l'épreuve du désir: Une lecture de *Polyeucte,*" *Poétique* 10.37 (1979): 83–90, finds heroism deflated in the play.

The opposing camp includes Tobin, Sweetser (1979, 125–26), and several others who insist on the synthesis of Cornelian heroism and the Christian message. See, for example, Jean Rousset, *Forme et signification* (Paris: Corti, 1964), 9; Lawrence Harvey, "The Role of Emulation in Corneille's *Polyeucte,*"

PMLA 82 (1967): 314–24; Joseph Pineau, "La Seconde conversion de Polyeucte," *Revue d'Histoire Littéraire de la France* 75 (1975): 531–54; François Lasserre, *Corneille de 1638 à 1642, Biblio 17,* vol. 55 (Paris, Seattle, Tuebingen: Papers on French Seventeenth-Century Literature, 1990), 184–258.

32. Thomas Pavel, *L'Art de l'éloignement: Essai sur l'imagination classique* (Paris: Gallimard, 1960), 87; hereafter cited in text.

33. Jean Chapelain, *Opuscules critiques,* ed. A. C. Hunter (Geneva: Droz, 1936), 130. In his preface to Pichou's *La Filis de Scire* (Paris: François Targa, 1631; no page numbers), Isnard states that the primary subject of tragedy should be bloody executions. La Mesnardière, in his influential *Poétique* (1640; reprint, Geneva: Slatkine, 1972), says that tragedy must have an unhappy ending, with the catastrophe precipitated by the hero's tragic flaw (8).

34. The original reads: "Sa [tragedy's] dignité demande quelque grand intérêt d'État, ou quelque passion plus noble et plus mâle que l'amour, telles que sont l'ambition ou la vengeance; et veut donner à craindre des malheurs plus grands, que la perte d'une maîtresse. Il est à propos d'y mêler l'amour, parce qu'il a toujours beaucoup d'agrément, et peut servir de fondement à ces intérêts, et à ces autres passions dont je parle; mais il faut qu'il se contente du second rang dans le poème, et leur laisse le premier" (*OC,* 3:124).

35. Among those in agreement with Corneille were Saint-Évremond, in his "De la tragédie ancienne et moderne" (173–81) and "Sur les tragédies" (245) (*Oeuvres en prose,* ed. R. Ternois, 4 vols. [Paris: Didier, 1969]), and Samuel Chappuzeau in *Le Théâtre françois,* ed. G. Monval (1674; reprint, Paris, 1876), 25. L'Abbé d'Aubignac's influential *La Pratique du théâtre* (ed. P. Martino [Paris: Champion, 1927]), published in 1657, uses Corneille as the exemplary author of tragedies—although he was so incensed that Corneille did not cite him in the *Discours* that his later writings became highly critical of Corneille. In *La Pratique,* Aubignac specifically says that it is a mistake to call a play a tragicomedy rather than a tragedy just because of a happy ending; for him, heroic protagonists are what make a play a tragedy (147–48). In his *Discours de la tragédie* (Paris, 1663), the playwright Jean-François Sarasin concurs that bloodshed and disaster are not necessary endings for a tragedy (338).

36. René Rapin, *Réflexions sur la poétique de ce temps et sur les ouvrages des poètes anciens et modernes,* ed. E. T. Dubois (Geneva: Droz, 1970), 98; André Dacier, *La Poétique d'Aristote* (Paris, 1692), viii–ix. Racine addressed the question of the nature of the tragic hero in most of the prefaces to his plays; see in particular the preface to *Andromaque* in 1668, in his *Théâtre complet,* ed. J. Morel and A. Viala (Paris: Garnier, 1980), 130–31.

37. Gustave Lanson, "Le Héros cornélien et le "généreux" selon Descartes," *Revue d'Histoire Littéraire de la France* 1 (1894): 397–411. See also Lanson's *Corneille* (1898; reprint, New York: AMS Press, 1977).

38. Jacques Maurens, *La Tragédie sans tragique: Le Néo-stoïcisme dans l'oeuvre de Pierre Corneille* (Paris: A. Colin, 1966); hereafter cited in text.

39. Robert McBride, *Aspects of Seventeenth-Century French Drama and Thought* (London: Macmillan, 1979) treats this question in his chapter "Doubt and the Cornelian Hero," 7–36.

40. Harriet Stone, *Royal DisClosure: Problematics of Representation in French Classical Tragedy* (Birmingham, Ala.: Summa Publications, 1987), 9; hereafter cited in text.

41. Mary Jo Muratore, *Cornelian Theater: The Metadramatic Dimension* (Birmingham, Ala.: Summa Publications, 1990), 2–3; hereafter cited in text.

42. Judd D. Hubert, "Plénitude et théâtralité dans l'oeuvre de Corneille," *Papers on French Seventeenth Century Literature* 17 (1990): 63–64.

43. Timothy J. Reiss, *Toward Dramatic Illusion: Theatrical Techniques and Meaning from Hardy to Horace* (New Haven, Conn.: Yale University Press, 1971), 1; hereafter cited in text.

Chapter Four

1. The role of Cliton was written for a well-known comic actor, Jodelet, whose flour-covered face, thick eyebrows, enormous moustache, and high-pitched, nasal voice would have added to the spectator's laughter. Jodelet later became a member of Molière's company (*OC,* 2:1220–21).

2. Mallinson disagrees, viewing Dorante as the creator of harmony, of order out of chaos (1984, 207). He sees in Dorante a solution to the leftover tensions in the denouements in the early comedies, whose characters are often unable to adapt to the demands made of them (209).

3. Claude Abraham in his *Pierre Corneille* (New York: Twayne, 1972) sees *Le Menteur* as a Cornelian self-parody, with Dorante recalling her heroes of the tetralogy in comic form (81–83); hereafter cited in text. Théodore Litman agrees (203).

4. *The Compact Edition of the Oxford English Dictionary,* 1971 ed., s.v. "recognition."

5. See chapter 11 of Aristotle, *Poetics,* trans. Leon Golden, ed. O. B. Hardison Jr. (Englewood Cliffs, N.J.: Prentice-Hall, 1968), 19–20.

6. Judd D. Hubert, "The Function of Performative Narrative in Corneille's *La Mort de Pompée,*" *Semiotica* 51 (1984): 115–31; hereafter cited in text. See Antoine Soare, "*Pompée* ou le machiavélisme de l'innocence," *French Forum* 13 (1988): 187–203, for another article that takes a skeptical look at heroic claims in the play, but with an emphasis on the historical and political context. Soare sees Machiavelli's influence on Corneille's theater back through the tetralogy and forward from *Pompée* until *Oedipe* in 1658. He exaggerates Corneille's political cynicism, in my view.

7. See Françoise Jaouën, "Pompée ou la fin de l'histoire," *Biblio 17,* vol. 89 (Paris, Seattle, Tuebingen: Papers on French Seventeenth-Century Litera-ture, 1995), 249–63, for an insightful reading emphasizing that the interpre-tation of history is an essential instrument of power in the play. She also sets the

play in its political context, specifically with regard to Corneille's relationship with the recently deceased Richelieu, and the new first minister, Mazarin.

8. It is interesting to note that *Le Menteur* and *Pompée* were created during the same period, the winter of 1643 (*OC*, 2:1215–16).

9. A letter from the dead Emperor Maurice, the conflicting stories of Léontine, and rumors among the people had only confused the identity question. It is perhaps significant that the authenticating letter is written by a woman, the Empress Constantine. The role of the female characters in this tragedy deserves separate study for which there is no room here, but see the discussions in particular of *Rodogune, Théodore,* and *Nicomède.* Of course, Corneille's female characters are always intriguing.

10. John D. Lyons, *A Theatre of Disguise: Studies in French Baroque Drama* (Columbia, S.C.: French Literature Publications, 1978), 120; hereafter cited in text. See also pp. 115–18 for a full discussion of *la voix du sang* in *Héraclius.*

11. Some critics read *Pertharite* as a site of conflict between bourgeois values (e.g., merit over birth, and conjugal fidelity) and their aristocratic opposite. See Baker, 89; Starobinski, 87; and Dort, *Corneille dramaturge,* 164, for example. Whether Corneille espoused aristocratic values or not remains a subject of controversy; see chapter 1.

12. This vocabulary, in lines 1027–28, disappears with the 1660 edition of the play. Baker notes that "never before in French classical drama had such nouns . . . been attached to royalty" (73–74).

13. See Carlin 1990 for a detailed discussion of Corneille's use of *bienséance* and *vraisemblance.*

14. Marc Fumaroli, "Apprends, ma confidente, apprends à me connaître: Les *Mémoires* de Retz et le traité *Du Sublime,*" *Versants* 1 (Fall 1981): 31; hereafter cited in text.

15. Mitchell Greenberg, *Subjectivity and Subjugation in Seventeenth-Century Drama and Prose: The Family Romance of French Classicism* (Cambridge: Cambridge University Press, 1992), 112.

16. Stone uses a psychoanalytic approach, suggesting that Antiochus is stuck in a unresolved oedipal phase of development: "The child who accedes to the throne remains unable to separate himself from his mother" (1987, 38–39). Although the psycho-criticism of Corneille's theater can produce very insightful interpretations, many of Stone's observations are valid even without this theoretical underpinning. She also has recourse to René Girard's work on ritual in his *La Violence et le sacré* (Paris: Grasset, 1972).

17. See Couton's detailed examination of reaction to the play in *OC*, 2:1313–17.

18. A. Donald Sellstrom, *Corneille, Tasso, and Modern Poetics* (Columbus: Ohio State University Press, 1986), 87. Sellstrom proves his point by showing how Corneille often "rectified" his source material in Tasso and other authors of the Renaissance and antiquity, which was frequently more violent or scandalous than his own treatment of the same subjects.

19. Mary M. Rowan, "Corneille's Orphaned Heroines: Their Fathers and Their Kings," *French Review* 52 (March 1979): 594–603; Larry Gregorio, "Double Standard and Double Bind: Social Constraints on Women in Corneille's Tragedies," *Papers on French Seventeenth-Century Literature* 16 (1989): 195–210.

20. Charles C. Ayer, *The Tragic Heroines of Pierre Corneille* (Strasbourg, 1898); Maria Tastevin, *Les Héroïnes de Corneille* (Paris: Champion, 1924).

21. Marie-Odile Sweetser, "Les Femmes et le pouvoir dans le théâtre cornélien," in *Pierre Corneille: Actes du colloque de Rouen,* ed. Alain Niderst (Paris: Presses Universitaires de France, 1985), 605–14.

22. Alice Rathé, *La Reine se marie: Variations sur un thème dans l'oeuvre de Corneille* (Geneva: Droz, 1990).

23. Timothy J. Reiss, "Corneille and Cornelia: Reason, Violence, and the Cultural Status of the Feminine: Or, How a Dominant Discourse Recuperated and Subverted the Advance of Women," *Renaissance Drama* 18 (1987): 3–41; hereafter cited in text.

24. Mary Jo Muratore, *The Evolution of the Cornelian Heroine* (Madrid: Studia Humanitatis, 1982); hereafter cited in text.

25. Harriet Ray Allentuch, "Reflections on Women in the Theater of Corneille," *Kentucky Romance Quarterly* 21 (1974): 97–110. See also her article "The Problem of Cinna," *French Review* 48 (1975): 878–86.

26. Critics are divided over Rodogune's sincerity when she tells Séleucus and Antiochus that she will marry whichever one kills their mother. At the end of the play, Cléopâtre's suicide has much more impact than any hope for a social renaissance, although Rodogune does manage to save Antiochus's life by preventing him from drinking his mother's poison.

27. Perry Gethner, "*Andromède:* From Tragic to Operatic Discourse," *Papers on French Seventeenth-Century Literature* 6 (1979–1980): 64–65; hereafter cited in text.

28. See Claire Carlin, "Louis XIV héros mythologique: une mise en scène numismatique," *Biblio 17,* vol. 80 (Paris, Seattle, Tuebingen: Papers on French Seventeenth Century Literature, 1994), 363–75.

29. Terence Cave declares that Corneille's "claim to have invented a new genre, the *comédie héroïque,* may be a ruse to evade the suspect category of tragi-comedy; it certainly displays his embarrassment" (313). If Corneille were indeed embarrassed by the new genre, however, he would not have continued to experiment with it in *Tite et Bérénice* and *Pulchérie.*

30. For a detailed exploration of the links between Corneille's plays of 1648–1652 and the Fronde, see Georges Couton, *Corneille et la Fronde* (Clermont-Ferrand: Publications de la faculté des lettres, 1951).

Chapter Five

1. It should be noted that the union of the young couple is not without complications in the tetralogy. Doubt lingers about the marriage of

Rodrigue and Chimène in *Le Cid*, even though she leaves the door open to it, while Camille and Curiace are united only in death in *Horace*. Only Cinna and Émilie form an apparently untroubled couple at the end of the play. In *Polyeucte*, Pauline's bond with her husband is strengthened by her conversion, but this only occurs at his death.

2. H. T. Barnwell, *The Tragic Drama of Corneille and Racine: An Old Parallel Revisited* (Oxford: Clarendon Press, 1982), 129.

3. Harriet Stone takes the opposite view when she states, "Like Oedipus, Corneille's character accepts the identity that others give him. In this sense, too, he is committed to a final misrecognition which in heroic terms translates as a lack of distinction—the failure of heroism itself" (1987, 53). But if heroism is defined in the terms of the Cornelian text, the approbation he receives after the denouement helps to constitute his status as a hero.

4. See Harriet Ray Allentuch, "Is Corneille's *Oedipe* Oedipal?" *French Review* 67 (March 1994): 571–79; hereafter cited in text. This article, like most of Allentuch's work, uses as a point of departure Charles Mauron's analysis of Cornelian theater in *Des Métaphores obsédantes au mythe personnel*. The pattern of violence against the father, followed by solidarity with him and exculpation of the son, is complicated in *Oedipe* because usually, the father figure is doubled in order to aid in the attenuation of the son's guilt (575). The miracle of the denouement thus becomes necessary in *Oedipe* since there is no doubling of Laïus to make Oedipe's crime something other than parricide (577). The heroine as the son's accuser, who then validates him as the curtain falls, is another constant of Corneille's theater, according to Mauron, seen here in Dircé's pardon of Oedipe, says Allentuch (575).

5. Christian Biet, "Oedipe dans la tragédie du XVIIe siècle: Mémoire mythologique, mémoire juridique, mémoire généalogique," *Papers on French Seventeenth-Century Literature* 21 (1994): 507; hereafter cited in text.

6. John C. Lapp, "Magic and Metamorphosis in *La Conquête de la Toison d'or*," *Kentucky Romance Quarterly* 18 (1971): 178; hereafter cited in text.

7. Jacques Morel, *La Tragédie* (Paris: A. Colin, 1964), 47–48, defines tragedy in terms of the insoluble dilemma that remains unresolved as the play ends.

8. Pocock emphasizes the divided nature of the world of the play (122), and Lyons specifically explores Sertorius's inability to pin down the meaning of "Rome" and the ambiguity of his position, which leads to the comparison between Sertorius and Sylla in act 3, scene 1 (1996, 148–52).

9. See also Judd D. Hubert, "The Greatest Roman of Them All: Corneille's *Sertorius*," *L'Esprit Créateur* 4.3 (1964), 161–68. Hubert paints Pompée as "a relativist" whose "skill at compromise leads him perilously close to bad faith" (163). Pocock's view better reflects the context of the entire play, although ambiguity certainly characterizes *Sertorius* and opens the play to interpretation.

10. See Jean Starobinski, "La Rochefoucauld et les morales substitutives," *Nouvelle Revue Française* 14 (1966), 14–34, 211–29, and Bénichou,

128–48, for a discussion of how post-1660 literature reflects the sociopolitical situation of the elite under Louis XIV's growing absolutism. Bénichou also discusses the influence of Jansenism on these developments, a subject to be addressed later in chapter 5.

11. See Jean-Claude Joye, *Amour, Pouvoir et Transcendance chez Pierre Corneille: Dix Essais* (Berne, Frankfurt, New York: Peter Lang, 1986); hereafter cited in text. In his analysis of the political philosophy expressed in *Sertorius,* Joye states that skepticism, pragmatism, and indeed the absence of any political system based on unshakable ideals characterize Corneille's political thought at this point in his career (84–85). Legitimacy can accrue after power is obtained thanks to a wise and magnanimous government like that of Sertorius, although wisdom and magnanimity may be less effective than a lack of scruples when it comes to acquiring power in the first place (84)—as shown by Sylla's rise. In the context of my analysis, the source of Sertorius's difficulties is precisely the absence of any fixed political belief system. Pompée, on the other hand, adapts to a political situation in flux, as shown by his statements about choosing a political master "following chance or necessity" in a climate in which the more virtuous party is impossible to discern (3.1.849–54).

12. Corneille had offended Aubignac in the *Discours* by taking issue with certain of the Abbé's comments in his *Pratique du théâtre* of 1657, and this without mentioning Aubignac's name, the worst possible insult. In response, Aubignac wrote three very critical treatises about *Oedipe, Sertorius,* and *Sophonisbe.* In the prefaces to *Sertorius* and *Sophonisbe,* Corneille again defends himself against the attacks without mentioning d'Aubignac by name.

13. H. T. Barnwell, "Corneille in 1663: The Tragedy of *Sophonisbe,*" *Papers on French Seventeenth-Century Literature* 11 (1984): 577–79; hereafter cited in text.

14. Baker remarks that "the conflict between the rival queens forms the very backbone of Corneille's plot" (99). Barnwell agrees on the importance of these episodes (1984, 582). See 1.3.170 for Éryxe's commonsensical attitude from the beginning of the play.

15. See Roy C. Knight, *Corneille's Tragedies: The Role of the Unexpected* (Cardiff: University of Wales Press, 1991), 90, for an evaluation of Othon's "do-nothing" lack of heroism.

16. One of Othon's best-known exploits while with Nero was to seduce Poppea in advance of Nero's marriage to her (*OC,* 3:1501). In the play, there is only a veiled reference to this incident (2.4.593–96), and thus the ambiguity surrounding Othon's virtue and status as a possible hero is underscored. Nevertheless, the weight of evidence in the play points to a more morally upright Othon than the man portrayed in historical sources.

17. The notion of bargain and economic exchange occurs often in the play, leading Baker to remark, "The confusion of worth, price, power, and license is one characteristic sign of the nascent possessive market economy which forms the backdrop of all of Corneille's theater" (133). The question of

bourgeois versus aristocratic values in the oeuvre is an interesting and controversial topic worthy of exploration, although it is not the focus of this study.

18. Helen Bates McDermott, "Uses of Irony in *Othon*," *French Review* 51 (1978): 649; hereafter cited in text.

19. *Cinna* is the most obvious example of such a dilemma for the monarch. Germain Poirier, in *Corneille et la vertu de prudence*, examines this theme in the tetralogy, and Marie-Odile Sweetser interprets *Agésilas* from this angle (1977, 219–22).

20. Georges May discussed the resemblances between the early comedies and the late tragedies 50 years ago in *Tragédie cornélienne, tragédie racinienne* (92).

21. Jacqueline van Baelen, "The Rhetoric of Theatricality in the Later Tragedies of Corneille," *Papers on French Seventeenth-Century Literature* 4 (1977): 73; hereafter cited in text.

22. Stegmann highlights these lines as a sign of Aglatide's "tranquil insolence" and the "grinding comedy" of the play (1968, 2:632).

23. Jean-Marie Apostolidès, in "Attila, le fléau de Dieu," *Parabasis* 1 (1989): 69–79, provides a political reading of the play as a presentation of Louis XIV as the rightful heir to the Roman empire (71).

24. François Dragucci-Paulsen, "L'Héroïsme féminin dans *Attila*," *Papers on French Seventeenth-Century Literature* 21 (1994): 95–112, examines the heroines' relatively greater energy in the play but concludes that both male and female characters end as representatives of the failure of aristocratic individualism.

25. Lyons notes: "This improbable conclusion, a *deus ex machina* if it had not been historically justified, is precisely a *deus ex historia*—salvation through events that are outside of human foresight and control" (1996, 176). In terms of Corneille's comic schema, the source of the conclusion remains a *deus ex machina*. Historically, there is some doubt as to how Attila died. As Corneille notes in his foreword, the historian Marcellin claims that Ildione killed him on their wedding night (*OC*, 3:641).

26. Apostolidès describes this process in which the sacrificer becomes the sacrificed as part of the providential view of history presented in the play ("Attila, le fléau de Dieu," 76–77).

27. See, for example, Pocock: "Corneille respected moral virtue—that is, the moral order outside poetry—and the characters of the nationalities he portrayed—that is, the external truths of behaviour; Racine failed in both respects—that is, he turned away from the main concerns of naturalism—and subordinated everything to passion—that is, to the unconscious, the irrational and amoral world of myth"(307).

28. See Blaise Pascal, *Les Pensées*, ed. Ch.-M. Des Granges (Paris: Garnier, 1964); and La Rochefoucauld, *Maximes*, ed J. Truchet (Paris: Garnier, 1967); hereafter cited in text.

29. André Stegmann, "L'Humour et l'ironie tragiques de Corneille," *Papers on French Seventeenth-Century Literature* 11 (1984): 323–48, provides many examples of this element of Corneille's theater.

30. For a stylistic rather than thematic comparison of the two plays, see G. Antoine, "Pour une stylistique comparative des deux *Bérénice,*" *Travaux de linguistique et de littérature* 11.1 (1973): 445–61.

31. Jonathan Mallinson, "Du Jeu de l'amour et de la politique dans *Tite et Béréncie,*" *Parabasis* 1 (1989): 81–96, sees all the characters prepared to fool themselves as well as each other (82). For the specific remarks on Tite, see p. 94; hereafter cited in text. Marie-Odile Sweetser, "Amour et renoncement: renouvellement de l'art cornélien dans la dernière période," in *Onze études sur la vieillesse de Corneille dédiées à la mémoire de Georges Couton,* ed. Madeleine Bertaud and Alain Niderst (Paris: Klincksieck, 1994), 95–122, provides an example of an extremely positive interpretation of the conduct of both Tite and Bérénice (111–13); hereafter cited in text.

32. Domna Stanton, "Power or Sexuality: The Bind of Corneille's Pulchérie," in *Gender and Literary Voice,* ed. Janet Todd (New York: Holmes and Meier, 1980), 236–47, says in her interesing feminist reading that Pulchérie is attracted to Léon because she is not subservient to him. His love, his tears, his youth all symbolically deny his manhood (241); hereafter cited in text.

33. I include Pulchérie among the "young lovers" even though she is not in the first bloom of youth. She has to be at least 30, which in the seventeenth century was considered middle-aged. Léon is younger than she.

34. Stanton comments that "[b]y avoiding feminine sexuality, Pulchérie hopes to attain phallic power, even though the latter is predicated on the former and, thus, essentially compromised" (239). She goes on to say that "Pulchérie upholds and perpetuates the Law of the Father, which defines power in woman as 'degenerate blood' " (242–43). Sweetser counters this reading with the observation that in the seventeenth-century context, Pulchérie's compromise represents a real victory for female power, just as the virginity of Elizabeth I of England had served her political purposes in the sixteenth century (1994, 119–20). These perspectives illustrate the different results arising from a reader-centered method versus a historically based one. Each has the merit of illuminating the text and making it richer for the reader.

35. Although I share Forestier's interest in the dramatic structure of the oeuvre, his genetic study leads to some differences in the details of the analysis. Helen Bates McDermott, "Politics and Amibiguity in Corneille's *Suréna,*" *French Forum* 2 (1977): 205–13, also addresses the question of *Suréna*'s "Racinian" qualities, seeing them as "useful to a point," but fundamentally inadequate for dealing with this "profoundly original work," which "belongs in the Cornelian tradition of dramaturgical experimentation and investigation into the nature of power" (206). The question of the nature of power is not underscored in my interpretation, but I echo many of McDermott's observations.

36. Critical opinion as to Suréna's murderer varies. For instance, Pocock believes Orode orders the assassination (143–48), while Nadal blames Pacorus (262), and McDermott mentions the possibility of a sort of suicide (213), a notion with which I agree much more than her suggestion that "Suréna . . .

imagines that his death might be the work of chance" (212); her quotation from act 5, scene 3, is out of context.

37. Forestier notes that Palmis's presence allows Corneille to use once again the schema of young couples whose union is blocked (45).

38. Greenberg sees symptoms of Freudian pathological melancholy affecting all the characters of the play in their lack of interest in the external world, their lassitude, their criticism and disdain for each other, and their expectation of punishment. All this is a sign of the malaise of absolutism in crisis (1986, 153–65).

Chapter Six

1. The playwright's own striving for recognition of a heroic effort is evident in his drama theory: he argues with the majority and insists on his right and his capacity to be original. See Carlin 1990.

2. H. T. Barnwell, in *The Tragic Drama of Corneille and Racine,* notes that in Cornelian tragedy, the audience experiences enlightenment at the end, rather than the protagonist, as was the case in Racinian and in Greek tragedy (238).

3. Corneille's views on aristocratic versus bourgeois values are more difficult to determine; they have inspired much critical debate and illustrate the open-ended quality of his theater. This debate is all the more understandable given the state of turmoil within and between the two classes during the seventeenth century. Erica Harth, *Ideology and Culture in Seventeenth-Century France* (Ithaca, N.Y.: Cornell University Press, 1983), describes the instability and mobility that characterize the bourgeoisie and the nobility.

Selected Bibliography

PRIMARY SOURCES

Principal Editions of the Works of Pierre Corneille

Oeuvres complètes. Bibliothèque de la Pléiade. Edited by Georges Couton. 3 vols. Paris: Gallimard, 1980–1987. Now the definitive edition of the complete works, including the theoretical writings, poetry, and correspondence. Couton uses the first published version of the early works, thereby retaining their verve. Extremely thorough documentation throughout; the edition used here.

Oeuvres complètes. Grands Écrivains de la France. Edited by Charles Marty-Laveaux. 12 vols. Paris: Hachette, 1862–1868. Until the 1980s, the standard edition of Corneille's works. Now superseded by Couton, Marty-Laveaux nonetheless provides interesting historical insights. Based on the 1682 edition, the last prepared by Corneille himself, Marty-Laveaux should not be used for the comedies, which Corneille revised heavily.

Oeuvres complètes. L'Intégrale series. Edited by André Stegmann. Paris: Seuil, 1963. The only scholarly edition of Corneille's complete published works in one volume. The introductory material for each play is often insightful.

Théâtre complet. Edited by Alain Niderst. 6 vols. Rouen: Publications de l'Université de Rouen, 1984–1986. Prepared for the tricentenary of Corneille's death, this edition of his theater is remarkable for its listing of and numerous photographs from modern productions of Corneille's plays. The bibliographies and introductory remarks for each play are valuable.

There are also excellent editions of individual plays available, some of which are mentioned in the notes for this study.

Translations of the Theater of Corneille

The Chief Plays of Corneille. Translated by Lacy Lockert. Princeton, N.J.: Princeton University Press, 1957. Includes *The Cid, The Horatii, Cinna, Polyeucte, Rodogune,* and *Nicomedes.*

Le Cid: A Translation in Rhymed Couplets. Translated by Vincent Cheng. London and Toronto: Associated University Presses, 1987. The most satisfying translation yet of Corneille's most famous play.

The Cid, Cinna: The Theatrical Illusion. Translated by John Cairncross. 1975. Reprint, Harmondsworth, England: Penguin, 1985.

Moot Plays of Corneille. Translated by Lacy Lockert. Nashville, Tenn.:Vanderbilt University Press, 1959. Includes *La Mort de Pompée, Héraclius, Don Sanche d'Aragon, Sertorius, Othon, Attila, Pulchérie,* and *Suréna.*
Seven Plays. Translated by Samuel Solomon. New York: Random House, 1969. Includes *The Cid, Horatius, Cinna, Polyeucte, The Liar, Rodogune,* and *Surenas.*
Three Plays: Le Cid, Cinna, Polyeucte. Translated by Noel Clark. Bath: Absolute Classics, 1993.

SECONDARY SOURCES

The Corneille bibliography is far too vast for every worthwhile book to be included here, to say nothing of the hundreds of articles his oeuvre has inspired. Only the most influential books and collections of articles are listed here. Books not at least half devoted to Corneille have in most instances been omitted. See the chapter notes and the following bibliographies for further references.

Bibliographies

A Critical Bibliography of French Literature. David C. Cabeen and Jules Brody, general editors. *Volume 3: The Seventeenth Century.* Edited by Nathan Edelman. Syracuse, N.Y.: Syracuse University Press, 1961. An invaluable tool for an overview of three centuries of criticism.
A Critical Bibliography of French Literature. Richard A. Brooks, general editor. *Volume 3A: The Seventeenth Century.* Edited by H. Gaston Hall. Syracuse, N.Y.: Syracuse University Press, 1983. An update of the 1961 edition.
French 17: An Annual Descriptive Bibliography of Seventeenth Century Studies. Edited by J. D. Vedvik. Published for the Seventeenth Century French Division of the MLA by Colorado State University, Fort Collins, Colo. Contains the most complete evaluative annotations for scholarly work on Corneille and the seventeenth century.
Klapp, Otto. *Bibliographie d'histoire littéraire française.* Frankfurt: Klostermann, 1956–. A very complete annual bibliography.

Books, Parts of Books, and Collections of Articles

Baker, Susan Read. *Dissonant Harmonies: Drama and Ideology in Five Neglected Plays of Pierre Corneille.* Études littéraires françaises, vol. 48. Tuebingen: Gunter Narr, 1990. Stimulating examination of *Clitandre, Théodore, Pertharite, Sophonisbe,* and *Othon* using Marxist, reader response, feminist, and psychoanalytic approaches.
Bareau, Michel L., ed. *Pierre Corneille: Ambiguïtés.* Vol. 1, *Parabasis.* Edmonton, Alberta: Alta Press, 1989. Eight excellent articles.

Barnwell, H. T. *The Tragic Drama of Corneille and Racine: An Old Paralell Revis-ited*. Oxford: Clarendon, 1982. An excellent aesthetic study of how the two dramatists constructed their plays.

Bénichou, Paul. *Morales du Grand Siècle*. Collection Folio/Essais, vol. 99. Paris: Gallimard, 1948. A classic study that places Corneille and other impor-tant seventeenth-century authors in the historical context of the period between feudalism and modernity. Describes the gradual destruction of the heroic aristocratic ethic Bénichou finds in Corneille's theater.

Bertaud, Madeleine, and Alain Niderst, eds. *Onze études sur la vieillesse de Corneille dédiées à la mémoire de Georges Couton*. Boulogne: ADIREL, and Rouen: Mouvement Corneille/Centre International Pierre Corneille, 1994. These 11 articles form an invaluable contribution to the study of the somewhat neglected area of Corneille's theater after 1660.

Clarke, David. *Pierre Corneille: Poetics and Political Drama under Louis XIII*. Cam-bridge: Cambridge University Press, 1992. A detailed study of the links between dramatic theory and the political situation in the noncomic plays from *Clitandre* through *Pompée*.

Conesa, Gabriel. *Pierre Corneille et la naissance du genre comique (1629–1636)*. Paris: SEDES, 1989. Excellent for the context in which Corneille began to write his comic theater.

Corneille comique. Edited by Milorad R. Margitic. *Biblio 17*, vol. 4. Paris, Seattle, Tuebingen: Papers on French Seventeenth-Century Literature, 1982. An important collection of articles on the comedies.

Couton, Georges. *Corneille*. Connaissance des Lettres. 2nd rev. ed. Paris: Hatier, 1969. The most succinct but rich biography of Corneille, this revised ver-sion of Couton's 1958 work draws on his other more specialized bio-graphical studies of Corneille.

———. Introduction to the *Oeuvres complètes,* by Pierre Corneille. Vol. 1. Paris: Gallimard, 1980. A convenient source for details not included in the 1969 book.

Dort, Bernard. *Corneille dramaturge*. Paris: L'Arche, 1957. Emphasis is on the sociopolitical context in this Marxist approach.

Doubrovsky, Serge. *Corneille et la dialectique du héros*. Paris: Gallimard, 1963. An indispensible breakthrough in Corneille scholarship upon its publication, still very influential. Cornelian heroism seen in terms of the Hegelian master-slave dialectic.

———. "Corneille: masculin/féminin, réflexions sur la structure tragique." In *Autobiographiques: De Corneille à Sartre,* 11–41. Perspectives critiques. Paris: Presses Universitaires de France, 1988. Doubrovsky totally revises the view of *Le Cid* he proposed in 1963, here using a psychoanalytic approach.

Forestier, Georges. *Essai de génétique théâtrale: Corneille à l'oeuvre*. Collection esthétique, vol. 59. Paris: Klincksieck, 1996. A superb examination of the construction of Corneille's plays.

————. *Corneille: Le Sens d'une dramaturgie.* Collection "Les Livres et les hommes." Paris: SEDES, 1998. Completes Forestier's 1996 study with an examination of moral and political issues in Corneille's theater.

Fumaroli, Marc. *Héros et orateurs: Rhétorique et dramaturgie cornéliennes.* Histoire des idées et critique littéraire, vol. 277. Geneva: Droz, 1990. A collection of important articles, mostly published between 1968 and 1984, with an emphasis on Corneille's Jesuit formation.

Garapon, Robert. *Le Premier Corneille: De "Mélite" à "L'Illusion comique."* Paris: SEDES, 1982. A well-respected look at Corneille's youthful works.

Gasté, Armand, ed. *La Querelle du "Cid."* 1898. Reprint, Geneva: Slatkine, 1970. An invaluable collection of the diatribes written for, against, and by Corneille during the quarrel.

Goulet, Angela S.-M. *L'Univers théâtral de Corneille: Paradoxe et subtilité héroïques.* Harvard Studies in Romance Languages, vol. 33. Cambridge, Mass.: Harvard University Press, Department of Romance Languages and Literatures, 1978. A penetrating study of Cornelian plot construction.

Greenberg, Mitchell. *Corneille, Classicism, and the Ruses of Symmetry.* Cambridge Studies in French. Cambridge: Cambridge University Press, 1986. Authority, power, and sexuality in *Médée,* the tetralogy, and *Suréna* are examined from the perspective of Foucault, Freud, and feminist critics. This stimulating but densely written study remains controversial for the application of contemporary literary theory to seventeenth-century texts.

Hubert, Judd D. *Corneille's Performative Metaphors.* EMF Monographs. Charlottesville, Va.: Rockwood Press, 1997. A study of Corneille's poetics and especially his use of the play within the play and similar theatrical references.

Joye, Jean-Claude. *Amour, Pouvoir et Transcendance chez Pierre Corneille: Dix Essais.* Berne, Frankfurt, New York: Peter Lang, 1986. Provocative political analyses.

Kerr, Cynthia B. *L'Amour, l'amitié et la fourberie: Une Étude des premières comédies de Corneille.* Stanford French and Italian Studies, vol. 20. Saratoga, Calif.: Anma Libri, 1980. Violence and egotism in the early comedies are examined. One of the first important books in the renewal of study of the comedies in the late 1970s and 1980s.

Knight, Roy C. *Corneille's Tragedies: The Role of the Unexpected.* Cardiff: University of Wales Press, 1991. Contains seven previously published articles. Not a systematic study, but provides fine insights on Cornelian dramaturgy.

Lanson, Gustave. *Corneille.* 1898. Reprint, New York: AMS Press, 1977. A classic study, against which all other interpretations were written for at least 70 years. Sees the Cornelian hero as a creature of unshakable will, unaffected by passions once decisions are taken.

Lasserre, François. *Corneille de 1638 à 1642: La Crise technique d'Horace, Cinna et Polyeucte. Biblio 17,* vol. 55. Paris, Seattle, Tuebingen: Papers on French Seventeenth-Century Literature, 1990. Studies Corneille's innovations as a playwright. Contains useful appendices on the social context and the question of dramatic genre.

Litman, Théodore A. *Les Comédies de Corneille*. Paris: Nizet, 1981. A solid contribution to the several books on Cornelian comedy in the late 1970s and 1980s, although there is too much emphasis on the potentially tragic elements of the comedies. Litman tends to see the comedies as precursors rather than plays with interest in their own right.

Lyons, John D. *The Tragedy of Origins: Pierre Corneille and Historical Perspective*. Stanford, Calif.: Stanford University Press, 1996. A superb analysis of *Horace, Cinna, Polyeucte, Sertorius,* and *Attila.* Lyons examines how Corneille uses the confrontation of past and present in history to tell the tragic story of the birth of new social and political order, in situations as relevant to our time as to Corneille's.

Mallinson, G. Jonathan. *The Comedies of Corneille: Experiments in the Comic*. Manchester: Manchester University Press, 1984. By far the best study in English of Corneille's comedies.

Margitic, Milorad R. *Essai sur la mythologie du "Cid."* University, Miss.: Romance Monographs, 1976. An important contribution to the renewal of criticism of the play, this study uses a methodology based on Roland Barthes's *Mythologies.*

Marthan, Joseph. *Le Vieillard amoureux dans le théâtre de Corneille*. Paris: Nizet, 1979. A detailed examination of the theme of the elderly man in love, present throughout the corpus but especially important in the final plays.

Maurens, Jacques. *La Tragédie sans tragique: Le Néo-stoïcisme dans l'oeuvre de Pierre Corneille*. Paris: A. Colin, 1966. Places Corneille in the philosophical currents of his time.

May, Georges. *Tragédie cornélienne, tragédie racinienne: Étude sur les sources de l'intérêt dramatique*. Urbana: University of Illinois Press, 1948. One of the earliest books to concentrate on Cornelian aesthetics.

Méron, Évelyne. *Tendre et cruel Corneille: Le Sentiment de l'amour dans "Le Cid," "Horace," "Cinna," et "Polyeucte."* Paris: Nizet, 1984. Sees Corneille as the poet of "pain, lack, solitude" as he depicts couples in crises of misunderstanding.

Mongrédien, Georges. *Recueil des textes et des documents relatifs à Corneille*. Paris: Centre National de Recherche Scientifique, 1972. An extremely useful collection of seventeenth-century documents about Corneille.

Muratore, Mary Jo. *The Evolution of the Cornelian Heroine*. Madrid: Studia Humanitatis, 1982. One of the only books dedicated to Corneille's heroines. They are divided into four nonchronological categories: idealists, individualists, reactive heroines, and public servants.

———. *Cornelian Theater: The Metadramatic Dimension*. Birmingham, Ala.: Summa Publications, 1990. Studies the theatricality present throughout the corpus, and sees the plays as a continuing reflection on the nature of the theater.

Nadal, Octave. *Le Sentiment de l'amour dans l'oeuvre de Pierre Corneille.* Collection Tel. Paris: Gallimard, 1948. A seminal work on the theme of love in the whole of Corneille's theater, carefullly placed in the seventeenth-century context.

Nelson, Robert J. *Corneille, His Heroes, and Their Worlds.* Philadelphia: University of Pennsylvania Press, 1963. One of the best overviews of Corneille's theater in English.

Niderst, Alain, ed. *Pierre Corneille: Actes du colloque de Rouen.* Paris: Presses Universitaires de France, 1985. Contains dozens of valuable articles.

Pavel, Thomas. *La Syntaxe narrative des tragédies de Corneille: Recherches et propositions.* Paris: Klincksieck, 1976. The only linguistic, narratological study of Cornelian tragedy; an original perspective on its structures.

Picciola, Liliane. *Esthétique de Corneille.* Paris: SEDES, forthcoming. A detailed introduction to the principles governing Corneille's dramaturgy, grounded in what the author calls *une esthétique de l'éclat.*

Pocock, Gordon. *Corneille and Racine: Problems of Tragic Form.* Cambridge: Cambridge University Press, 1973. A stimulating contrast of Corneille's "naturalistic techniques" and Racine's more poetic approach to tragedy.

Poirier, Germain. *Corneille et la vertu de prudence.* Geneva: Droz, 1984. A learned study emphasizing the allegorical aspects of Corneille's theater.

Prigent, Michel. *Le Héros et l'État dans la tragédie de Pierre Corneille.* Collection Écrivains. Paris: Presses Universitaires de France, 1986. Emphasizes the political dimension, in a movement toward the destruction of the hero by the State. An important contribution to Corneille criticism, but its narrow focus at times deforms the author's readings of the tragedies.

Rathé, Alice. *La Reine se marie: Variations sur un thème dans l'oeuvre de Corneille.* Histoire des idées et critique littéraire, vol. 289. Geneva: Droz, 1990. A study of queens and their power or lack thereof in Corneille's "matrimonial" tragedies.

Reiss, Timothy J. *Toward Dramatic Illusion: Theatrical Techniques and Meaning from Hardy to Horace.* New Haven, Conn.: Yale University Press, 1971. Especially interesting on spectator psychology.

Sellstrom, A. Donald. *Corneille, Tasso, and Modern Poetics.* Columbus: Ohio State University Press, 1986. A penetrating study of Corneille's intellectual roots.

Starobinski, Jean. *L'Oeil vivant.* Collection Le Chemin. Paris: Gallimard, 1961. Contains "Sur Corneille," an extremely important essay on the concept of *éblouissment* (the overwhelming "first sight" of an impressive personage) in Cornelian theater.

Stegmann, André. *L'Héroïsme cornélien: Genèse et significtion.* 2 vols. Paris: A. Colin, 1968. Volume 1 contains a very complete intellectual biography of Corneille. The second volume, over 700 pages, continues to develop the seventeenth-century context from several angles (literary, political, philosophical) and analyzes all of the noncomic plays in detail.

Stone, Harriet. *Royal DisClosure: Problematics of Representation in French Classical Tragedy*. Birmingham, Ala.: Summa Publications, 1987. Examines questions about mimesis representation raised by the tragedy of Corneille and Racine, drawing on feminist and psychoanalytic criticism, as well as on the work of Louis Marin and René Girard.

Sweetser, Marie-Odile. *La Dramaturgie de Corneille*. Geneva: Droz, 1977. One of the most comprehensive studies of Corneille's theater. Very valuable for students.

Venesoen, Constant. *Corneille apprenti féministe de "Mélite" au "Cid."* Paris: Lettres Modernes, 1986. An interesting contribution to the rash of books concentrating on Cornelian comedy.

Verhoeff, Han. *Les Comedies de Corneille: Une Psycholecture*. Paris: Klincksieck, 1979. Using a Freudian psychoanalytic approach based on the work of Charles Mauron, Verhoeff finds the fear of women to be a driving force behind the dramatic structure of Corneille's comedies.

———. *Les Grandes Tragédies de Corneille: Une Psycholecture*. Archives des lettres modernes, vol. 201. Paris: Lettres modernes, 1982. Using the same psychocritical approach as his book on the comedies, Verhoeff examines the tetralogy.

Yarrow, Philip J. *Corneille*. New York: St. Martin's Press, 1963. One of the few general studies of Corneille available in English.

Index

Abraham, Claude, *Pierre Corneille,* 99–100, 160
Alarcón, *La Verdad sospechosa,* 78
Albanese, Ralph, 47, 154
Allentuch, Harriet R., 100, 110–11, 144, 156
Antoine, Gérald, 166
Apostolidès, Jean-Marie, 165
Aristotle, *Poetics,* 7, 9, 11, 16, 56, 82–83, 96, 108, 139, 160
Aubignac, François Hédelin, abbé d', 116; *La Pratique du théâtre,* 150, 159, 164
Ayer, Charles, *The Tragic Heroines of Pierre Corneille,* 99, 162

Baker, Susan Read, *Dissonant Harmonies,* 39–40, 43, 90, 95, 100, 119, 153, 161, 164
Barnwell, H. T., 116–17, 119, 164; *The Tragic Drama of Corneille and Racine,* 107, 163, 167
Baro, Balthazar, *Célinde,* 154
Barthes, Roland, 54
Beaujour, Michel, 158
Bem, Jeanne, 158
Bénichou, Paul, *Morales du grand siècle,* 18, 49–51, 93, 144, 151, 163–64
Bertaud, Madeleine, editor, *Onze études sur la vieillesse de Corneille,* 149, 166
Biet, Christian, 110, 163
Bilezikian, Monique, editor, *Homage to Paul Bénichou,* 149
Black, Cordell W., *Corneille's Dénouements,* 155
Boileau-Despréaux, Nicolas, 123; *L'Art poétique,* 150
Bossuet, Jacques Bénigne, 70

Cairncross, John, 158
Calder, Andrew, *Molière: The Theory and Practice of Comedy,* 151
Carlin, Claire, 9, 16, 31, 48, 150, 161–62, 167

Cave, Terence, *Recognitions,* 56, 83–83, 89, 109, 111, 153, 162
Chapelain, Jean, 71–72; *Opuscules critiques,* 159
Chappuzeau, Samuel, *Le Théâtre français,* 159
Cheng, Vincent, translator, *Le Cid,* 155
Clarke, David, *Pierre Corneille,* 39, 42, 64–65, 153
Cognet, Louis, *Le Jansénisme,* 151
Conesa, Gabriel, *Pierre Corneille et la naissance du genre comique,* 23, 151
Conti, Prince de, *Traité de la comédie,* 16, 158
Corneille, Pierre: Academy, French, 4, 8, 52, 71; Alexander VII, Pope, *L'Imitation de Jésus- Christ* dedicated to, 18; Anne of Austria, relations with, 5, 6, 105; Condé, Prince de, relations with, 5, 105; Corneille, Marthe (sister), 12; Du Parc, Thérèse "Marquise," inspires love poetry, 13; "Five Authors" group, 3; Fouquet, Nicolas (patron), 6, 108, 124; Fronde, 5–6, 89, 101, 124; Hôtel de Bourgogne, 10; Hue, Catherine (first love), 12; Jansenist influence on Corneille, 130, 138, 141, 145; Jansenists, relations with, 15–18; Jesuit influence on Corneille, 15–19, 39, 53, 110, 130, 138, 143–45; Lampérière, Marie de (wife), 12; Longueville, Duc de, *Clitandre* dedicated to, 39; Louis XIII, relations with, 2, 3, 93; Louis XIV, influence on Corneille's theater, 4, 6, 17–18, 110, 120, 134, 141, 144; Louis XIV, relations with, 11, 101–2; Marais (theatrical company), 11; Marillac, Maréchal de, subject of *Clitandre,* 39; Mazarin, Cardinal, relations with, 5, 101, 105; Quarrel, Ancients vs. Moderns, 11; retirement from theater, 89; Richelieu, Cardinal, influence on Corneille's theater, 50, 62, 93;

Corneille, Pierre (*continued*)
Richelieu, Cardinal, influence on theater in general, 4, 6, 7; Richelieu, Cardinal, relations with, 3, 8, 12, 39;
Rouen, life in, 2; *Sentiments de
l'Académie Française sur la tragi-comédie
du Cid, Les,* 53; social status, 2, 4, 6,
12

CONCEPTS AND THEMES IN WORK
admiration for hero, 9, 31, 49, 74–75,
88, 96–98, 105, 109, 119, 139
amour-propre, 115, 130, 133–34, 141
anagnorisis, 22, 56, 75, 82, 90, 103–5
audience, onstage, 114, 143, 146; role of,
22, 31, 36, 40, 44, 48–49, 57, 66,
74–75, 77, 79–85, 87, 89, 93, 96,
105–6, 140, 142, 145, 147
baroque, 35–36, 46
bienséance, la, 10, 37, 42, 58, 91, 94–95,
110, 116
Christianity, 15–18, 39, 53, 66–71, 73,
94–95
comedy: classical, 21, 27, 32, 45, 48, 78,
97, 104, 107, 143; comic schema or
structure, 21–23, 26–27, 31, 34–36,
39, 48, 49, 57, 62, 71, 74–77, 79,
83, 86, 93, 95, 97–98, 101, 103,
105–10, 114–20, 125, 128–29, 133,
141, 142–45; definition of, 12, 22,
32–33, 39, 62, 75, 98; heroic comedy,
11, 33, 77, 101, 103–5, 124, 131,
135, 144
conversion, 64–65, 69–70, 109–11,
133–34, 141–42
death: in battle, 58; in duel, 50–52; execution, 69; false announcement of, 24,
38, 52–53, 123; fear of, 103, 122;
fratricide, 128; infanticide, 87, 92,
128; martyrdom, 66, 68–70, 94;
murder, 58–61, 83–84, 87, 92–94,
139–41; parricide, 86–87, 89, 92;
regicide, 86–87, 92, 128; suicide
(realized), 92–94, 109, 119; suicide
(threat of), 51–53, 58–60, 63–64,
136; threat of, 38, 46, 50–51,
63–64, 84–85, 87, 89, 92–93,

96–97, 121–22, 132, 143, violent,
127–28
didacticism, 31, 30, 42, 80, 142
distinction, desire of hero for, 19, 23, 25,
30, 32, 35–36, 40, 48, 62, 66, 73,
76, 89, 108, 117, 132, 141, 145, 147
duty, 41, 43, 51–52, 58, 61, 65, 69, 90,
104, 131–32, 135–36
farce, 20–21, 24, 26, 32, 45
feminine, the, 43–44, 55–56, 66–67,
73, 90, 92, 98, 127, 139
free will, 18, 32–33, 39, 72, 108, 110,
130, 138, 145
générosité, 83–84, 90, 94, 97, 126, 133
genre, theatrical, 11, 33, 71, 103, 106,
110
gloire, 52, 54, 59, 61–62, 65, 69, 84, 89,
93, 113, 116–19, 132–34, 140; definition of, 51
glory, 24, 26, 49, 58, 62, 63, 66, 72, 99
hero, as social servant, 49–50, 57, 59,
72, 70, 76–77, 79–80, 82, 88, 96,
106–7, 110, 112, 115, 129, 131,
136–37
heroism, 19, 29, 44, 53–54, 60–62,
68–69, 72–75, 84, 102–4, 109,
141; of Corneille, 123, 144; failure of,
99, 108, 116, 120, 122–23, 132,
133, 144; refused, 90
honor, 16, 28, 41, 49, 50–52, 58–59,
61, 63–64, 80–81, 84, 128, 140
illusion, characters' creation of, 22, 24,
33, 40, 44–45, 48, 49, 56, 78, 88,
120, 143
instruction, 40, 48, 80–81
irony: in comedy, 30, 32–33, 81; dramatic, 88, 104; in tragedy, 63,
65–66, 69, 109, 118, 123–26,
128–30
language, comic, 20–21; of female characters, 55; of heroism, 126; *précieux,*
13–14, 110, 124; *stances,* 124; in
tragedy, 57
love, 141, 144; cause of suffering, 13, 17,
90, 103; in Cornelian comedy, 12, 20,
23–29, 31–33, 38, 45, 78–81;
courtly, 19, 52, 67, 137; false, 122,

The Author

Claire L. Carlin holds a Ph.D. from the University of California at Santa Barbara (1984). She has been an assistant professor of French at the University of Victoria (British Columbia) since 1989, and from 1984 to 1989 was an assistant professor at Washington State University. She has published numerous articles on the theater of Pierre Corneille, including "The Woman as Heavy: Female Villains in the Theater of Pierre Corneille" (*French Review,* 1986) and "Corneille's *Trois Discours:* A Reader's Guide" (*Orbis Litterarum,* 1990). She has also published articles on Racine, the medallic history of the reign of Louis XIV, the baroque, la préciosité, and feminist psychoanalytic literary criticism. She was the 1996–1997 president of the North American Society for Seventeenth-Century French Literature (NASSCFL) and is the editor of the proceedings of the 29th annual conference of NASSCFL in the Biblio 17 series.

The Editor

David O'Connell is professor of French at Georgia State University. He received his Ph.D. in 1966 from Princeton University, where he was a National Woodrow Wilson Fellow, the Bergen Fellow in Romance Languages, and a National Woodrow Wilson Dissertation Fellow. He is the author of *The Teachings of Saint Louis: A Critical Text* (1972), *Les Propos de Saint Louis* (1974), *Louis-Ferdinand Céline* (1976), *The Instructions of Saint Louis: A Critical Text* (1979), and *Michel de Saint Pierre: A Catholic Novelist at the Crossroads* (1990). He has edited more than 60 books in the Twayne World Authors Series.